SLUMBOY
FROM THE
GOLDEN CITY

From Zenani Mandela

Uncle Paul and Aunt Adelaide Joseph are second parents to me and in that way their story is inseparable from mine.

They were activists against apartheid in South Africa with my parents, Nelson and Winnie Mandela, and they all paid the price for this. But before I could even start school, these beloved adult figures were ripped from my life.

I was just a tiny little girl when my father was sent to prison in 1962 and only five years old when the Josephs left South Africa for a life of exile in England.

I have such fond memories of going to play at their house in the Johannesburg suburb of Fordsburg, especially the times I spent with Zoya and her late twin brother, Anand. With them, Tanya and later Nadia, who was born in England, I formed another family and they became like brothers and sisters to me. Brought together by our parents, we children formed a close bond that has lasted over half a century.

Uncle Paul and Aunt Adelaide opened their home to me and whenever I visited London they would put me up and shower me with love. I remember the delicious meals Aunt Adelaide would cook in her warm kitchen and how she would serve them along with snippets of our history and anecdotes of their escapades and friendship with my parents.

My wish for the readers of this book is that they learn something of the remarkable men and women, like Paul and Adelaide Joseph, who are not known throughout the world, who are not recipients of many accolades, but who played a vital role in the struggle that brought democracy and freedom to our country, South Africa.

Paul Joseph

SLUMBOY
FROM THE
GOLDEN CITY

MERLIN PRESS

First published in 2018 by
The Merlin Press Ltd
Central Books Building
Freshwater Road
London
RM8 1RX

www.merlinpress.co.uk

ISBN 978-0-85036-750-8

The moral right of the author has been asserted

Front cover photograph: Paul and his comrades released from prison after the state of emergency following the 1960 Sharpeville massacre. Left to right: 'Fats', a member of the ANC; Alfred Nzo, later Secretary General of the ANC; J.B. Marks, President of the Transvaal ANC and chairman of the African Mineworkers Union; Lionel Morrison, Coloured People's Congress, and Paul Joseph, Transvaal Indian Congress. OWLS000151-6

Portrait on back: Photo taken during the time of the Treason Trial by Eli Weinberg, printed with kind permission from Mayibuye/UWC

The copyright holders for some of the photos that feature in this book are unknown despite extensive research. Applications were made to the IPO and licences granted under the Orphan Works Licensing Scheme.

A CIP record of this book is available from the British Library

Printed in the UK by Imprint Digital, Exeter

Contents

Acknowledgements

I was first prompted to write following the death of my older brother Peter.

I wanted to pay tribute to his quiet and unstinting contribution to the South African liberation struggle. I soon realised that in honouring him I inevitably touched on the lives of numerous South Africans who, in my mind, also deserved to be acknowledged.

I was unsure how to develop the work and spoke to a longtime friend, Professor Lionel Caplan, who advised me to simply write as many recollections as possible and seek help with the structure later. I thank him for this practical advice.

I later showed samples of my writing to my friend, Dr Pat Logan, who I first met through Bill and Celia Pomeroy. The Pomeroys had been involved in the Hukbalahap liberation movement in the Philippines and were supporters of our struggle in South Africa.

Pat took on the mammoth task of typing up my handwritten notes. I suggested that if he had difficulties he should hold the notes up in front of a mirror or ask his local chemist to read them. I thank him for his time, skills, patience and constant encouragement.

As the project developed I called upon the help of yet another friend, Katherine El-Salahi, an experienced editor of books relating to Africa.

Katherine had also played a part in the liberation of South Africa. She was one of the 'London Recruits'. This was a body of daring people who smuggled arms and other materials to the MK cadres is South Africa.

Katherine showed no hesitation when I asked her to assist me. I am so grateful for her knowledge and editorial expertise in helping to shape my writing into a book. Her commitment to the project was immense and I truly value her friendship. She later collaborated with our daughter Nadia.

Nadia had been actively involved in the Anti-Apartheid Movement and the ANC in London. She was one of the 25 freedom marchers who walked from Glasgow to London to mark Mandela's 70th birthday.

When we reached the stage of looking for publishers, Nadia was thankful for the encouragement she received from Professor Gus John and Linton Kwesi Johnson.

She later selected photos from our personal collection to include in the book. She tried to ensure the images were of the best possible quality as well as researching copyright for their use. She was gratefully assisted by the following; Tracy Clayton, Pete Muller, Sahm Venter and Georgia Atienza.

Final thanks goes to the publisher Tony Zurbrugg who Katherine found. I would like to thank all the staff at Merlin for their work in enabling me to share my memoir with you.

Paul Joseph

Dedication

For my dear wife Adelaide, Barberton's finest and most resilient daisy. She has stood by me for more than 60 years.

During the early years she not only looked after our children; the twins Zoya and Anand and later Tanya but also had to cope with me being on trial for treason, imprisoned, under banning orders and house-arrest.

My mother and sisters supported us through these times as did all the women in the lives of my fellow freedom fighters. Adelaide was also engaged in her own important political work.

Life in exile brought a different set of challenges but Adelaide remained steadfast.

This memoir is for our comrades, relatives and friends and those we have lost along the way, in particular our son Anand. It is also for the living and with love for our daughters Zoya, Tanya and Nadia and our grandchildren Shura, Catriona and Arjuna.

Foreword

I first heard of Paul in my capacity as a human rights lawyer practising in Johannesburg, when I was briefed on behalf of his wife, Adelaide, to bring a habeas corpus application to the Supreme Court in Johannesburg to have Paul brought to court from solitary confinement in which he was being held under the 90 days detention without trial law in South Africa. Evidence in support of the application case was very slender, based on a bloodied shirt worn by Paul, which the police had allowed to be taken for laundering at Paul and Adelaide's home on the understanding that it would be returned to the jail the next day properly laundered. The police were fortunately intimidated by a threat from me to call every policeman in the security branch to submit to cross-examination on the bloodied shirt, which I suggested must have resulted from torture by the police to obtain a confession. The prospect of a large number of the special branch police being cross-examined about torture worked and Paul was then released. In the event, it emerged that the blood on the shirt had arisen from Paul cutting himself while shaving, but he could not tell me this because under the 90 day detention law he was not allowed contact with anyone, including his lawyer!

Paul was subsequently re-arrested and charged with other statutory crimes of protesting against the apartheid system. Somehow or other I managed to secure his release so that he could continue with his nonviolent onslaught on the apartheid system.

A few years later I emigrated to the United Kingdom and Paul later managed to escape from South Africa. We met up again in London, where I was able to secure him a job as a filing clerk in a company for which I worked, which was called Abbey Life. There were grave concerns amongst some of my colleagues in employing a communist but I pointed out that South African communists were very well organized and competent and that Paul would be a real asset to the company. I was correct in my judgement and Paul eventually rose to head up a department of about thirty clerks, which was one of the most competent departments in the company. Paul never allowed his communist activities to adversely affect Abbey Life. Our close friendship continued, and when one speaks of Paul one immediately includes Adelaide because they are as one, so that our families got to know each other and were always pleased to meet.

In the UK Paul continued with his peaceful communist activities and got to know and befriend a large number of British people as well as a large number of refugees, many of whom found employment with our company. Paul had and has an astonishing network of friends at all levels of society, all irrespective of race, sex, politics or prejudice and was the one person I always turned to when I wanted information about anybody. With his bubbly and thoughtful personality he was very popular, helped many individuals, supported many organizations and made and makes a significant contribution to the community, both where he lives and beyond. He gave lectures on human rights at universities and was invited abroad to speak and, all in all, was and is an exceptional human being whom Vanetta, my wife, and I are very proud to know and love.

I look forward to seeing the book about Paul published, because I think it is a remarkable story of a remarkable human being.

Joel Joffe, 2017[1]

---

1 The foreword was written by Joel Joffe a short time before his death in 2017.

Acronyms and Abbreviations

ANC	African National Congress
ARM	African Resistance Movement
BCM	Black Consciousness Movement
COD	Congress of Democrats
CP	Communist Party
FEDSAW	Federation of South African Women
GDR	German Democratic Republic
IDAF	International Defence and Aid Fund
MK	Umkhonto we Sizwe
NIC	Natal Indian Congress
PAC	Pan-African Congress
PIDE	Portuguese secret police
SACPO	South African Coloured People's Organization
SAIC	South African Indian Congress
SAN-ROC	South African Non-Racial Olympic Committee
TIC	Transvaal Indian Congress
TIYC	Transvaal Indian Youth Congress
Wits	Witwatersrand University
YCL	Young Communist League

Glossary

Blerry	bloody
Boesman	Bushman, derogatory term for the San, the first nation people of South Africa
Buti	brother
Dagga	marijuana
dhaniya	coriander
indunas	security guards
Jamal koteh	powerful laxative
Kavadi	Hindu religious ceremony
Knobkerries	thick wooden clubs with knobs on the top, used as weapons
Kofia	brimless cap with flat crown
Koolie	coolie
Mapoisa	security guard, watchman
marrela	whitewash
mealie(s)	maize
morogho	wild spinach
mutiman	traditional medicine man
nyanga	traditional medicine man
opskit	Afrikaans dance of quicksteps and swirls
pap	stiff maize porridge
rasam	a type of hot pepper soup. British soldiers in India made a version which they called Mulligatawny, from *mallaga* (chillie) and *tawni* (water)
samosas	triangual deep-fried snacks filled with curried meat or vegetables
Shebeen	illicit bar
Sjambok	heavy leather whip
Skokiaan	locally brewed beer (known as '*Kaffir* beer')
Varkkop	Pighead
Voortrekker	Afrikaans and Dutch for pioneer

List of Names

Gamat Jardine	police plant
Abdulhay Jassat	TIC, MK activist
Joel Joffe	lawyer
Vanetta Joffe	Joel Joffe's wife
Solly Jooma	TIC leader
Adelaide Joseph	activist, author's wife
Anand Joseph	author's son
Chella Iyer	author's sister
Darley Iyer	author's sister
Daso Joseph	author's brother
Helen Joseph	women's leader
Nadia Joseph	author's daughter
Peter Joseph	author's brother
Tanya Joseph	author's daughter
Ramsamy Iyer	author's brother
Violet Joseph	author's sister
Zoya Joseph	author's daughter
Sam Kahn	CP, MP, *New Age* journalist
Ahmed Kathrada	ANC activist, Rivonia trialist
Harold Kingsman	childhood friend
Dave Kitson	MK operative
Wolfie Kodesh	MK operative
Moses Kotane	ANC and CP leader
Colin Legum	jounalist, writer
Margaret Legum	writer
Dr Ahmed Limbada	Unity Movement leader
Alan Lipman	COD activist
Chief Luthuli	Leader, president of the ANC1952-60
Mac Maharaj	ANC activist
Nelson Mandela	MK leader, Rivonia trialist
Winnie Mandela	ANC activist, married to Nelson Mandela
J.B. Marks	CP, Chairman African Mineworkers Union, President Transvaal ANC leader
Matselane aka Rosie	domestic help
John Matthews	MK operative
Solly Matthews	code name for Mac Maharaj
Ismail Meer	TIC, ANC
Ronnie Michael	lawyer
Wilton Mkwayi	Deputy Commander of MK
Ruth Mompati	ANC, MK activist

Mosie Moola	ANC activist
Dr G.M. 'Monty' Naicker	ANC leader
H.A. Naidoo	CP
Indres Naidoo	MK operative
Ramnie Naidoo	TIC, ANC activist
Steve Naidoo	ANC activist
Shanti Naidoo	CP, TIC activist
Shirish Nanabhai	MK operative
Sergeant Nayagar	Durban security police
Lindiwe Ngakane	ANC activist
Lilian Ngoyi	ANC, FEDSAW leader
Duma Nokwe	ANC leader
Henry Nxumalo	*New Age* journalist
Aggie' Ahmed Patel	the TIC secretary
Vella Pillay	SAIC, ANC, CP leader
Ivan Schermbrucker	*New Age* circulation manager
Reverend Michael Scott	activist
Dawood Seedat	SAIC, CP activist
Ralph Sepel	lawyer
Reverend B. L. Sigamoney	TIC supporter
Eric Singh	ANC activist
J.N. Singh	CP leader
Walter Sisulu	Secretary-General of the ANC
Nana Sita	passive resister
Joe Slovo	CP, ANC leader
Robert Sobukwe	PAC Leader
Marcus Solomon	Unity Movement
Brian Somana	ANC, *New Age* journalist
Major Spengler	head of the Johannesburg security police
Helen Suzman	MP
Captain Swanepoel	Security police
I.B. Tabata	Unity Movement leader
Dick Taverne	lawyer
Mo and Irving Teitelbaum	Irving was a lawyer, Mo worked for Amnesty International
Reverend D. C. Thompson	priest

Ben Turok	activist
Stanley Uys	journalist
Reggie Vandeyar	CP, childhood friend
Eli Weinberg	*New Age* photographer
Bert Williams	alias Robert Govender
Sophie Williams	women's leader
Harold Wolpe	CP, Lawyer
Dr A.B. Xuma	President of the ANC in the 1940s
Elsie & Isaac Yudelman	bookshop owners

Part 1: South Africa

1

Beginnings

My mother was born at the end of the 1890s in the village of Vazhakulam, near Muvattupuzha in the district of Ernakulam, state of Cochin-Travancore, now known as Kerala in South India. Her name was Annamall Veghese.

When I was still in my teens I remember talking to my mother about her family history. By my calculation it went as far back as 250 years. In 1980, I went to India and visited the family living in the house where my mother was born. I was shown the very room in which she was born. I met several related families in the locality. I also visited Bangalore and met academics from Catholic educational institutes. Slowly I was able to build a picture of my mother's background.

I learnt from one of them, a Jesuit brother who was steeped in the history of Catholicism in India, that Verghese was one of the names of two hundred Brahmin families who were converted to Catholicism by St Thomas of Assyria.[1]

In another village I met more relatives of my mother. They were a prominent family in the Catholic church, called Thevasia Purakal. One of their daughters, Susheela, was a nun in the Order of The Little Sisters of Jesus, which was founded in Algeria in 1939. Susheela was an amazing source of information. By her account there were something like 72 relatives who were nuns. She lost count of the brothers and priests who had moved to various parts of India and the States. It turned out just before I left India that the academic I met in Bangalore was related to me.

In her novel, *The God of Small Things*,[2] Arundhati Roy wrote about my mother's people in the district of Ernakulam.

My mother was brought to South Africa when she was about seven years old by an aunt and uncle who were childless. It seems they virtually kidnapped the little girl from her extended family, saying they were taking her for a visit to Madras. Within days Annamall was on a boat with the aunt and uncle, bobbing on the high seas to Delagoa Bay near what was then Lourenço Marques (now Maputo) in Mozambique. She made her way with them from there to Johannesburg, totally unaware of the upheaval and anguish she left behind in Muvattupuzha and the surrounding villages.

The ancestral home in Kerala was dubbed 'The African House', probably because the aunt and uncle were among the first people to leave Kerala for South Africa. There were only two other families, both Catholic, who landed in Natal around the same time. My mother believed she was an orphan until she was well into her sixties. She was brought up by her relatives with love and affection.

She often recalled her childhood days in the village. She remembered the little schooling she got in the Malayalam language and that it was the wish of the Maharajah of Cochin-Travancore that all his citizens be educated. She remembered how she used to go with her aunt to the river to wash clothes, and watched in fascination the elephants at work, clearing boulders and shifting logs. At festival time the elephants were decorated. Going to church was very much part of the life of the villages.

The one aunt she was attracted to was blind. This aunt led the singing by the river. When my mother went back to Kerala after more than sixty years, the blind aunt was well, and nearly 94 years old. The Verghese family, she found, still observed the Catholic code of conduct. My mother, who had become fluent in Tamil in South Africa, was quite lost initially in Malayalam, but within a week everything she learnt as a little girl came back, so for the three months she was there she was able to talk in Malayalam.

She remembered there was no animosity between Christians, Hindus and Muslims. There was, however, a deep prejudice towards the lower castes.

My mother's arrival in the Transvaal was just before the outbreak of the South African War (she still called it the Boer War). They lived at various times in the towns of Pietersburg, Bloemhof and finally Johannesburg. The uncle was a peddler in clothes and later he ran a shop, with little success.

The increasing anti-Indian sentiments and a string of anti-Indian laws affected their means of livelihood and their freedom of residence and movement in the Transvaal Republic. The British government cited the ill-treatment of the Indians in the Republic as one of their reasons for engaging in the war against the Boers, although the real reason was the country's abundance of gold.

Mother told us of how White people treated them with taunts and disdain. There were no recreational facilities for any black people except a zoo and the surrounding gardens. To reach there they had to go on foot as they were not allowed on the trams. From where they lived, in Johannesburg's slum Ferreirastown, it was about five miles to the zoo, so mother, aunt and uncle would set out early in the morning with a packed lunch. At the zoo they had to make sure they stood behind the White people to watch the animals, and make doubly sure they did not bump into any White people.

Johannesburg was never really a planned city. It had sprung up in the days of the gold rush in 1867. What town planning there was applied mainly to the commercial centre and the White suburbs. They led organized lives compared with the Africans, Indians, Coloureds, Lebanese and Chinese crowded into slums and having to make do with whatever was available.

The Africans were mainly enclosed in locations and in single-sex coal- and gold-mining hostels. These were set in complexes of compounds in various parts of the city, in which municipal, domestic and railway workers lived under the strict control of the pass laws.

My mother told us myths about the Chinese. Such myths were widespread: that they were mainly gamblers, ate strange food, and should not be interfered with because they would cut up people and preserve them in four-gallon paraffin tins. To get children to behave they were told horror stories about the Chinese.

She also told us about the thousands of Chinese men who were brought in to work in the gold mines. They were housed in compounds and from time to time there were outbreaks of violence. Gambling and drinking seemed to be the cause of the violence. There were no women, as the few men who did have families did not work in the mines. Then one day there were only the shopkeepers and market gardeners. The rest were shipped back to China.

The Lebanese (who were referred to as Syrian but were actually Catholic Maronites), though White in appearance, spoke mainly Arabic. The authorities treated them as 'Asiatics'. Most of them appeared to be occupied in bootlegging and running *shebeens* through their shops and houses. Their houses seemed to contain only the bare necessities, except for lots of tables and chairs. These were for the drinkers. Their homes were often subjected to raids by the liquor squad. Virtually every house had a big picture of Jesus or Mother Mary. There were enough Maronites to constitute a church of their own as well as a school. As kids, we attended their church.

The fast-developing mining industry needed all available skills, so batches of Coloured and Malay workers were sent to Johannesburg. These people settled in what became known as 'Malay Camp' in Ferreirastown. It would appear that the name 'Malay Camp' came about after a settlement of 'Cape Malays', descendants of the slaves brought into the Cape from Batavia by the Dutch colonizers. In time they became skilled carpenters, blacksmiths, masons and builders. Some were tailors. Their skills were much in demand by the booming mining industry in Johannesburg.

There were also many African men in the locality, but there was no established African community and there were no African families. These men were odd-job workers, menial workers or domestic servants.

There was a settlement of old Jewish men. They lived apart from the other communities. They ran second-hand furniture and clothes shops. Some were pedlars in odds and ends. Sunday was the big trading day. In time they either moved out to Doornfontein or simply died of old age.

The Indians were scattered around Ferreirastown. They were mainly Gujaratis, Hindus and Muslims. The rest were Tamils, Christians and a smattering of Hindi-speaking people. The Hindus and Muslims were shopkeepers in the main. The Tamils and Tamil-speaking Christians were waiters who came from Natal, the offspring of the indentured labourers from the sugar plantations.

Ferreirastown had a vibrancy of its own. There was a synagogue, a mosque, a Maronite church, an Anglican and a Presbyterian church, two battered cinemas, and any number of *shebeens* where hard liquor or an African brew was available. There was an Indian market, an Indian school, a Coloured school, and the small Chinese community had a school of their own. There was no shortage of gambling dens, brothels, or *dagga* sellers. The locality was bustling and weekends were noisy with shouting, singing, and plenty of fights with horrendous results. It was in this environment that my mother lived with her aunt and uncle, and it was here that we were all born.

Annamall was not aware of any political development except that people talked in awe about a clever man in the neighbourhood who was a lawyer named Gandhi. She once saw him. There was talk of meetings about the hard life of the Indians. The meetings were mainly attended by men.

We were never really able to work out at what age my mother got married. It could have been between thirteen and sixteen years of age. It was an arranged marriage to one Dorasamy Iyer, a high-caste Hindu priest from Madras, who doubled up as a clerk by day and on off-days as a priest. Later he was employed as a horse-drawn tram driver. He could very well have been the tram driver who passed my mother, aunt and uncle on their way to the zoo. Soon after the marriage, the aunt and uncle left for India. There is no account of how they faced the families of the village of Mupativazim.

This marriage of a Hindu priest to a Catholic woman was most unusual. Besides, one only spoke Tamil, the other Malayalam. We thought the marriage was agreed to because Dorasamy was from a high caste and my mother, though a Christian, had a Brahmin caste background. Otherwise, under the usual caste category my mother would have been regarded as low caste.

From this marriage she bore five children, two sons and three daughters. Then Dorasamy died after a short illness. The world seemed a lonely place. There were no relations in Johannesburg, just her and her brood and some friends. Swift decisions had to be made. Chellamall, the eldest, had to be taken out of school and sent out to work. She worked for a Greek confectioner called Piryacos, six days a week. Fortunately the workplace was within walking distance from home.

Piryakos the confectioner was always a suspicious character. He thought the few staff he had were stealing his sweets and if any of us happened to peer over the fence he scowled at us. We would see him carrying huge basins of confectionery. Each step he took was with a grunt. He always looked old and tired, cursing and his head moving from side to side. Then Piryakos died and with him Chellamall's job.

Ramsamy, the second eldest, was also taken out of school and sent out as a flower-seller. Handsome like his father and with fair skin, which enabled him to enter office buildings from the front entrance, he could use the lifts to offices where the White female staff were shown the neatly arranged bunches of flowers. The women were also taken in by his charm and smart appearance, unaware that he was actually an Indian. Later he worked as a waiter and in some places he had to wear a turban. A 'White man' in a turban, he looked odd.

He also managed to supplement the family income through bootlegging for the Lebanese *shebeen* owners, as he could pass for White and purchase the liquor. For that he got a commission.

Ramsamy, who was conscious of his responsibility to the family, was afflicted by a compulsion to gamble. His specialities were billiards and horse-racing. At times when broke he would bundle up his suits to sell to the dealers in West End Chambers. I remember my mother pleading with him not to sell his clothes. It seems the conflict of gambling and the poverty of the family pained him. And like most gamblers he always lost.

Third of the five children was Letchmee, who died from an illness as a teenager, then Darley, whom my mother kept in school and saw through college to qualify as a teacher.

The local Indian community, even though working class, was quite conservative. They showed their displeasure at my mother for allowing Darley to continue schooling beyond primary education. The women came on a deputation to dissuade my mother from letting Darley go for further education. They told her that a young girl should be prepared for marriage, and besides, at this particular college there were 'Native' and Coloured men.

Mother asked Darley in front of them how she felt about continuing her studies. Darley said she loved to study and her ambition was to become a teacher. Mother turned to the women and said that now they had heard her daughter's decision they should support her. The women left in a huff. Darley became one of the first two Indian women teachers in the Transvaal.

The last of the brood of children was Gopal. He was a bright and talented lad in sports and 'academically promising', as one of his teachers described him at his funeral. He died of a football injury to his brain which was not picked up at the time. He was thirteen years old. His funeral was large, with schoolmates, teachers, neighbours and a Boy Scouts guard of honour. We took a basket of food and milk to five of the African gravediggers. It was said they would care for the grave. Besides, they earned very little money.

Hovering in the wings was a hotel chef by the name of Veeraswamy. He came from Pondicherry in South India. He was single, and quite prepared to take on a ready-made family. My mother's beauty was legendary. Petite, clad always in a saree and blouse and wearing beautifully designed gold earrings from the time of her marriage, she cut an impressive figure. As a widow she fended off approaches from men, especially married ones. She succumbed to Veeraswamy because he was a Catholic from India and he showed a genuine interest in her and her children.

Hotel owners and managers had a tendency to dub European names on their workers. If a waiter had a name they found difficult to say then they called them Sammy. It appears that because Veeraswamy was Catholic, in the hotel where he worked they called him Joseph.

From this union my mother bore the second batch of five children. There were two sisters, Elizabeth and Violet, and three sons, Peter and me and then Daso. Our actual Indian names were Thevarajh, Navarajh and Thasarajh.

I have no real recollection of my father apart from a few vague images of a man with a long drooping moustache and a walking stick. I remember him once helping me gently to get off a horse-drawn cab. He was cooing in my ears. I was about two or three years old.

One day I heard my sisters talking in hushed tones of my father having gone to India on a visit and of having received a message that he died there. I recall that in a quiet manner he had gone to see his other family there, of which he had made no disclosure.

This development did not seem to create any distress. If anything it brought the family closer. Our older sisters and brothers showed great concern, love and attention to the family. We were never referred to as half-brothers or half-sisters. Neither did we see them in that way. I only became aware that they had a different father at the age of twelve and it was not a problem.

2

Growing up in Ferreirastown

We were all born in the vicinity of West End Chambers, the Indian market, the gold mines and its sand dunes, commonly called the mine dumps. This was Malay Camp in Ferreirastown. We lived there until I was about eleven years old. Then suddenly circumstances changed. The whole community was evicted and the houses were demolished for the construction of a complex of magistrates courts, the biggest ever built in the country.[3]

The evicted families had to fend for themselves. They scurried all over for shelter. My family found two small rooms in the lower end of the westerly part of Malay Camp, in a compound where many families lived in candle-lit rooms with two outside taps and two toilets. Passers-by as well as hundreds of drinkers made use of the facilities. The houses were built of zinc, wood, mud bricks and iron. Some of the houses were built in the days of the gold rush.

Most of the properties were owned by Jews and Lebanese, and our quarters were owned by 'Oubaas' Chaitowitz. 'Oubaas' (Old Boss) was a pleasant, religious, soft-spoken man. He would call once a month on a Sunday morning to collect the rent. Never a sharp word was said to my mother when she was behind or short of the rent. He would give her time. He always gave her a receipt. We never knew of anyone who was evicted from any of his properties. Nor did he bump up the rent even during the war years when accommodation was scarce.

On rent Sunday we were sure to get a penny from 'Oubaas' Chaitowitz. Chaitowitz had the reputation of being the largest owner of slum properties in many parts of Johannesburg. The properties were maintained by his son Abee, who was a man of few words. When he did speak it was in monosyllables which sounded like grunts. He had powerful shoulders and arms, acquired from the constant shifting and fixing of iron pipes, bricks, timber and boulders. His fingers were thick. He was always scratching his body. He twisted pipes with ease.

Abee knew a great deal about building repairs. Nothing was replaced with new parts. The material was picked up from demolished sites and put on a horse-drawn cart. He never seemed to be in a hurry. He walked slowly and drove his cart slowly. Abee never gave the horse forage. It was fed from the leftover corn after the beer was brewed and sifted. The drink was called either 'Kaffir beer' or skokiaan. That explained why Abee's horse swaggered from side to side. Quite often Abee gave me a ride on the cart when visiting some of the properties.

Abee's staff consisted of two other men. One was the yard sweeper. His job was specifically to sweep up the yards of the Chaitowitz properties. The yard sweeper was called 'Mr America'. He was tall and very dark, with shifty large black eyes that had a scary look, and his face was heavily painted with white cream. Mr America wore layers of clothes. On his head he wore a woolly hat and sometimes another hat on top of that. He never spoke to anyone. Occasionally he would stop and rest his broom to take a pinch of snuff. The talk was to avoid Mr America. Even the liquor squad never asked Mr America for his pass.

The other worker was the painter. His job was to marrela (whitewash) the properties. The painter's eyes were bloodshot and watery. My mother said it was from the lime in the whitewash. The painter came around periodically to paint the rooms in our compound. He, too, was a man of very few words. The only sounds that could be heard were the sucking of his pipe and bouts of coughing. I did hear him say once to my mother, 'This job is hard and I get fucking little pay.'

Quite often when the toilets and drains were blocked and the spillage covered most of the yard, then Mr America would try to shore up the muck, and 'Ikee', as Abee was known, would arrive with the painter. The crew of three would work on the operation of clearing the blockage. Not a word would pass between the three men. The stench would linger for days.

Ikee had a brother, Sidney. He was never seen around. Sid was a lawyer. He became well known in the administration of White football. I always felt we helped Sid become a lawyer from the rent his father collected.

Our neighbourhood was friendly and protective towards us. There was the occasional nervousness when brother Ramsamy appeared. They took him to be some kind of White official who had come to check them out. Some were puzzled that in a relatively dark Indian family there was the 'White man' in their midst. Odd stories circulated about this White man. The more daring would ask my mother or sisters who was the father of this White man.

From Friday to Sunday evening there was buzzing as the booze trade thrived, with heavy drinking, arguments and brawls resulting in gruesome stabbings. An assortment of bricks, stones, clubs and iron bars were used. The police would arrive in their pickup vans to conduct brisk raids on gamblers, drinkers and possible victims of pass law breaches. They would arrive with sharp, long iron bars with which they would stab the ground to pierce any tin drums of the illicit brew of African beer. The buried tins of beer would be unearthed, spilled out and the tins would be smashed. If it happened on the days when the toilets and drains were blocked, the splash of the *skokiaan* added to the stench.

The leader of the police raiding party was a huge White man who had a large and oddly cropped head. He was nicknamed *Varkkop*, Pighead. He was fearsome. A blow from him would send his victim sprawling. When word reached the drinking yard that Varkkop was coming, drinking parties and the dice dens would melt away.

The inhabitants of our compound yard were made up of flower vendors, waiters, factory workers, a teacher (my sister), unemployed, tramps and prostitutes and the people who ran the *shebeen*s and sold *dagga*. There was a young boxer who marked off a little space for his shadow boxing.

A woman whose husband was stabbed to death in one of the weekend brawls lost her mind. She would take her chamberpot and stand in the middle of the yard and look into the pot asking 'Jonnie, waar is jy?' ('Johnny, where are you?') a number of times until she was overcome with sobbing.

As we grew up we spoke less Tamil. There were no Tamil-speaking families around us. We spoke more and more English and acquired a smattering of Afrikaans. My brothers, apart from Ramsamy, were not fluent in Tamil, though we understood it. My mother and sisters spoke fluent Tamil. A lot of the English we spoke contained Afrikaans and African words or expressions.

It was very much later when I went to school that I discovered the English we spoke was understood only by our peer group from the neighbourhood. The teachers had quite a task in correcting us. We spoke of totoobikes (for motorbikes), fire magates (for fire brigades), ouchie and skelm (for the goody and baddy in the movies).

One day Barney Desai, who was one of our classmates, brought in a little bespectacled boy to us, saying, 'Hey, manne, listen to this oke for what is the right word for puss and cunt.' He went on, 'Tell them Suli, tell them!' Suleiman blinked, then uttered the word 'vagina'. There was a momentary silence. We were astonished. Barney said, 'Is he not blerry clever?'

Ferreirastown and Fordsburg had some goldmines distinguished by the mine heads and the mine dumps. The crushed rock was washed for gold and the remains came out in the form of slurry, which was pumped on to the adjoining ground. Over the years it hardened and formed a flat sort of pyramid. The other process was to take the crushed grit and pile it high, looking almost like low-lying hills. Brick-making firms bought it for construction. The dumps were a common sight, as were the mine dams.

These became our playgrounds, which carried certain risks, like the sudden falling and movement of large quantities of sand. A child of one of our neighbours died from such a sand shift. Another play spot was the mine dam. The older boys who could swim showed off their skills. Some who were not so skilful drowned. We smaller ones stayed near the embankment to only splash in the water.

Another hazard, which was a great discomfort that people experienced on windy days, was the wind carrying the mine sand over the residential areas. The grit which fell was like a sandstorm, sometimes lasted for days. It went into the houses, settling on the beds, furniture, utensils, and into the eyes, ears and nostrils. The streets and pavements were covered in it. This did not seem to bother the mine owners or make them take preventive measures.

Most of our playtime was in the streets or on waste ground belonging to a mining company. Our games did not last long. Soon enough the *mapoisa* – a watchman, whose uniform gave him the appearance of a policeman – would emerge with a *sjambok* to drive us off.

One evening one of our mates, a girl, was not so lucky. She was cornered by a *mapoisa*, who whipped her all over her body. The *mapoisa* had to go into hiding when her family and angry neighbours came to beat him up.

A more daring effort would be made by a gang of us, especially during the sweltering hot days. We would creep into the 'showers'. This was a maze of overhead pipes from which jets of warm water shot out. The pipes were near the mining plant. They were thoroughly enjoyable since none of us had showers or bathrooms at home. We knew how to move out of sight of the *mapoisa* or, if he did spot us, we made sure we were in the middle of the jets. We could see the *mapoisa* waving his *sjambok*. We knew he would not venture into the showers. We made sure our scanty clothes and underwear were piled in a suitable place for a quick snatch and getaway. Quite often we would be running naked with our clothes under our arms with the *mapoisa* in pursuit, much to the amusement of commuters in passing trains.

Once a group of us were wandering around the streets. We were being led by my older brother Peter. On the steps of an unused building we saw a man asleep in a sitting position with his mouth wide open. Peter did not say anything to us. He picked up a handful of sand, stood above the man and poured the sand into the man's mouth. Peter sprinted. We sprinted as well. The man screamed and wriggled with shock. For some days we never ventured near the area.

Some Sunday afternoons we went to the 'Fighting Grounds'. This was a clearing on mine property waste ground. Here gangs of *Amalaitas* came to spend Sunday afternoons in physical combat. They were decorated with animal figures, wearing *tekkies* (sandshoes), loose shirts, and thick-studded bangles.

They would set out in groups in various parts of the White suburbs, converge into larger groups, partly trotting and partly dancing rhythmically in unison to the shrill sounds of whistles and tiny mouth organs. They looked frisky and raring for combat. They would finally settle in gangs on the edge of the battleground. The referees were White plainclothes police. The fights would take the form of head-butting, banging, kneeing, fisticuffs and the use of the thick-studded bangles to the face and heads.

The men would have blood-splattered shirts, broken teeth and noses, gaping wounds and swollen heads and ears. Some walked in agony as if their testicles were damaged. These scenes we watched lying on our stomachs and peering over the edge of the sand dunes. There was no singing, dancing or trotting on departure, but the sight of men dishevelled and dragging themselves home.

Weekends in Ferreirastown were a violent time. My mother was very watchful of our movements. She kept us indoors late afternoons and evenings when clashes would break out. All sorts of projectiles came into use. Men got disembowelled, women got battered and molested.

My friends were Coloureds, Lebanese, and Indians. We went to the cinemas, wandered into the city to frequent the department stores, and made for the cake and biscuit stalls. There we pilfered by stowing what we could get under our shirts. Another spot was the Indian market. The shopkeepers used the pavements to stock their supplies of fruit and vegetables. We would choose the buying period. We walked in file. The chap in front would use a razor blade to cut a bag of oranges and the rest of us would catch the oranges rolling out and stuff them into our shirts. This was done with lightning speed.

The one time I got caught was when there were only two of us. It was a sweltering day and we thirsted for watermelon. I asked my friend David Jack to select a watermelon. His job was to keep an eye out. David selected a large one. I picked up the watermelon and walked off. Just about a block away from the school I felt a tap on my shoulder. It was the shopkeeper. He asked me where I was taking the watermelon. I said I was taking it to my teacher to show him. I was quite baffled when the man said I should carry it back to his shop. Had he asked me to take it to the teacher, whose reputation was one of sheer terror for corporal punishment, I was sure to be skinned alive. Sensibly David Jack disappeared.

3

Mother

My mother struggled to clothe us. At times her friends helped out with cast-offs for us. There was a bakery about half a mile away. If we got there in time, we could buy some fresh broken loaves of bread for a few pence.

The bakery in our neighbourhood was owned by the Edelsons. Edelson Bakery baked bagels, rye and chollah breads, cakes, rolls, bread puddings and tarts. The puddings and tarts were baked in long trays. Serving behind the counter was the father of the Edelson family. We would ask for a penny cake, which was on the far end of the shelf. By the time old Mr Edelson shuffled there and back with the penny cake, a couple of trays of pudding and tarts would have been spirited out. After gorging ourselves it was expected that one of us would leave the empty trays, leaning them against the window display.

We would walk along the railway lines to pick up lumps of coal and go to the fields to pick wild spinach. This spinach was also known as *morogho*, which Africans collected. Mother made a lovely meal by adding some spices and garlic. This, with dhal, potato curry and *pap* (stiff maize porridge) and a bit of chutney, made a delicious meal.

Our mother was frugal, and skilled at cooking any kind of vegetable, or river crabs and dried or fresh snook, into different kinds of curry. This type of skill was typical of a lot of mothers in our locality. There was always just enough for one meal in the evenings. We dared not waste any food when eating. A clip or two around the ears soon put that right.

For a time relief came in the form of a weekly ration for some of the poorer Indian families. This ration consisted of a bar of blue soap, a tin of condensed milk, some packets of dried beans, flour and sugar, salt and *mealie* meal. This we got through the initiative of the Reverend B.L. Sigamoney, an Anglican priest and a militant figure with a background of being the first Indian to join the Socialist Party in 1918. Together with a social worker by the name of Sister Katz, he cared for the poorer Indians. Apparently at the time the term 'sister' was also applied to a social worker.

These two people, concerned for the poor, got relief through the Rand Aid Association sponsored by the provincial council.

Later, when I got involved politically, the Reverend veered to the right and we were highly critical of him, but my mother had a lasting respect for him. When she heard us being critical of him, she was most upset. She chided us for our scathing remarks and for being ill-considered in forgetting that when we were hungry it was Sigamoney who helped us. It was my first lesson in how to be critical and yet not to be offensive to people like my mother, since she was a typical member of the poor and oppressed who needed to be reached.

We had no idea how ill-nourished we were until were taken for medical examination to the school doctor. The three of us had bandy legs and it was then I first heard the word rickets being used. We heard it being said that we lacked vitamins, another new word for me.

The doctor prescribed cod liver oil, and once a week the poorer children got a dollop of malt. A school feeding scheme was introduced. We got a daily mug of milk, with a bun or a slice of brown bread. Our mother prepared an oil application to our legs every night. She was assisted by our sisters. An improved diet and massaging soon straightened us out.

There were nine of us living in one room and a kitchen. The room was our bedroom, bathroom, eating room and a small portion set aside at night for a waist-high bench for Darley's study. We had a couple of rickety chairs and little benches. The kitchen was about a third of the size of the bedroom-cum-eating room. In the kitchen we had two packing cases. Shelves of a kind were on the top box, and the bottom had cupboards with doors held by pieces of leather as hinges. This completed our kitchen dresser. We had a small coal stove and a primus stove.

At mealtimes we sat on hessian mats and sacks on the floor. The food was dished out in portions into enamel plates. We ate neatly and, when finished, the mats were shaken out, rolled up and put under the bed until night time. We had a family-size iron bed, which Mother, Darley, Violet and Daso slept in. Peter, Chella and I slept on the floor on the hessian mats, which were rolled up each morning and stored under the bed again. Ramsamy had a single iron bed.

Periodically, and especially at Christmas, Easter and Diwali times, my sisters gave the house a thorough going-over. This was quite an involved operation. All nooks and corners were cleaned and tidied. The two tiny windows were cleaned. The iron beds and mattresses were taken into the yard. Boiling water was poured over the springs and irons and insecticide sprayed all over the mattresses. The floors were thoroughly scrubbed and the crevices sprayed. Mother's revered pictures of Adam and Eve, the crucifixion and the Virgin Mary were cleaned of the fly droppings and bugs. The brassware, cutlery and the mostly chipped and cracked crockery came in for a good soak, wash, rinse, and polish with ash. The last stage was making attractive our cut-outs from newspapers or brown paper for the shelves, which had a display of crockery and enamelware.

The smell of insecticide pervaded the house for several days. It was a pleasure nonetheless to have a spruced-up house, but within weeks the bugs and cockroaches came back. The whole compound was infested. Sometimes the authorities moved in to fumigate the compound.

On festive occasions mother made sure we got some meat and fish dishes. My sisters baked cakes and biscuits. The boys got new shorts and a shirt and sometimes a pair of shoes. We were sent to the barber's for a close-cropped haircut, which cost a sixpence. Mother's reasoning was we would be free of lice. We thought otherwise. Once in three months she would spend one shilling and sixpence.

Only Peter was allowed to grow his hair, because of his job as a bellboy. We were all astonished when he grew a crop of wavy hair. So Daso and I asked our mother to allow us to grow ours. She relented. In a matter of months our hair grew wavy. We now had the pleasure of throwing our hair back, which was the fashion then.

In spite of our crowded conditions, my mother was always prepared to help out some unfortunate woman with a couple of children. This meant making sleep space available as well as food. I remember a woman arriving with three children. The next day a young mother arrived with a set of twins. Then, at another time, another young mother with three children.

We did not raise any objections. It was not the done thing. On one occasion I did ask my mother who these women were. The explanation was, 'These women are the daughters of my sisters.' We knew that was not possible because we had no relatives whatsoever, but we dared not say so.

We would overhear our sisters talk about how these women were abused by their husbands or abandoned. It was also said that the mothers of these women were friends of our mother who in turn gave support to her during her hard times.

Our mother had strong ideas about not wasting food. Our sisters were told not to throw any food away. Leftovers were placed in an enamel bowl and covered. She believed there would always be someone in need of food. Invariably someone turned up, and somehow there was food available. The poorer people in our yard would come at night and knock gently at the door, asking in either English or Afrikaans, *Ou mama het my n bikkie kerry cos?* ('Old mother, have you got a bit of curry food?')

Our mother had her quota of superstitious ideas about luck and misfortune. We were told never to sweep the dirt out of the house at night, never to give anyone from outside salt at night or break mirrors as that would bring seven years of bad luck.

Peter would test these ideas without mother's knowledge. He would sweep out the dirt at night, and then sit down waiting for some bad luck to happen. He would call out to passers-by in the yard and hand them salt and wait for a result. But with mirrors there was a problem. There was no mirror to break. Instead he had a chat with mother about the seven years of bad luck. The way he put it was, 'Ma, what about the man who makes mirrors? He must break some and he is still in business.' That did keep her thinking.

We did our washing and bathing in our bigger room. In wintertime we had a bola fire, fashioned out of a four-gallon oil drum, to warm up the tank and prepare hot water. A small tin of water was carefully placed on the bola.

My sisters were not as methodical and careful as mother in preparing hot water for bathing. One day Darley had prepared the bathwater for herself. First she poured the boiling water into the galvanized bath, then she went to the outside tap to get a tin of cold water. Whilst she was out Daso came charging into the room from playing outside. He tumbled into the bath of boiling water. He was rushed to hospital with serious burns. Darley got quite a few clips around the ears.

Another time we were sitting around the bola. Daso stubbornly chose a high rickety chair and rocked in it. He toppled on to the bola. By now Daso was a familiar figure at the General Hospital. The hospital was a long way away with a very poor public transport system.

Our mother, who was illiterate, had a good knowledge of home remedies, partly from the tradition of village life in India brought to South Africa by her aunt and uncle. The added knowledge was from the other Indian mothers in the neighbourhood. A lot of it was based on ginger, garlic, cloves, cinnamon and turmeric. She had a variety of ointments, tablets, emulsions, iodine and bandages, cough mixtures, laxatives and the dreaded castor oil. Most of these medicines were well out of date. The stock of the miscellaneous items was in a medicine chest, which was actually a knocked-up box with compartments and leather-hinged doors.

Whenever one of us got ill, mother would treat us with home remedies of something from her collection of drugs. She would bring out the 'kusen salts' (kruschen salts), 'fixin syrup' (syrup of figs) and the 'cardliver oil' (cod liver oil). Constipation was easy to handle. We would be woken up early and given a tablespoon of castor oil. A milder purgative was 'Absent'

(Epsom) salts. There was a joke around the yard, 'Absence makes the heart grow fonder, but "absent salt" makes it disappear.'

She knew what was poisonous and what was not. One evening one of us took ill and mother asked Darley to bring some kind of powder. Darley went to the medicine chest with the candle and returned with something. When mother took the little packet she scolded Darley, 'Do you want to kill your brother with poison? Can't you read?' Mother hurriedly left her bed for the medicine chest and in the dark she picked out the non-poisonous packet of powder.

Of all the young ones in our household I was the one most prone to stomach bugs which led to diarrhoea and vomiting. This would last for a couple of days, leaving me weak. The one thing that seemed to work was *rasam* soup. The other was the constant love and affection she gave me.

Once there was a bout of diarrhoea which seemed to have worried her. She sent for one of her close friends for help. They gave me the usual home remedy treatment. I heard them talking in Tamil. They said that my guts had fallen out of position and that had worsened the diarrhoea. My mother took out one of her sarees and doubled it lengthwise. I was put in the middle, my mother at one end and this 'aunty' at the other. They picked up the saree and gently rolled me from one end to the other while at the same time singing Tamil lullabies. That apparently settled me and the diarrhoea stopped. My guts were put right.

Most of the time we went without shoes. We would come home with cuts and bruises from broken glass, nails, tins and wood splinters. This was generally attended to by our sisters. Once Peter did not realize that a piece of glass had got embedded in his foot. After some days he complained of pain. He had a fever and a swelling full of pus. Our mother told an old friend of hers. He asked her to prepare a compound of garlic and some sort of seeds. She was also to heat some oil and have some bandages ready.

He told her that what he was going to do would be painful but only for a few moments. She and a sister were to hold Peter down. All this was discussed quietly in Tamil and my sisters understood. Peter's foot was raised and the old friend made an incision in the swelling and pressed his hand around the foot. The hot oil with the compound was poured into the incision. Peter yelled and the bandage was quickly wrapped around. The fever came down. By the next morning he was unbandaged and a piece of glass came out.

Talking to medical friends years later, I learnt that being gently rolled in the saree and hearing the lullabies had the effect of settling me psychologically. The saree and the songs became my safety net. But in Peter's case apparently the operation was not necessary. The pus was a sign that left untouched it would have naturally rejected the piece of glass. We agreed that with the lack of resources, poverty and lack of knowledge, poor people did what they thought best.

We still retain some of the home remedies and some of the medicinal qualities in certain dishes. The most popular is *rasam* soup. This wonder drink was good for diarrhoea, constipation, colds, fever and for men to clear their hangover.

Mother was quite enterprising. She would buy a box of tomatoes, a bag of potatoes or green beans and a fair-sized snook. She would portion out enough for home use. The rest was put into enamel bowls for us to sell from door to door in the neighbourhood. In this way she recouped her capital investment and came off with a small profit each week.

The actual purchasing of vegetables and the making of our furniture was done by a family friend whom we called Lingam Thata. *Thata* means 'grandfather' in Tamil, and for a while we really thought he was our grandfather. Each time some old person turned up we were to call them grandfather or grandmother. The younger adults were called aunts and uncles. Those below them were either big brothers or sisters. Though we knew them not to be relatives, we dared not call them by their names.

We heard that Lingam Thata was a passive resister with Gandhi and was thrice imprisoned and thrice deported to India. To know someone had been in jail was considered bad, so we did not talk about it. Many years later we realized how heroic Lingam Thata was.

There was another Thata. He was called Nanthe Thata, crab grandfather. His speciality was catching river crabs, which he brought alive to our doorstep in hessian bags. His hands were almost White from the clawing he got from the crabs. Mother made a strong delicious curry from them.

One evening mother bought some crabs and placed them in a paraffin box. She went to the kitchen to prepare some boiling water for killing the crabs. Whilst she was busy she heard the tin of crabs topple over. The crabs scampered all over the room. Mother got us to the kitchen and went to the room to retrieve the crabs. As we stood waiting in the kitchen we heard a great yell. We rushed in to see her on her knees screaming in agony. A huge crab which she had tried to remove from under the bed had his pincers firmly around her fingers. Relief came when one of my sisters whacked the crab with a broomstick. The crabs were all retrieved and duly prepared for a sumptuous meal. We ate in silence until mother broke out in a fit of laughter. She said she was foolish in the way she went looking for the crabs.

Generally we bought our meat from the local Muslim butcher. On occasion we ventured into town or the Newtown market to the White-owned butcher shops. At these butcher shops there were the usual separate queues for White and Black people. Under the trestles were galvanized baths with notices saying 'Boys' Meat' and 'Dogs' Meat'. The 'Boys' Meat' was for the African domestic servants and the 'Dogs' Meat' was for the White people's pets and guard dogs. The dogs' meat was clearly of better quality than that for the domestic servants. We bought some of the dogs' meat. We noticed Africans handing in notes from their madams saying, 'Please hand bearer x pounds of particular meat and a separate supply of dogs' meat.' Thus they came off with better meat.

Similarly we sampled the dog biscuits from the department store. They, too, proved to be of a better quality. Quite often we bought packets of broken biscuits. The White assistants on occasion were quite generous, they would put lots of the finest and unbroken biscuits into our threepenny bags.

It was not unusual to see a notice in the classified section of a newspaper, 'Dog for sale. This dog can smell a native.' This idea put out by Whites was picked up as true by some Coloureds and Indians.

Once we were playing football in a quiet street in Westage, an area adjacent to Ferreirastown. My brother Peter went to retrieve the football, which had landed in the grounds of a private company. The African watchman grabbed Peter, took him to the police depot a block away[4] and handed him over to a White policeman.

Someone raced off to inform our mother in a house where she was visiting. She and her friends hurried to the depot. There she asked for an explanation why Peter was being held, since he was under twelve years old and had not done anything wrong. The policeman became abrupt and aggressive towards our mother. He then reached for his baton and threatened to hit her.

At that moment a man appeared. He was known to us. He was a cousin of Shanti Naidoo. The man was Govindasamy, whose father was a contemporary of M.K. Gandhi, who led the first passive resistance campaign. He was outraged at the attempt by the White policeman to assault our mother and threatened him that if he hit our mother he would deal with him.

The policeman put back his baton. Instead he marched Peter to the Marshall Square police station, with our mother and some of her friends and us trooping behind. The desk sergeant asked why the little boy was brought in. The policeman said Peter had trespassed on private property to take a football back. The sergeant was annoyed, and told the policeman to let Peter go. He asked our mother to take Peter home.

The sight of our mother about to be beaten was very disturbing. It never left me.

4

Wartime

When the Second World War broke out, a lot of the lads in our neighbourhood enlisted for service. They were camped in an area called Crown Mines. This military camp was only for Coloureds and Indians. We heard that in Cape Town there was a Coloured and Malay corps. The Africans of course had their own corps.

Some Sundays we would go there in the hope we would see the soldiers from our area. At various points of the camp and at the main gate there were soldiers on guard duty. They marched in style and when they stopped at some point, or changed guard duty, it was quite a performance. When they came to a halt, they stomped their feet and switched arms. It was not a rifle they carried but wooden staves, the sort used for pickaxes. The government did not allow these soldiers to carry arms. Those who were sent to North Africa and Italy were stretcher-bearers, ambulance drivers or batmen to do the domestic chores for the White officers.

Two men in our neighbourhood reached the rank of sergeant-major, the highest rank for a black man. Another on demobilization got a bursary for a university degree by correspondence. The Africans got bicycles.

Some of our neighbours encouraged us to collect scrap iron. They said it was for the war effort. They told us that tanks, bullets and guns could be made from scrap iron. We collected enthusiastically, especially when the local Communist Party (CP) arranged with the local cinema for a show where admission was by a collection of jam tins.

The war was a regular subject of conversation. Very few people had radios. Most of the information came from newspapers. We heard how clever the Germans were and how good they were at war. Similar stories were told about the Japanese. The Japanese were showing the world that they were as good as the Europeans and would soon drive them out of Asia. Some were excited that the Japanese were near India. Some people thought the Japanese would come to South Africa. My eldest sister Chella said that as a matter of fact it was written in the Bible that one day the 'yellow race' would rule the world. That notion was fairly widespread in our locality.

Amongst the many friends I had in the neighbourhood was John Aaronson. He was plucky and daring in pinching fruit and cakes from the shops. He had a bullying streak, though never towards me. One of his unpleasant habits was teasing people beyond the power of endurance. He, a Coloured, was especially nasty towards Africans.

One evening he entered an Indian corner shop. The shopkeeper employed an African cleaner who also acted as watchman. John taunted the African in ugly racial terms, one of which was 'Hey, you blerry stinking *Kaffir*.' This went on for some time until the man snapped and lunged at John, who moved swiftly out of range and fled. The cleaner gave chase and John darted out like a buck. He ran in and out between parked cars still laughing and calling out further taunts. He ran into an oncoming car and was killed instantly.

We went to his funeral with sorrow and anger, because we thought he was foolish. The African labourer went into hiding, as some of the older Coloured youth were keen to deal with him. Fortunately John's parents accepted that their son was foolish in his pranks.

The taunting of Africans by Coloureds seemed to bring some kind of delight. But not so one Sunday morning when a couple of Africans, off-duty domestic workers, had come out of a *shebeen*. A group of Coloureds baited them. They retaliated by bringing down their *knobkerries* on any non-African passerby.

They went on the rampage. We were sitting on our haunches around our mother on our doorstep when the two infuriated Africans raised their sticks. Our mother looked up and was very calm. They then lowered their sticks to their sides and walked away.

As children we were all infected by the notion of colour that overwhelmed our lives. Racial terms of abuse like 'Bushy', 'Coolie' or '*Kaffir*' were of common usage. The worst insult was to call someone a *Kaffir* or to suggest that one's colour, hair or facial features were that of an African. It seemed at that time like harmless fun to racially insult one another.

I was often puzzled when a husband and wife who lived across the road from us got into an argument. The Indian husband would shout out aloud to his Malay wife, 'You blerry Malay dog' or '*Boesman*'. The wife would respond, 'You fucking dem koolie.' They continued living with each other and had a string of children. The slanging matches never abated.

In both Ferreirastown and Fordsburg there were some junior schools. The city council provided one for Indians and a separate one for Coloureds. There was a private school for the Lebanese and one for the Chinese.

For the Indians and Coloureds the schools were quite run down. As the Lebanese community dwindled, we got their school. Similarly, as the White working class dwindled, the Coloureds got their school, ironically called *Die Goedehoop Skool* (the Good Hope School), most likely named after one of the three ships that sailed into Table Bay in 1652 with Jan van Riebeeck on *Die Goede Hoop*. The Indian school I attended in Ferreirastown was made up of mainly Indian children but a lot of Malay and Coloured children were smuggled in as Indian.

Among my playmates was a girl called Trixie. She was of African and White parentage. Trixie could have been taken for a White girl. We used to go to catechism and to church. Once a year we attended the Corpus Christi procession. The same forms of racial categories were applied. On one occasion, as we were getting ready for the procession, a couple of White nuns came towards us. They asked Trixie to come out. She was steered to the African contingent. We constantly exchanged perplexed glances.

We had quite a number of Catholic families in our neighbourhood. We could attend the cathedral in the city, a church in a White working-class suburb bordering Fordsburg, or the Maronite church in Fordsburg. Assigned to look after the local Indian and Coloured flock in our area was an Italian priest, Father Abrahama, whom the local women came to adore. He was strikingly handsome and relished the attention he got.

Once a week Father Abrahama came to the house of a prominent Indian family, where he conducted catechism classes. My mother suggested we attend the classes, thinking we might learn something. At the first class Father Abrahama asked me, 'Who made you?' I said 'My mother and father.' He slapped me across the face shouting, 'No! No! God made you.' Holding my hands ready to slap me again he asked, 'Who made you?' I safely said, 'God'. Had he not slapped me I might have believed God did make me. I disliked him and refused to attend catechism classes after that.

There was talk that Father Abrahama was frequenting that house more than once a week. The householder was a beautiful woman and so were her daughters, and with the women swooning around this priest the allegations seemed plausible. Father Abrahama's reputation seemed to have preceded him when he was assigned to the Coloured township of Coronationville. Years later when I worked in a furniture factory, a Coloured worker told me about a certain Father Abrahama. I was curious to know what he was up to. The Casanova Father got into a spot of bother. He was caught in a compromising position with one of his parishioners by the woman's husband. In anger the wife got a wallop, the Father a knock and the altar a kick. Father Abrahama was banished to Australia, where my co-worker hoped the Aboriginal women would be safe.

With the war on there were groups of people coming into our neighbourhood. These people, some Indians, Africans and Whites, were carrying placards and handing out handbills. It said the people should not join the war, we should get our freedom first. There were some banners about the CP. We were puzzled. There were soldiers walking about and we were collecting scrap iron for the war efforts. Only a handful of people listened to the speakers. A few stray dogs came and smelled each other's behinds, peed and walked off. Those who listened seemed to be friends of the speaker and at various times they would say 'Hear, hear'.

One afternoon I was playing in our yard when a friend came to tell me something was happening at the Osrin cinema. He said there were lots of Indians shouting and getting angry and, more unbelievable, there were more cars than they had ever seen in the streets.

We went out to see the unusual throng of people and cars. We saw groups of people arguing, waving their hands and frequently mentioning the names of S.M. Nana and Dr Yusuf Dadoo. Then we heard the noises increase. There were shouts, screams and bottles, bricks and pieces of wood being hurled. We heard people saying, 'It's the Kajee gang', and the name of someone called 'German West'.

It seemed that name struck terror. 'German West' was actually a Somali who was not from German West Africa but from East Africa. He was part of the Kajee gang, it was said. Shortly thereafter we heard anguished screams. A man was being helped out of the cinema. His stomach was ripped open. We fled in terror to hide behind parked cars.

Then we heard the name of Dr Dadoo being mentioned again and again. Suddenly, someone said, 'There he is. That's Dr Dadoo.' We had known of White doctors; never an Indian. Seeing an Indian doctor was strange. He was dressed in an open-neck cream shirt, a sports jacket, grey trousers and brown shoes, for some reason called golfers. He was tall and good looking. He walked hurriedly accompanied by a group of men towards a crowd around the injured man.

I had never seen that many Indians at any one time, and never that many wearing *kofias* of black and maroon. Apart from the women in the nearby streets, who were there more out of curiosity, the people at the gathering were only men.

5

Fordsburg

One evening a man arrived at our house. He was tall. He wore a black suit and cloak and carried a fancy walking-stick. He was a Bengali friend of my mother, whose name was Prawasi and was said to be a Brahmin. He was a bookkeeper and a palmist. For this work he called himself 'Professor Prawasi'.

He came quite often, bringing sweetmeats. He smoked cigars, sometimes switching to *ganja*, and drank only whisky. We heard from bits of conversation between him, my mother, older sister and brother Ramsamy that he had come to arrange for the marriage of Ramsamy to a woman in Louis Trichardt (now Polokwane) in Northern Transvaal. She was the daughter of a well-known farmer by the name of Tommy Narsoo.

A date was agreed and my mother, sister and Ramsamy set off for Louis Trichardt. Ramsamy had been there before to visit the Narsoo family. The marriage took place, with Prawasi acting as the Brahmin priest. It sounded as if it was quite a social event in the town.

They returned to a newly rented house in Hubert Street, a couple of blocks away from where we had been living. It had three bedrooms. We had a room, as did the sisters and mother. Ramsamy and his bride Letchmee had their own room. Living in this house was sheer luxury. Apart from being spacious, it had a bathroom and a kitchen and toilet. This was paradise compared to No. 7 Main Street.

Sadly, our comfort and luxury were short lived. Ramsamy and his wife decided to move out. Letchmee was not happy living with the family. Darley's salary was barely sufficient to sustain a family of seven.

My mother and sisters went house-hunting. Once again it was Lingham Thata who came to our aid. He found a small house in Fordsburg. It had two rooms and a tiny kitchen, with an outside tap and toilet to be shared with three other families. The property had a corner shop.

This property was owned by the Chaitowiz family. We saw a lot of Ikee, Mr America and the painter. As usual the drains were periodically blocked and the toilet spillage flowed through the narrow yard on to the pavement. Then sadly 'Oubaas' died, and with him our pennies.

Fordsburg had been one of the strongholds of the White miners. It came into the news in 1922 when the White workers went on strike against the mining companies, which wanted many of the jobs transferred to Africans at a lower rate of pay. The strike was brutally suppressed by General Smuts. The workers were shot, assaulted, imprisoned and bombarded. Smuts had cannons placed on the Hillbrow Hills to bombard the homesteads of the people in Fordsburg; all this in the interest of the Randlords, the capitalists of the mining industry. The major weakness of the strike was its failure to draw in the black miners in solidarity.

In 1927 the White workers of Fordsburg returned an MP from the Whites-only Labour Party. The 1929 worldwide economic depression took its toll on all workers in South Africa. Thousands of Whites were impoverished in the countryside and poured into the cities. As for the black people, their plight was worsened by class and racial oppression.

By the early 1930s most White people were moving out of Fordsburg for suburbs with better housing and civic amenities mainly in the westerly part of Johannesburg. Soon Coloureds, Indians and Africans were renting the vacated houses, which were owned by Jewish landlords. The houses were still in reasonable condition and many had electricity. There was an infrastructure of street lighting, pavements, tarred roads, a sewage system, two parks and a cinema for Whites only despite a fast-dwindling White population.

Fordsburg was the nearest black suburb to the giant Newtown Market, so there was always a flow of people heading for the market, some from as far afield as Soweto and Sophiatown. It was very much like District Six in Cape Town. There was a similarity in appearance – the little houses, the corner shops run by Indians and Chinese, several Muslim-run butcher shops, and a parade of spice and sweetmeat, vegetable and fruit shops.

Always there were the beautiful smells of food and incense wafting through the air. Sometimes one encountered the smell of *skokiaan* from a few backyards, and the smell of *dagga* was often in the air. On weekends the locality had Indian and jazz music and some *opskit* music blaring out from the radiograms.

Our community was made up of Indians, Coloureds, Maronites, a sprinkling of Africans and some Chinese families. There was a fair amount of buzz from people going to the mosque, to a Hindu temple tucked away in an old house, or to a couple of Christian churches, one of which was mainly for the Maronite community.

Amongst the Indians who moved into Fordsburg were people whose parents were involved with M.K. Gandhi, the Non-European United Front or the Nationalist Bloc, a left-wing faction led by Dr Yusuf Dadoo in the Transvaal Indian Congress (TIC). These included the Asvats, Cachalias, the T.N. Naidoo clan, the Ali family, the Baroochis and the Nagdees.

The advent of the Second World War saw once again the rise of militancy in Fordsburg. The war in Europe and Asia infused the progressive movements. Many of the sons and daughters of the previous campaigns were now in the forefront of the latest outbreak. This new surge was for the fight for national liberation, socialism and to improve the quality of life for the hard-pressed and racially discriminated-against people. The left-wing element in the TIC captured the leadership of the organization. The CP declared an open space in Fordsburg as the Red Square.[5] The square became a place for lots of meetings (in the Natal Indian Congress [NIC] the anti-segregation council did the same where an open space in Durban was also dubbed the Red Square).

In June 1946 the progressive leaders of the South African Indian Congress (SAIC) launched a passive resistance campaign. Within months the African miners came out on strike with a ten-shillings-a-day demand. The strike was suppressed by police brutality. Eight miners were shot dead and hundreds injured.

We lived in Avenue Road. The streets were tree-lined, the roads tarred, there were pavements of stone slabs and there were street lights. The house did not have electricity. For a time we were the only Indian family amidst mainly Coloured and a few African families. Some of the Coloureds said they were Malays. Many of these people were dark and made it known they were not 'natives'. They spoke mainly Afrikaans. Some of them passed themselves off as White people. We could tell immediately they were not, as their accents did not match that of the Whites.

Those who looked like Africans were often stopped for passes and they were at pains to convince the police that they were not 'natives' for fear of being hauled off to prison. These darker people were also rejected socially by the Coloureds. They were at the receiving end of racial insults. Yet the Africans called them *Boesman*.

Several months later an Indian Moslem family moved in next door to us. They also acquired the corner shop. The father was known variously as Ali Bhoulai, Mia or Mr Mee. The eldest son, Essop, had a violent streak towards Africans, whom he would not hesitate to brutally assault with the flimsiest excuse.

The father looked like a rat, with protruding ears and narrow eyes and narrow fine teeth. He also had a violent streak, especially towards children other than his. He showed open contempt for us, whom he considered to be 'Madrasi', little knowing my folks did not came from Madras, and he seemed unaware that a lot of Tamils were also Moslem.

This family had an intense dislike of dogs. Our pet dog and that of our neighbours were always being booted by Mia and Essop. One morning we found one of the dogs with an eye gouged out. We knew it was Ali who did it. The dog was treated by my mother but eventually we had it destroyed.

I soon found many Indians just as affected by race issues. They also had gradings amongst them. This was prevalent among Moslems, Hindus, and Christians. Whilst most Indians thought themselves better than Coloureds, they did not hold back from marrying Coloured women, so it was fairly common to see such mixed unions. There were hardly any instances of a Coloured man married to an Indian woman. As for African men married to Indian women, it was unheard of.

The locality still had pockets of poor White families. They kept apart from the black people. There were some Chinese families, mainly shopkeepers and runners of gambling dens. The Maronites were somewhat scattered; a number were concentrated between Fordsburg and Mayfair. They had a string of houses in Park Drive. Every house in the street was a *shebeen*. Some years later in jest I called Park Drive the Gaza Strip. The name stuck. It even featured in the novel *The Golden City* by Enver Carim.[6]

In Fordsburg we soon got to know Indians in the Catholic and Anglican churches, Hindus and Moslems. My interest and attendance in the Catholic faith went into decline by the time I was thirteen years old. Father Abrahama's face slap and the treatment of Trixie contributed to it. The final departure came when I questioned the youth leader of our Catholic group. I asked her to explain why we were not allowed to sit in front at church, or anywhere we chose. Why should Indians and Coloureds sit at the back and Africans have to stand behind?

I could see her annoyance. She said there were no restrictions. We could sit wherever we wanted to, but 'You will feel very uncomfortable'. I did not accept that and pointed out that the Maronites also treated us the same way as the White churches and yet they were 'Asiatics'.

Instead I continued going with my brothers and sister Violet to the Hindu temple in Melrose in the northern White suburb, a fashionable White neighbourhood. We were most welcome there. On special religious days the events were quite spectacular, with food, music, incense and *kavadi*. This was a ceremony when men and women took vows and fasted, and on the day of the festival would go into a trance and waltz until they collapsed, when soothsayers would revive them. The worshippers would then bathe in the nearby stream and we all joined in.

The festival event at the Melrose temple was something to look forward to. The women wore colourful sarees, the men were in suits and the children were spruced up in fine clothes. The boys looked as if they were sweating, but it was the excess of coconut oil seeping down from their heads. The other attraction for us was the stream we could splash in, where there were lots of garden plots. The Chinese were the market gardeners. They grew the greens. The aroma was from the mint, parsley and *dhaniya* (coriander) cultivation.

Topping the attraction was the delicious vegetarian food that was served after the religious programme was completed. The favourite was the sweet and sour rice, followed by sago pudding and papadoms (large circular pieces of thin, spiced bread made from ground lentils and fried in oil). All this delicious food was served on banana leaves. When the feasting was over there would be an auction. The money was for the temple. Well-groomed men competed as to who would lay out the largest sum of money. There were usually only a handful of people who had the money. Their wives and female relatives flaunted their jewellery.

Leading the bidding was a wealthy businessman by the name of 'Fatty' K. Thambi. He was bloated, and sweated in his tight-fitting suit. As he went higher in his bidding, he looked like he was going to burst any moment as his eyes widened. His wife was also plump. She wore a garland of gold sovereigns. Whenever she got up from her stool she looked as if she was going to topple over from the weight of the gold jewellery.

At one of the festivals a group of us decided we would not follow the devotees to the well for the final part of the ritual. We had noticed people leaving coins in the oil lamps in the temple. We stayed behind and when everyone was away we helped ourselves to the coins. Someone said that if we took the coins we would be struck dead. After a quick discussion we decided we would not clear all the coins. Besides, the priest would later return to collect the coins and would discover what we had done. We scampered off to the stream and waited in suspense in case one of us dropped dead. Our expectations declined with each passing day. We of course dared not tell anyone else for fear if the gods did not get us the priest or a temple official would skin us.

I noticed at these gatherings that several families I knew were not invited. They belonged to the so-called pariah sections of the community. It was an accepted norm that they could not attend the service at the Melrose temple. The pariahs went to their own little temples in backyards or in an old dilapidated house converted into a temple.

We were never ostracized at the Melrose temple. We were always invited to all the social events of the community, which was mainly of South Indian origin. The people referred to us as the children of the Iyer family. The Iyers of India were from the Brahmin caste. As my mother had been married to a Brahmin, we seem to have qualified. Nobody seemed to have known that our father was a Catholic from Pondicherry.

My mother hardly went to church, neither did she frequent the temple. She never forced any religious instruction on us. She was wise enough to know when people were phoney in their religious conduct. She kept some Christian pictures, and Indian brassware used for special occasions related to certain Hindu customs in the house.

The neighbour on the left side of our house was Willy the herbalist, variously known as the *nyanga*, the *mutiman* or medicine man and sometimes ridiculously called 'the witch doctor'. Willy was a Venda, coming from Duiwelskloof.[7] He was a pleasant and warm friend.

I was always curious about the way he prepared his compound of skins, fats, oils, and concoctions from roots and plants, which he bottled or placed in the horns of animals and pouches. These were sold to a steady stream of customers claiming to suffer from all kinds of maladies. Some wanted treatment for luck with jobs, men for problems with women, or women for problems with men. Some wanted to 'fix' someone out of jealousy. Many came with medical problems which the White doctors, they felt, could not treat.

His other skill as a *nyanga* was fortune-telling. This was known as 'throwing the bones'. These were the bones of different kinds of animals, which he kept in a pouch made of animal skin. Willy would blow a couple of times on the pouch and throw the bones on an animal skin. He would then develop a story from the layout of the bones, much to the astonishment of his client. This was a popular request. He would earn five shillings a session.

Whilst Willy's clients were mostly Africans, there was the odd Indian who slunk in through our backyard or sometimes knocked on our door instead of Willy's. Some of the Indians frowned on Africans, so when we discovered an Indian client of Willy's we would ask, 'Are you looking for the witch doctor?' We could see the discomfort on their faces.

Sometimes I would go with Willy on one of his evening calls. I would carry his bag. One evening he asked me to accompany him on a visit in the neighbourhood. When we arrived there we realized that this particular house was that of a well-known Indian Catholic family. When the householder answered the door, Willy was received. Willy was a large fellow and the householder did not see me behind him. As Willy walked in I followed immediately after him. The householder looked a bit startled. She asked Willy what I was doing there. In his charming way he told her that I was merely carrying his medicine bag.

She then whispered to Willy and Willy said I should sit on the couch. The woman led him to a room. The door was ajar and I noticed another woman propped up in bed. She was the younger sister of the householder. I remembered the talk in the neighbourhood that this woman was to have been married to a man from Durban. Just before the marriage the man fled, leaving the woman with a nervous breakdown. The family had gone to great lengths to get her treated medically, with no apparent success.

So that evening they were going to try out Willy's talents. Willy asked the householder to leave the room. He shut the door. After some time there was considerable coughing. Later he opened the door of the bedroom and some smoke billowed out. The woman went into another bout of coughing. Willy called for the householder, who hastened to see her sister.

This time the door was left open. I heard Willy say, 'You see these seeds? Someone has tricked your sister so that she does not get married.' What Willy had actually done was burn some roots on a tray and place it under her nose. He asked her to inhale deeply. The smoke almost knocked her out and Willy had sneaked some seeds on to the tray. Both sisters were convinced of Willy's talents and for the services rendered Willy earned five pounds, which was a considerable amount of money at the time.

One day I told Willy that the teacher was caning me quite regularly. Could he find a way to stop the beating? Willy took some fat from a horn and said I should keep it in my trouser pockets to stop the beating. Some days later I called on Willy to tell him that the beatings had not stopped. If anything they were more painful; besides my pockets were smelly. Willy burst out laughing. He said no magic would help me. I should get my schoolwork right. I improved my schoolwork and the caning was reduced.

Behind Ali Bhoulai's shop was another occupied by three Africans. One, Brown, was a cobbler; another, Hamilton, a tailor; and the third, Themba, was a dry-cleaning agent. Brown did not seem to do much business. He was always engaged in heated conversations with a string of African deliverymen who left their bicycles outside the shop for a chat and a mug of tea. Neither did Hamilton do much tailoring. He spent a lot of free time writing music. His income came in at weekends when 'Hamilton and His Music Makers', written across the bass drum, played in crummy, smoke-filled and overcrowded dance halls converted from rundown warehouses or churches. Hamilton played the saxophone in the combo. Jimmy, a Coloured, had a very wide cleft chin with an equally divided moustache which did not seem to cover his teeth and gums. He played the banjo with gusto.

Some Sunday afternoons we accompanied Hamilton to the dance hall. One dance hall that was popular was at the former Maronite church in Diagonal Street. This was the hub for the African bus and tram commuters. It was known as 'the native bus stop'. To this hall came the domestic and manual workers in their Sunday gladrags. Some wore bowler hats, carried walking sticks and on their breast pockets displayed the British ensign or badges of the king and queen. They would strut around the hall to the beat of the music as others would applaud, 'Hey British Empire'. The dancers only wanted music with a fast beat and the occasional waltz. There were not many women, so those that were there would dance to exhaustion. Many of the men danced on their own. A dance session could last for three to four hours. It was from Hamilton that I learned about jazz and on Hamilton's gramophone was introduced to the leading performers.

Themba was the most astute of the three. He was disciplined and hard-working, putting several days and evenings into his dry-cleaning agency. He started with a push-bike, then on to a motorbike and later a car. He was an elegant dresser and had a polished command of Tswana and English.

Themba's customers were mainly clerks and municipal workers. Some days and evenings we accompanied him to the various municipal compounds to deliver the clean clothes. These were compounds and hostels mainly for the municipal workers and some that housed workers for factories and construction companies. They were relatively free in that they could move around in certain parts of the city, provided they had their passes and did not stay out beyond the daily curfew time of 9 pm. Admission to the compound was strictly controlled. The *indunas* (security guards) knew Themba and so he did not have to show a permit.

Sometimes we got into the mining compounds, which were within the precincts of the mines. The miners were confined in these huge complexes. They could only move about in the complex and down the mine shafts. The only glimpse they had of Johannesburg was when they alighted at a railway station some miles away from the city centre and were escorted to the compounds by the *mapoisa*, the companies' private security guards. The guards carried *knobkerries* and *sjamboks*. They had a reputation of being ruthless. Most of the miners seemed very young and wore blankets. It was said that they came from the 'native reserves' in remote parts of the country. We had no idea what and where the reserves were.

One of the largest compounds was in the British-owned Crown Mines. The other was the Robinson Deep. I saw the kind of conditions these men lived in. The dormitories had concrete bunk beds. There were communal kitchens, toilets and showers, and a football field, which at times was used for tribal dancing. There was a zoo, giant canteens, a hospital, post office and an open-air cinema and, most important of all, the beer hall, where miners could spend time drinking *skokiaan*. Sunday afternoons were also a treat for the White tourists who came to see 'the natives in the raw', which included a display of tribal dancing.

Some of us were able to get into the compounds on the pretext of helping with deliveries or helping some of the Indian flower-sellers who were going to the White miners' married quarters. We could only make eye contact with the miners since there was a language barrier. It was always said one can speak with one's eyes, which happened as they broke into smiles. Perhaps this was their first sighting of Indians. Our parents never knew about our venturing into those prohibited and risky areas.

The contrast of lifestyles was seen on weekdays when I would go with some friends with a pushcart selling flowers to the White householders living in the special-quartered cottages.

Sometimes Brown asked us to make the tea in the afternoons. There was a lot of animated conversation in Xhosa, Tswana, English and Afrikaans. We were sent out to buy the newspaper. Hamilton would read aloud the items on the war situation. Through this we learned about the faraway places in Europe, Africa and Asia.

This led my curiosity to deepen. After school I would go off to the steps of City Hall. Displayed there were two very large boards showing the theatres of war, in Europe on one, and in Asia on the other. In the course of the day a man would come to shift the positions of the contending armies. I found this exercise most fascinating. So Hamilton and the display boards sustained my interests.

It was at this site that there was a recruiting depot. One day I asked the uniformed woman whether I could join the army. She smiled and suggested I should come back when I was eighteen. By the time I got to fifteen the war was over.

At Willy's shop I met someone he described as 'a home boy'. This was a Mr Dipoko. He was a foreman in a brushware factory in the neighbourhood. He looked more like a scholar in his fine-lensed spectacles, and had excellent command of the English language and knowledge about the African trade union movement. It was through Dipoko that I and my brother Peter learned about the sinking of the SS *Mendi* in 1917 off the Isle of Wight[8]. As a consequence we attended the annual memorial service held at the Bantu men's sports ground in Loveday Street. The service was chaired by Dr A.B.

Xuma. Our presence caused a mild stir since we were the only Indians present.

Soon after we moved into Fordsburg the kids on the block taunted me and at times threatened to work me over. One evening they lay in wait for me. I ran back into the house and returned with a butter knife. I shouted, 'Now come and get me', waving the knife, which shone in the darkness. The gang scampered in all directions. By the next day I had established a reputation as a tough guy. Some of the lads came to shake my hand. Others were still peeved and did not accept me. I was challenged to fight. I beat my opponent, who cried hysterically and vowed he would kill me. His friends sneered at him. I was accepted and was regarded as the leader.

We roamed the open spaces, checked out derelict buildings, went to the cinemas by collecting bottles and hessian bags to sell for the fares and tickets, and pinched fruit and cakes from shops. Some evenings we scaled the fences to play in one of the two places reserved for White people. The park was hardly ever used except by old down-and-out Whites who used the benches. Once we entered the park with saws and hammers to break the locks and chains on the swings and merry-go-round. Here we played for a couple of hours.

The following day the White park attendant, whom we called Parkee, would be on his bike followed by a pick-up van cruising parts of Fordsburg in search of the vandals. We made sure we did not look like the sort that caused damage. Parkee was a scary-looking person. He was thin and tall, with sunken eyes and jowls. His head swivelled as if it was loosely screwed on, and his eyes shifted like a chameleon's. He looked disgusted.

After some years there were no White people left in the area to use the park. Even the old and lonely died out. The only White settlement, of poor Whites, was some mile and a half away on an estate called Octavia Hill. Their nearest park was derelict and had no attraction for us. Finally the municipality gave up the Fordsburg park for a municipal bus parking lot, rather than give it to us.

The only other park left in Johannesburg was several miles away. This was Joubert Park. We were only allowed to walk through the park. We were not allowed to sit on the benches. The African women childminders were allowed to sit on the lawn. The fame of Joubert Park was that it also housed an art gallery. We never saw any Blacks venture into it. We did. There was no law as such to prevent us. The Blacks teeming past the gallery were more concerned about earning a crust. The gallery did not seem to attract White working-class people either.

One of the other public places we ventured into was the Transvaal

Museum above the Whites-only public library. The museum displays were mostly about White people's clothes, pictures, furniture and artefacts depicting their pioneering days and struggles against the African people. Their paintings were of heroic Boer men and women in their *voortrekker* garb and oxcarts, slaughtering the blacks, and items belonging to that 'treacherous' Zulu chief Shaka. There was a painting of the battle of Blood River.

All this aroused an instinctive anger in us. We cut some of the Boer women's period clothes and broke some of the samples of what were supposed to be Shaka's stool. Fortunately the guns and daggers were encased in glass. We would have had no hesitation in stealing them.

6

School

My primary school was opposite our house in Main Street, Fordsburg. It was the Ferreias Indian School. The day my young brother Daso and I were admitted we were looked after by a Coloured woman we called Aunty Nelly, a loveable, large, dark woman, whose husband, a Mr Wilson, was said to be a proper Englishman and not just a local White man.

We were brought before a teacher for admissions. Aunty Nelly said we were Joseph's children. I never knew we had such a name. The teacher dutifully put down with great difficulty our Indian forenames of Navarajh and Thasarajh, followed with a flourish of Joseph. When we had a piece of paper in our hands we could not make out the Indian names, but Joseph was clearly distinct. I only discovered some years later that it was the name dubbed on my father by the boss of the hotel where he had worked.

Aunty Nelly got her daughter Gloria, whose actual surname was Wilson, into the same school by calling her Gloria Pillay.

Our primary school had several men and women teachers who looked White or fair. The women were heavily powdered, at times leaving darker patches near their necks. When they spoke they did not quite sound like 'Europeans', especially when they spoke to us. It was there I heard the term 'play Whites' in use by my sisters and neighbours. I was curious where these 'play White' teachers lived, since most Indian and some Coloured teachers lived in the same areas as us.

By the time I entered junior school in Market Street, which was still part of the Ferreias Indian School, I discovered that play-White teachers were living in White working-class suburbs. A few were not so fortunate; they had to make do living on the fringe of Fordsburg, bordering on Mayfair where the White workers lived.

At junior school we were sent for woodwork lessons to another part of the school in Main Street. The head of the woodwork school was a Coloured, a Mr Cookman. He had been in charge for many years. His understudy was Dick Ferguson, an active member of the Transvaal Indian and Coloured Teachers Association (TICTA).

The head of both the primary and junior schools was a Mr K.L. Desai. He styled himself as a staunch Hindu, never one for meat, tobacco or alcohol and at the same time a disciplinarian and an unhesitant believer in corporal punishment, which he administered with relish. We called him Hitler because of his looks and manner. His other obsession was grovelling to White people, especially people in authority in the education department, or the mayor and mayoress of the city. Whenever he invited these people around, we were asked to contribute for gifts and garlands. If a White official was retiring we were expected to make higher contributions. I reluctantly gave a penny or two. Then one day we contributed for a gift and were astonished when the senior schools inspector was presented with a huge solid writing desk, as well as a reception and the usual garlands.

Later we heard that the woodwork teacher, Mr Cookman, was retiring. There was no talk of a gift or a reception. This angered us. So a group of us decided to approach the teachers to vent our feelings. We asked for permission to have a collection, which was agreed without the blessing of Desai. We raised enough money for a leather briefcase, which Cookman was quite pleased with.

Several years later a friend of mine qualified as a teacher and was on Desai's staff. He also acted as Desai's personal assistant. One of his functions was to escort Desai to his home. Desai was increasingly getting stoned. From being escorted, he was now being carried home, which was about two blocks away from school. Desai, the staunch Hindu and disciplinarian, died eventually from drug addiction.

On Sunday mornings neatly dressed friendly and polite White people came into the area to collect the children for Sunday school lessons. They would be given coloured religious cards and taught hymns. For the hard-worked mothers in crowded houses this was a boon to get the children off their hands for a couple of hours. Periodically a 'Bible Tent' was set up and a lantern show was presented.

Once there was a 'faith-healing week'. People with physical handicaps and/or ailments would be given special attention. We went one evening to see what was happening. On the platform was a group of White people. Each took a turn telling the people that their problems were due to sin. A list of sins was rattled off. We were assured that, if we gave ourselves to God, we would be cured.

The crowd was asked to kneel and pray. The man leading the prayer had a booming voice. He spoke as if he was in a trance. At the height of the frenzy he asked those using walking sticks or crutches to discard their aids. The crowd stood up amidst a lot of 'Amens' and 'Oh Jesus'. Then the preacher said, 'Open your eyes and walk.' There were cries of joy and one man, our local celebrity drunk, shouted 'I am cured! I am cured!' He thanked the Lord with outstretched arms and immediately keeled over. He was totally drunk. When the preacher and his team started packing up, the ailing people were looking for their walking sticks and crutches.

Apart from the Sunday school there were also the meetings of the CP. These meetings were interesting. The speaker spoke about racial segregation, the pass laws, trade unions and about people fighting for freedom in India, Indonesia and China. They talked quite a lot about the Soviet Union and about a man called Hitler. They described him as a murderer who killed millions of people especially Jews. It was said that if Hitler could be defeated, we black people would get our freedom. They asked the people to support the war.

It was at these meetings we heard the names of Dr Yusuf Dadoo, who was in jail for fighting against the pass laws, Paul Robeson, the Red Army of the Soviet Union, the Red Army of China and the name of Pandit Nehru.

What was unusual about this group of people was its mixture of Indians, Whites, Africans and Coloureds. They were friendly at these meetings and seemed completely at ease the way they spoke to each other. Whilst the meetings were on there were people selling *The Guardian*[9] for a penny and handing out leaflets.

The Sunday CP meetings did not attract a lot of people. There were some students in their university blazers, some drunks, and children wandering in and out, sometimes gaping at the speakers and those Whites present. Stray mongrels would also wander in, sniffing each other's backsides and trying to mount one another until someone would shout *voertsek* ('scram') and give them a kick.

A number of the Party members were people living in the locality or from Ferreirastown or Vrededorp. Many of them wore red ties. The speakers spoke with a lot of anger and gestures. They would ask a question and immediately answer it themselves and there were shouts of 'Hear! Hear!' We soon picked up the chorus and joined in the 'Hear! Hear!' even though we did not quite grasp the point.

Then there was question time. Most of the questions were from the Party members. There were handshakes and laughter. It was here that I saw Ismail Meer and J.N. Singh. They wore university blazers. They were widely spoken of as leaders of the Indian community and were regarded as clever law students.

My interest in what was happening in the country and in the world was being further aroused by some of my school teachers. I noticed some of them also wearing red ties. Amongst themselves they spoke about TICTA, and I saw copies of TICTA bulletins, which carried reports on low wages, poor training facilities and the poor conditions of the schools.

The name that often cropped up in their discussions was that of George Carr. They spoke of him with high regard as a brilliant writer, sportsman, chess player and the first Coloured man in the Transvaal with a BA degree. He wrote short stories for the weekly *Outspan* under another name which the editor assumed was a White man. The educational authorities saw George Carr as a radical and had him transferred to a school in Pietersburg in the Northern Transvaal, some two hundred miles from Johannesburg.

What caught my attention was the appearance of the *Cape Standard.* It was the journal of the Teachers League of South Africa, mainly a Coloured teachers' organization. I was impressed by the layout, the standard of language and the critical way it dealt with race discrimination. Occasionally it carried reports on the Transvaal educational issues.

When I mentioned my interest in the *Cape Standard* to one of my teachers, he looked quite surprised. He asked me whether I would be interested in helping to distribute the paper, which came out fortnightly, to the houses of some of the members in various parts of the suburbs. For this service I got a few shillings.

As I took more interest in TICTA and the *Cape Standard* I did not quite understand why there were separate teachers' unions in the country for Coloureds and Indians and that the Africans had their Transvaal African Teacher's Association. I thought if there was one body then the union would be stronger.

Having heard so much about George Carr I wrote to him raising the question of unity. He wrote back and invited me to take tea so as to discuss the question. I had not realized just how complex it was on account of the numerous laws controlling the lives of the people in each province. The point Carr made was that, given the difficulties of unity, we should not stop trying to improve the conditions of the people in their day-to-day lives.

Whilst I was still increasing my knowledge of the world at war with my regular visits to the City Hall steps, there developed within the Indian community a considerable amount of political activity. This was being generated by the factions within the TIC. There was to be an election meeting on a Sunday at the Bantu men's sports ground. Once again the names of Dr Yusuf Dadoo and S.M. Nana were being bandied about.

On the election day my brother Peter and I went to the sports ground. We were shocked at the vast number of Indians present. We had never seen so many thousands at one time. The crowds were separated by a thick rope.

The supporters of Nana were cordoned off from those of Dadoo in the opposite section. Those supporting Nana appeared to be Muslims, many wearing the fez. There were also a lot of my schoolmates on the Nana side. There was a handful of Tamils, mainly from the C.K. Thambi Naidoo clan. As always 'Fatty' K. Thambi was sweating and looking like he was bursting from his tight double-breasted suit. His equally large wife, this time minus her garland of gold sovereigns, looked like she could do with a giant fan.

On the Dadoo side were Muslims, Hindus and Christians and a noticeable presence of women. Many of the people I recognized were shopkeepers, shop assistants, tailors, teachers – several from my school – and the communists I saw on the Red Square. This was a much more friendly and cheerful atmosphere. I was particularly excited when I saw the Reverend B.L. Sigamoney. All the supporters were known as the Nationalist bloc.

Only those over eighteen were entitled to vote. I was thirteen and Peter was fifteen. But that did not deter me from participating in helping the women supporters. The mother of one of the teachers charmingly asked me to get her a bottle of cold water. Before I knew it I was to-ing and fro-ing with bottles of water for the womenfolk for the rest of the afternoon. I thought of a film I saw about Gunga Din, the chap who gave the British soldiers water while they were fighting the Indians.

After the vote was taken the Dadoo faction lost by a slight margin. Our disappointment was given a huge lift by Sigamoney. He made a brilliant speech urging the Dadoo supporters not to lose courage and said that the next time round the progressives would win.

In the 1946 TIC elections the Dadoo group won resoundingly. The opposition, this time without Nana, who had died, failed to turn up. I was elated, though still two years away from voting. Now my attendance at the Red Square meetings became frequent, and attendance in general increased. Ismail Meer and J.N. Singh often spoke at the gatherings. They were astute and well-spoken on and off the platform.

At one meeting I asked Ismail Meer a question on Poland. This was about the time when the United Nations Organization was coming into being in San Francisco. General Smuts was the most prominent figure in drawing up the United Nations Charter. Of all the allied countries, Poland was not invited and I was curious as to why not. I was quite shy in raising my voice and I put the question through Saleh Asvat, someone I knew from our immediate neighbourhood. He relayed my questions in a much louder voice, pointing out that it had come from me. I felt awkward. Whilst Meer was answering, a group of men, clearly members of the CP, looked bemused at me, a barefooted lad in short pants. It was J.N. Singh who lowered his head, suggesting I attend the Party meetings on Sunday nights on the City Hall steps.

Those meetings were a real treat. There I was to hear Sam Kahn, George Poonen, Issy Hayman, Issy Wolfson, J.B. Marks, Danie du Plessis, and H.A. Naidoo. These were impressive people, lawyers and trade unionists. There was an abundance of reading material in the form of pamphlets, newspapers and leaflets.

The City Hall steps meetings also drew another element who were brazenly opposed to the Communist Party of the Soviet Union. They openly flaunted their hatred against Jews, Indians and Africans. Tempers flared and skirmishes broke out as the elements from the pro-Nazi groups like the Grey Shirts and the *Ossewabrandwag* (the Oxwagon Sentinel) waded on to the communist platform. The Party members retaliated with amazing vigour. Two of the outstanding defenders were the Marcus brothers. These brothers possessed enormous strength. They would pick up a fascist above their heads, spin him around and throw him down the steps. When the police saw the fascists were coming off badly they would intervene.

One evening a couple of van loads of police arrived and, when it was evident the fascists were getting a trouncing, the police were ordered into formation and at a command they moved into the anti-fascists, flourishing their batons. People got hit over their heads, faces and backs. I was horrified. This was my first experience of this kind of violence.

The CP continued to use the City Hall steps. The number of defenders increased. When fights broke out, I and a couple of my friends would run down to the Cosy Café in the Indian quarters, where there was a regular gang of toughies who, though not political, had an intense dislike of the police and the fascists. We would tell them of the attack and say their support was needed. They came trotting and joined in the punch-ups.

Once Nathie Marcus held a man with his arms pinned behind. He announced that the man was Weighardt, the leader of the Grey Shirts. Weighardt was clearly in agony. I went up to a White woman supporter and asked to borrow her hatpin. I took the pin and shoved it into Weighardt's behind. He clenched his teeth and did not yell. It was an impulsive hatred that made me do it.

Quite often the speakers, supporters and ordinary black people passing through the city centre were waylaid and brutally assaulted. Whenever possible members of the Springbok Legion, an ex-servicemen's organization, came in their army jackets to lay into the fascists. It was quite a spectacle to see Joe Slovo, the Marcus brothers and other Whites joined by Coloured trade unionist James Phillips, Enver Baroochi, Saleh Asvat and Ahmed

Kathrada, all Indians, in an integrated squaring up to the fascists. The fascists often shouted, 'You Jewish fucking communist capitalist bastards, we will get you!'

7

The Lyric Cinema and the Hassim family

At about the period we moved into Fordsburg, the second oldest synagogue was being demolished. Most of the Jewish community had moved out to Doornfontein and the rich ones went further north. The waste ground where the synagogue had been, by now dubbed the Red Square, was littered with rubble, which made it look like a bomb site. It became a popular play area for the children. Soon it became a meeting place for political and religious gatherings. After some time the municipality levelled the ground and built a low brick wall around the square. The red sand was apt for the Red Square. The children just loved this open space. There were football games, races, and gangs just hovering around for fun. In winter a scanty funfair or circus was set up. Their lucrative business was in the summer months in the White suburbs.

Just two blocks away was the Lyric Cinema. For many of the young people growing up in Fordsburg, the Lyric Cinema and the Red Square became very much part of their lives. For older people the cinema was the only place they could go for relaxation and to enjoy the fascination of the movies. The Lyric seemed to attract more people than the other five cinemas for black folk in Fordsburg.

The Lyric had been a warehouse formerly owned by a Mr Sivaram Pather, an Indian in Vrededorp, who also owned a cinema called the Star Bioscope. Sometime in the early 1940s the warehouse was leased to the young Hassim brothers. They proceeded to convert it into a cinema they called the Lyric Cinema, in Lovers' Walk, Fordsburg.

The Hassim brothers were known to have come from a poor background. It was believed that their forebears came from South India. The Hassim brothers and their sisters lived modestly. They seem to have had a sheer sense of determination, discipline and unity. This was evident in the way they ran the cinema. The family had other relations in Vrededorp and Newclare. Though poor, they turned out a teacher, a clerk, a bookkeeper and eventually a lawyer. An uncle, known as Himdad Khan, was a successful bookkeeper. Another uncle made a living by selling *samosas* in the cinema.

Four of the brothers carried Mustapha as their middle name. Mustapha was the father's first name. Eusuph Mustapha, the eldest, seemed the most astute in business acumen. He also had a deep knowledge of films and the film industry and was widely read. The second eldest was Hashim Mustapha Hassim. Over the years, Hashim acquired managerial skills. They were followed by Akbar Mustapha, Abubakr Mustapha, Abdul Quadir, Mohamed Amin and their sister Fatima.[10]

Amongst the distinctive qualities of the Hassim brothers was their modesty, coupled with a noticeable degree of shyness. They were not short of intellectual depth. In vacations and school holidays all the brothers helped out at the cinema, either in the office, or ushering, or running errands. It would be several years before the Hassim family would see real progress in their small business venture.

The work at the Lyric Cinema was quite demanding, at times having to deal with noisy young people out of control. The cinema became even more popular in screening Indian films. It was also hired by charitable and political organizations. This was a rare achievement for the Indian community in the Transvaal. It was now the focal point for hundreds of people for a social outing, and Fordsburg was attracting an increasing number of Coloureds and Indians. Of the dwindling White population the one community that still remained was the Lebanese, who were mainly of Maronite (Catholic) stock. They were holding out because black people were patronizing their *shebeens*. They retained their houses in Fordsburg and bought plusher properties in the White suburbs.

During the war years we saw a host of anti-Nazi and anti-Japanese films. Many were powerful and dramatic and, as was customary, the American and British armed forces came out best. It was good propaganda. In our neighbourhood was a man called Sergeant-Major Maharaj. He was at the highest level a black man could go in the army. So when we saw films in which black men featured as soldiers or entertainers we were quite excited.

Round about 1943-44 there was a national campaign in support of the war effort in Europe and Asia, and the local Party branch hired the cinema for a fundraising event. This event was rather unusual because admission was by way of donating a lump of metal, metal cans or iron bars. The event was for children only. The puzzled children soon learned that the scrap metal would be smelted down to 'make guns and build tanks'. Some of us wondered how the mountain of scrap metal in the alley was going to be removed. That day's event turned out to be very enjoyable and successful for the CP. The use of the cinema was the Hassim brothers' contribution to the war effort.

There were other memorable events at the cinema. In 1952, the TIC held a mass meeting as part of the impending Defiance Campaign against unjust laws. In 1954 the Society for Peace and Friendship with the Soviet Union held an anniversary celebration of the Russian Revolution of 1917. That time there was no donation in the form of free use of the cinema. The political climate had changed. In anticipation that the security police would probe the management of the cinema, a fee was paid. Sure enough, the security police called. The hiring of the cinema was within the scope of the law.

The Lyric Cinema was one of the few to show a weekly serial. This proved most popular, especially *The Drums of Fu Manchu* and *Dick Tracy*, a fast-moving cops-and-robbers film with fisticuffs. The screening of films intended to be shown went through a maze of complex and mind-boggling censorship. The censors first determined what was fit for a White audience, then whether it was suitable for a Coloured and Indian audience, but not necessarily for Africans. Adult Africans' right to view a film was based on whether the film was suitable for eighteen-year-old or sixteen-year-old Whites. The other aspect of censorship was the cutting of scenes that might show White nudity or Blacks and Whites fraternizing. There was one film in which Frank Sinatra and Sammy Davis Jr did a dance routine. That was cut, as was a poster showing Sinatra and Davis holding hands. *Pinky*, with an all-star black cast, was totally banned. A smuggled copy, shown privately, showed nothing startling.

The few non-White cinemas used to get immediate second-release films. These tended to be musicals or versions of blockbusters. Always popular were the movies of the big American bands like Glen Miller, Duke Ellington, Count Basie, Cab Calloway, Tommy Dorsey and so on. The Lyric Cinema had wooden floorboards and one could feel them sagging to the rhythm of the music as the African patrons were keeping time with their feet.

In this diet of war films there were some that somehow the censors could not have clearly considered. One particular film was Charlie Chaplin's *The Great Dictator*. We saw most of Chaplin's films, in which he showed great sympathy for poor working men and women. Sometimes a film like *West Side Story* slipped in. After many years *Gone with the Wind* was released to us.

The Schlesinger Organization controlled the distribution of most of the films until Twentieth Century Fox appeared in South Africa. The

Lyric Cinema got Twentieth Century Fox and United Artists releases. In the late 1950s and early 1960s an Afrikaner film distribution company, STER, emerged. They seemed to have acquired a quantity of films that were considered harmless and of poor content. But what sometimes came out were anti-war films in which the only way the civilian population could fight an occupying force was through armed struggle. This was just at the time of the emergence of *Umkhonto we Sizwe* (MK),[11] the armed wing of the African National Congress (ANC).

African patrons were segregated from Coloured and Indian patrons. This practice was applied in most White or Indian-owned cinemas. There was, however, one cinema which was owned by an Indian stalwart of the Congress Movement, Hamid Bhyat, who bought the Good Hope Cinema and changed it to the UNO. There the seating was not segregated.

Attempts were made by the Transvaal Indian Youth Congress (TIYC) to make the management of cinemas allow mixed seating. The only management which agreed to meet us was the Lyric Cinema. Our delegation told them that seating should be integrated since there was nothing in law to enforce discrimination against African patrons. The management were sympathetic to our views but said they were prevented by their Coloured and Indian patrons, who did not want to mix with Africans. No doubt there was an element of truth in this. Still, we argued that it was totally unacceptable to pander to such people. What was clear to us in the TIYC was that, whilst this appeared to be an insoluble problem, its root cause was in the racially instituted system of divide and rule. Nevertheless we should continue our struggle against apartheid and, where and when possible, combat the prejudices within the non-White folk.

The location of the cinema, after several years in Lovers' Walk, shifted to Central Road in Fordsburg in the direction of Vrededorp. The Hassims acquired a corner plot of land to build their own cinema. Indeed it was a spectacular building. It had a cosy atmosphere with the most comfortable seating arrangements. In 1951 the Lyric Cinema won an international award as the best designed cinema in the world. Amongst the architects were Rusty Bernstein, later a Treason Trialist and a Rivonia accused. The other was Alan Lipman, a prominent member of the Congress of Democrats (COD).[12] These were not political appointments. It so happened that both men worked for the contracting firm of architects.

The running of the new cinema was much more demanding. This did not prevent the Hassim brothers from taking an interest in the developing political events in the country. They knew a number of people connected with the political movement. Besides us there were also some of their cousins and relatives involved in the Unity Movement (then known as the South African Non-European Unity Movement).[13] Some of the leading figures were brother and sister Enver and Dolly Hassim, and later Ghoolam Nabi. The only Hassim brother who was reasonably active was Abdul. For a period he was the treasurer of the TIYC.

One day I had a request from Hashim M. Hassim. He was interested in the subject of Marxism. I suggested that, rather than a one-to-one discussion, we have two other people so as to have a wider discussion and more points of view. I suggested it would be better to keep it small for personal and security reasons. We used a textbook *What Is Marxism* by John Eaton,[14] a British Marxist scholar. Apart from our pro-Soviet brand of Marxism, there was the pro-Trotsky brand of Marxism which was propounded by the Unity Movement. I never asked but often wondered why Hashim asked us and not his cousins. The Hassims were regular readers of our weekly *New Age*. I do not recall seeing a copy of the Unity Movement paper *The Torch*.

The house in which we held our study class was in the new mansion put up for the family in Mint Road, a street parallel to where the cinema was in Central Road. This was perhaps the finest house that any Indian person had in Johannesburg. The Hassims entertained and threw lavish parties, at which there was always a collection of interesting people. The presentation of Indian cuisine and the savouries became much talked about, and their gatherings were legendary. The Hassims were always the most charming hosts.

At one point I took Nadine Gordimer to one of the parties. On another occasion I asked the Hassims whether I could bring a friend along. This was someone I had met in the course of our political work. Her name was Sybil Garach. Sybil was an attractive woman, but poorly clad and without shoes. She lived with her mother and siblings in two rooms. Initially she was shy and just smiled a lot. She was nevertheless attentive and showed some interest in our political work. I made the occasional visit with our weekly paper. In the course of time she became active.

When I invited her to the Hassims, she was quite startled, and turned down the invitation. I suspected it was largely because she did not have the kind of clothes for such parties. I suggested that she come in simple clothes. There would be no reason not to join us. On the evening of the party I called to pick her up. When I saw her I was surprised. She had on a neat simple dress, her hair done up, a pair of shoes and no jewellery. She looked very attractive. We set off to Mint Road. Sybil looked a bit nervous.

After introducing her to the Hassim brothers and some of the guests I knew, I left her and wandered off to talk with other friends. When I glanced occasionally I noticed she was coping easily and had an air of confidence. Considering this was her first ever party where there were doctors, lawyers, business people, students and teachers, she was doing well.

After several days I heard Sybil had made quite an impact on Hashim. Now they were dating and not long afterwards they got married. We were delighted when we got a postcard from Hashim and Sybil on their honeymoon in Japan. Hashim knew that Sybil came from a very poor family, but the poverty of the Garach family did not put him off. Instead he provided the family with much of their needs and was a frequent visitor to their house. For Sybil people said it was like a fairy-tale experience. Hashim and Sybil lived happily together and reared a lovely family.

8

Real-world education and work

There were only two major political and industrial struggles in the mid-1940s. One was the Indian Passive Resistance Campaign in 1946, which petered out by 1948, the other was the African mineworkers' strike, which was smashed within a week by police brutality; the union and CP leaders were arrested and charged with sedition. The Native Representative Council, a dummy institution handpicked and made up of some of the older leaders of the ANC, resigned in protest against the shooting of the African miners.

Up to then the ANC had always been a very weak organization. It was mainly sustained by the involvement of the Africans from the CP, as was the case of the TIC and the Native Representative Council. The ANC was defunct for ten months of the year; towards December they would meet in conference in Bloemfontein, where a lot of steam was let off. Dr A.B. Xuma was the most distinguished leader of the ANC. He had a sense of organization and foresight, but the ANC was cut off from the mass of the African people.

This appeared to be one of the reasons why the African mineworkers' strike was smashed in so short a period. Because the miners lived in compounds, cut off from the settled population and the workers, they had no social relationship with the urban population, who themselves were not yet drawn into mainstream struggles, about which the ANC was hesitant and weak-kneed in any event.

The African and Indian members of the CP were mindful that neither the ANC nor the SAIC should be a communist organization but a true reflection of the needs of the oppressed people, which was not for socialism but for freedom from racial domination. I had not seen any pamphlets or leaflets from the CP demanding socialism for the oppressed.

At times there were confused positions from the CP. For example, it campaigned for its candidates on dummy institutions like the Native Advisory Boards, and never won a single seat. It was a seat for one of the three Native representatives in Parliament, who had to be a White person.

One of the most colourful MPs in the White parliament for the 'Natives' was the communist Sam Kahn.

While the party campaigned for this kind of parliamentary participation, the leadership of the SAIC successfully boycotted the elections of the White 'representatives' for Indians. The SAIC leadership was made up of very many distinguished communists like Yusuf Dadoo, Ismail Meer, and J.N. Singh, H.A. Naidoo and Dawood Seedat. For many of us young communists all this was mystifying, but loyalty and disciple demanded our best attention.

As for the Coloured people, their state of organization was virtually nonexistent. They lacked leadership or organization, and had a few disparate groups in some centres of the country. One that often featured was the African People's Organization. It had no clout, only a ghost of what was once a powerful organization in the early 1900s.

An anecdote that made the rounds in political circles at the time was in part reflective of the state of the organization. It was said that the White comrades would turn up on time for a meeting. The Indians came half an hour later, the Africans an hour later and the Coloureds never turned up.

The first study classes I attended were led by Vella Pillay; our textbook was the party's *Economics and Politics of South Africa*. The classes were held in Chancellor House, Fox Street opposite the Magistrates Court. Vella was regarded as one of the bright sparks of the CP. He was completing a Bachelor of Commerce degree at Witwatersrand University (Wits). He made the classes interesting and encouraged our participation.

We attended many of the Party and Young Communist League (YCL) meetings and functions. We were introduced to a vast range of literature from within the country and from the UK, the US, and India as well as books on the Soviet Union, China and Europe. It was then that I read about Dr Hewlett Johnson, known as the Red Dean of Canterbury, the *Daily Worker* from London, *Masses and Mainstream* from the States and the unrivalled collection from the Left Book Club.

I did not limit my reading to only communist and left-wing literature. I regularly read *Time, Life, The Christian Science Monitor*, the *Saturday Evening Post* and occasionally *Esquire* and *Harper's*. Nationally I read *The Forum, Trek*, and *The Forward. The Forward*, the organ of the Whites-only Labour Party, impressed me the most. The layout was attractive, the articles were well written. I was astonished when I heard that the editor was only 23 years old. His name was Colin Legum, who was well known in political circles. He was a councillor for the Labour Party in the Johannesburg Whites-only Council. The Labour Party had control of the city council.

It was to be another twenty years before I actually met Colin Legum in London. I was reading his articles in the *Observer*, which I got regularly in

Johannesburg. He wrote on African affairs in a manner, style and depth that I had not come across in many of the other journals I was reading. Our friendship lasted for over thirty years until his death in Cape Town in early 2003.

One of the exciting periods of my reading was a series of simple biographies of distinguished black people like Paul Robeson, Dr Edward Du Bois and Washington Carver. A number of prominent progressive South Africans wrote the biographies, which were published by *The African Bookman*[15] and sold for a sixpence. The editor was Dr Eddie Roux. This spurred me on to wider reading.

A lot of my reading took place in front of the Johannesburg City Hall steps. Indians were allowed to run flower stalls there. I worked on Saturdays for one of the stallholders for pocket money. I could earn five shillings, and if I continued till about nine or ten in the evening I could earn another five shillings. From my earnings, plus a few tips, I could buy newspapers and magazines and go to the cinema, as well give my mother some money. When there were quiet periods I would sit on my haunches or on an upturned tin and read. In any event most of the publications were only available in the city centre bookshops.

Selling flowers on a Saturday night was sometimes a hazardous experience. Crowds of Whites would flock to the cinemas and bars. The Café Bioscope appeared to be quite popular. The crowds on a Saturday night were robust, noisy and argumentative, and at times broke into fights amongst themselves. And if any black person happened to be walking past or stopped to look, he would be in for a belting.

There were times when they would come to us with their female partners to buy flowers. Some of them paid; some took extra bunches of flowers and paid less. Others in groups would call us names, threaten assault and, if the mood caught them, overturn all the flower tins and stands. We would retreat and wait for the orgy to be over, go back and pick up the spilt tins and flowers.

All the books and magazines I was reading were mind-boggling in terms of history, places and events, compared to the utterly dull and dreary White view of history taught at school, especially about South Africa and the world. The textbooks that we had to use at school were designed for the White schools. Fortunately we had some Indian and Coloured teachers who slipped in some interpretations from a black point of view.

We had the same problem with English literature. The closest I got to a semblance of anti-slavery literature was *Uncle Tom's Cabin*.[16] This was actually introduced by a White teacher in my first year in high school.

As a result I just had no desire to continue schooling, for sheer lack of stimulation. So I quit after one year.

I took on a number of odd jobs, selling flowers over the weekends whilst looking for regular work, which was not easy. I then got a job as a printer's assistant with an Indian-owned firm. This was one of the few Indian-owned print shops. Indians, Coloureds and Africans could not get qualifications in the printing industry, which was White owned, and the White typographical workers in the Transvaal were protected by the Whites-only trade union. But Blacks were not barred from buying print machines and operating them themselves, so the few Indian, Coloured and African printers were self-taught.

I was taught to operate the Heidelberg and the inking of some of the machines. I was keen to learn comping (setting type) but that was already well in hand and commanded better pay, certainly better than the two pounds a week I was earning for five-and-a-half days of work. The comper would set up machines for leaflets and run them off during the absence of the owner, have the packages delivered and collect the cash.

After my first week, the owner said he did not have enough money to pay me and that I would be paid the following week. This was my first lesson that exploitation did not come in the form of Whites only. Here was an Indian who sounded progressive. His co-director, who was not an active partner, held a fairly cosy job with a wholesale firm and was a member of the CP. I doubt he was aware of the shenanigans of the active director.

I was not getting much joy from being a printer's assistant either by way of experience or for the pay. I lasted three months with the Indian Caxton. I flitted from odd job to odd job. It then dawned on me with regret that I should have stayed on in school as long as possible and obtained some sort of certificate of higher education, which could have improved my work position.

In the meantime my education in the real world was progressing. I continued attending meetings and demonstrations. The Indian Passive Resistance was still on, and resisters were entering Natal from the Transvaal without a permit, also from Natal into the Transvaal. The site chosen for the Natal resisters was the Red Square, where a camp was set up. Fortunately our resisters were not attacked by White hooligan racists, presumably because it was in the heart of a black area. But our resisters were not so fortunate in Durban, where White hooligans physically attacked some of them. This particular episode was graphically described by the Reverend Michael Scott at various meetings. He and Zainab Asvat, a young medical student, witnessed the attack.

9

Bellboys and waiters

In 1942 on a trip to Port Elizabeth my eldest brother, Ramsamy, became ill with typhoid, and died within a few days, leaving behind his wife and young son. Shortly afterwards my brother Peter started working as a bellboy at the Orange Grove Hotel in an upmarket suburb of Johannesburg. He was fourteen.

He seemed happy at his job, even though the pay was low. This was supplemented by the tips he got from customers for running errands, carrying bags, and handling mail and telephone enquiries. The customers found him pleasant, friendly and reliable. I remember the kind of advice my mother, sisters and family friends gave him. He should remember when working for White people he must be neat, tidy, polite. He must appear to be trustworthy. Some said he must be careful of the White man. They would try to trap him by leaving a five-pound note lying about to see if he would steal it. He was not to touch it.

For the day shift he would work a week leaving home at 6 a.m. and returning at 6 p.m. The alternate week was the night shift, which started at 4 p.m. and was supposed to finish at midnight. Most nights he finished at two am. For the night shifts he was allowed to sleep in one of the rooms in the back of the hotel with the waiters.

Sometimes, during school vacations, my young brother Daso and school chums like Kenneth and Reggie Vandeyar, David Jack, Daniel Lazarus and I would walk to the Orange Grove Hotel to visit Peter in the waiters' quarters. He had no difficulty in persuading the waiters and chef to bring us generous helpings of the best dishes – spaghetti bolognese, roast beef or whatever was the special of the day – followed by scoops of ice cream. With this kind of nourishment the twelve-mile round trip from Fordsburg to Orange Grove was a pleasant experience.

Peter was always pleasant, helpful and polite. He was dressed in the bellhop's monkey suit and hat. The boss called him Sabu. The waiters wore white tunics, sashes and turbans and were invariably also called Sabu.

So there were quite a lot of Sabus around. The waiters called Peter Kutty (Puppy) to differentiate.

He led a very organized life. He gave our mother his wages and part of his tips. He opened a post office savings account, bought the occasional garment of his choice and regularly bought journals like *Time, Life, Picture Post* and the *Saturday Evening Post.* Each year without fail he bought a copy of *Pears Encyclopaedia.* He was also an avid reader of the daily papers. His social life was visiting a few friends, and going to the cinema.

When he came home he told us lots of stories about the strange behaviour of the residents, customers, the White staff and the management. He developed a friendly working relationship with the domestic African staff. Most of the White staff had to be formally addressed as Mr, Miss, Mrs or Sir. The White staff had to be waited upon for lunch and dinner before the dining room was opened to the customers. Peter's image of the White man as decent, all-powerful, upright and honest did not last long. He found them to be abusive, untidy, crooked, demanding, prone to excessive eating, and of low morals.

The hotel was owned by a wealthy English family, Tommy and Arthur Ellis and their mother. They were a well-known family; a street in Orange Grove was named Ellis Street, just off Louis Botha Avenue. Tommy Ellis was quite an eccentric person. He would have bouts of drinking and go 'native', engaging in stick fights with the Zulu domestic staff. It annoyed him when the bewildered Africans showed reluctance in hitting back. He could take quite a beating. When he sobered up after a stick session he was oblivious to what had happened. Then he was businesslike and kept his distance from the staff.

Arthur, the younger brother, was steady, pleasant and an effective manager. He got on well with customers and staff. But not well enough to raise the wages of the staff. Peter, for example, worked for thirteen days and nights before getting a day off. His starting wage was four pounds a month. Five years later he was earning eight pounds a month.

Through Peter I also got a job as a bellboy at the Orange Grove Hotel. When I started I earned five pounds a month. We were soon joined by our friends Reggie Vandeyar and David Jack. Most of the waiters were from families we knew from the neighbourhood.

I would walk into town to catch the bus at Juta's Corner. Juta's was the leading booksellers of mostly textbooks and limited quality novels. (I later learned that the original Juta was a Dutch Jew who had married a sister of Karl Marx. They went to live in the Cape, where he first set up a bookshop.) From this spot most of the buses headed for the White-populated northern suburbs like Hillbrow, Berea, Houghton, Orange Grove and Highlands North. These were some of the plushest and most expensive White areas.

When the bus left Hillbrow and made its way down Louis Botha Avenue, it was a beautiful sight. Vast tree-lined roads, beautiful gardens, spacious and attractive houses and there was an area called The Wilds. Everything looked so neat and tidy, with manicured gardens and uniformed domestic workers either cleaning the flats and houses or looking after little White children. Seeing the world passing by from the segregated upstairs deck of the bus, whilst seemingly pleasant, still irked me. Here I was from a heavily deprived area and living in confined spaces, travelling to a hotel to earn a pittance for the comfort of White people.

The Orange Grove Hotel was the most popular place for entertainment. For five nights a week the Coconut Grove, part of the hotel, was packed with dancers to the music of Roy Martin and his band. The resident singer was the petite and attractive Eve Boswell. The Roy Martin band played in the style of Glen Miller and was often featured on the radio. The hotel also boasted a first-class Chinese restaurant, the first of its kind for Whites. Trade was brisk. There were a number of bungalows at the back of the hotel suitable for singles, couples and families and they were much sought after. There were bars in various parts of the hotel complex and a grillroom run by a Mrs Parker, whose grilled steaks were very popular.

The clientele came from a cross-section of the White population. There were business people, professionals and, on Saturdays, rugby players in after their matches. For the evening dances the ones who appeared in formal evening wear were the Afrikaners. Invariably they wore ill-fitting dinner suits and dresses. They were generally rude, and poor tippers. Many, we could tell, were just workers trying to be big spenders.

It was not unusual to find they did not understand an *à la carte* menu as against an ordinary menu. They would ask for the best. The waiters would try to explain the difference, and if the customers displayed an unpleasant attitude the waiters would recommend the *à la carte* menu. When the bill came, a jaw would drop and the astonished customer would insist he did not ask for such an expensive meal. The headwaiter or manager would be called and it was clear the waiter wrote down what the customer asked for. The waiter would humbly explain the customer only wanted the best. The customer left stone broke.

Then there were customers who ordered food and drink and tried to avoid payment. That was soon resolved. The hotel bouncer was Norman Albright, who was just over five feet tall and weighed about 175 pounds. Norman would lift the evader bodily and carry him off to the hotel fountain for a solid dousing, and if there was any resistance he would ask the hotel's African night watchman to whip the man. This was the worst form of humiliation, having a White man whipped by a 'native' with a *sjambok*. Sometimes a more lenient Norman would take the culprit and place him behind the bar to wash up hundreds of drinking glasses till closing time.

Norman, who was English, seemed to have had a special dislike for Afrikaners. One night after we had finished the night shift Daniel Jack, Jacob the night floor waiter and I were cooling off on the edge of the hotel premises. Diagonally opposite the hotel was the Victory Cinema. There was still some late-night traffic on the main road and the odd couple strolling by. Standing in front of the cinema was a White policeman accompanied by an African policeman.

We were still in our white hotel jackets. From across the road the White policeman glanced at us and immediately made a charge towards us and specifically for Jacob. Jacob appeared to have committed the cardinal sin of being up and about in a White area. Africans had to have special permission to be in such an area after 9 p.m.

Jacob's initial reaction was to slink back, turn on his heels and run for it. The White policeman accelerated his speed and so did the African policeman. Jacob ran back into the rear of the hotel premises. We also ran with Jacob. Jacob was soon caught. I shouted at the policeman that Jacob was an employee at the hotel. My plea was ignored. Whilst the police were grappling with Jacob to try to handcuff him, I called out to Daniel to rush over to the bungalow of Arthur Ellis, where he and Norman were checking out the night's takings.

Norman immediately came bounding out at speed and shouted at the police 'What is going on?' When Jacob saw Norman, followed by the boss Arthur Ellis, he grabbed hold of the White policeman and head-butted him. The White policeman flew up into the air with a spin and went rocket-like into a window of about twelve inches square. His body was contorted and he was screaming. We were astonished. The African policeman was transfixed. Norman held the stuck policeman by the legs and gently unwound him from the frame.

Jacob was not to be seen. The White policeman was still in a state of shock, and shouted at Norman and Ellis, 'You let a *Kaffir* hit me!' Norman told him he had no authority to arrest any staff on the premises. In the meantime Ellis phoned the commander of the local police station and within minutes the commander arrived, profusely apologizing to Ellis for the conduct of his police, for which he said this particular policeman would be dealt with. We heard later that the policeman was formally reprimanded and cautioned. Jacob reappeared at the hotel a couple of days later, receiving a hearty welcome from us.

Generally the African and Indian staff had to watch their step in dealing with White people. One had to be obedient, polite and willing, never forgetting the 'Sir', 'Madam' or '*Baas*' address. It was not uncommon to respond to the clicking of fingers or answer to the call of 'Sammy' for attention. Neither was it uncommon to hear taunts of racial abuse.

The catering staff acquired a technique of retaliation. This took various forms. It was not difficult to foul their drinks and food, inflate the bill, or serve expensive drink and food. For residents known for their racial abuse and bossy attitude there was a special treat. They got a dose, and depending on the notoriety of the abuse, more than a good dose of *jamal koteh*.

Jamal koteh was a seed with a powerful laxative quality, which was sold in African herbal stores. The seed would be ground down into fine powder and for quicker results it was warmed in a pan. The powder used to be sprinkled into the soup, and again depending on the rank of the abuser it would be sprinkled on the main courses. The result would take about fifteen to twenty minutes. The victim would be seen leaving the table, returning, leaving and later running, leaving a visible trail.

Flanking the Orange Grove Hotel were blocks of luxury flats, landscaped with beautiful gardens. The complexes were kept in immaculate condition by 'flat boys', 'garden boys' and 'garden girls'. These were the names given to the domestic staff of African adults. July and December were the months when the occupiers motored to the coast, leaving behind some African staff, whilst some like the nannies were taken along to look after the kids. Those left behind stayed in quarters in the rooftop flats, which the Nationalist Party called 'locations in the sky'.

Some of the Indian waiters were dating the African domestic workers surreptitiously, and boon time was when the White occupants went in a throng to the coast. The waiters would snuggle into the pyjamas and gowns of the White occupants and enjoy some of the drinks and cigars. When Master and Madam returned, the flat was as immaculate as when they left. The clothes were neatly ironed and put away. The waiters were calmly working their shifts at the hotel.

Some of the waiters had the gift of the gab in either English or Afrikaans. One or two had a smattering of Italian. This would catch the attention of some of the White women residents. They would ask for room service and ask specifically for certain waiters by name. Two of everything was ordered, teas, drinks and snacks. The waiter would arrange for a stand-in until his service was completed, and return contented, plus a tip.

Indian waiters rarely ate the food at the hotel. They were always suspicious of its quality. Food was never prepared under proper hygienic conditions. Leftover food was turned into something else and given a fancy French name. At one hotel the proprietor would stand in the kitchen with a pair of tongs. As each waiter entered from the dining room, she would pick out pieces of leftover cold meats and salads which she placed on trays and put into galvanized baths and shoved into large fridges. The next day the rescued food was recycled and attractively laid out and garnished for the evening diners.

The waiters knew the White management mentality and worked on that. The trick was to praise the manager for his kindness and understanding of Indian religious tradition, telling him that they knew he or she was well aware that Indians, being Hindu, did not eat beef or pork. The response would be something like, 'Of course, my boys. I understand your religion. Go to the fridge and help yourself to some mutton.' The workers would help themselves to the choicest lamb cuts. A waiter would be delegated to cook a curry meal. The first plate of curry and rice, attractively laid out, would be presented to the manager, much to his delight. Then we would have our share.

The 'Hindu' ploy worked for many years, and the waiters, whether Hindus or Christians, who ate beef and pork and drank alcohol, were able to control how and where their food came from.

It was very important to have a good relationship with the kitchen staff. If the head chef was a White man, we would develop a special technique in getting on with him. If he was an Indian or an African, it was not too difficult. In this way we could secure fresh chops or steaks and prepare them ourselves. If all else failed we would settle for eggs fried in butter, toast, milk or coffee. When the request was not possible, the waiters would go home and have a cooked meal at ten o'clock at night rather than eat the poor-quality food of the hotel.

One of the things one learned in the catering trade was to work well in the hope of retaining one's job and topping up one's low wages by tips. Good tippers got good results. Receiving a few pence was not considered polite. Some of my waiter friends found various ways of dealing with rude and grumpy customers. On clearing a table a waiter might find a threepenny bit or a sixpence on the table. Should the customer decide to sit in the lounge the waiter would purchase a box of matches or a newspaper and present it on a tray to the customer. The waiter would tell the perplexed customer that he thought that was why the money was left. Another technique was to toss the coin to drop alongside the customer and hand it to him, 'Sir,

I believe you dropped this coin.' A common technique was to launch in subdued tones a tirade of abuse in Tamil and if asked he would say he was complimenting the customer for his kindness.

At the Orange Grove Hotel there was a varied collection of residents; barristers, lawyers, businessmen, retired wealthy people and couples. Some were pleasant, polite and tolerant. Others were nasty, brazen and demanding as of right, being White people. This element were bad tippers and gluttons who would eat their way through the menu.

The wealthy unmarried Kugelman sisters were rude and unpleasant and forever complaining of poor service. One evening the patience of one of the waiters was wearing thin. He decided the time had come to give these women some kind of special attention. One of the regular complaints was that the plates were never warm enough. On this evening he put two soup plates into the oven. When they were excessively hot, he used his napkins to withdraw the plates and pour the hot soup into them. They were placed on the table a little way beyond normal reach.

As the sisters pulled the plates towards them there were two loud screams, and the plates got tossed into the air. Waiters and fellow diners rushed to the women, who were in agony. The manager and the headwaiter called the waiter for an explanation. The waiter with a deadpan face explained that the madams always complained that the plates were cold. This time he warmed the plates. Now the madams were complaining that the plates were too hot. He said he was sorry but he did not know what to do. The management accepted his explanation.

The Kugelman sisters never again complained about cold plates. They did however continue to complain about other services. Finally the management suggested they leave the hotel since the service did not meet their demands. They left in a huff.

Whilst we depended on tips, we politely refused tips from people who were decent, polite and appreciative of our service. Quite often some of these people expressed surprise at our refusal. We explained that simple courtesy and politeness were preferable to tips.

On the whole the hotel residents were not particularly pleasant to us. There were, however, exceptions. The one man with whom we got on particularly well was Ronnie Michael. He was a partner of the law firm Hellman, Michael & Basner. They had a particularly large practice of African clientele. Hellman was a specialist in divorce law. Hymie Basner was a specialist in criminal law and civil rights. For some years he was the White elected senator for Africans, and was held in high esteem by the African community.

We developed a rapport with Ronnie Michael but were careful not to indicate that we were politically aware or that we knew of his partnership with Hellman and Basner. Clearly he knew of our political awareness but pretended otherwise. But most importantly we did not want the management to know that we were more friendly with Ronnie Michael than with any of the other residents.

Initially Ronnie would tip us for the odd jobs we did for him. But invariably we refused to accept the tip. This would annoy him. One day he asked us outright why we refused his tips. We explained that it was so rare to get a decent White man who was polite and always grateful, and that this to us was more acceptable than a tip. He said he tipped us because we were so poorly paid, but eventually he understood our attitude. He was the sort of man we would never dream of giving *jamal koteh.*

Some years later after I left the hotel I learned from Louis Joffe, who was the fundraiser for the African Mineworkers Union, that amongst the donors was Ronnie Michael. Ronnie's sister was married to Emanuel Baker, one of the three Baker brothers who were lawyers. Julius and Lewis were well-known members of the CP. I was rather quietly pleased to learn about Ronnie's support, something which I did not disclose to anyone else except to my brother Peter.

By the time he was twenty, Peter had graduated to becoming a waiter and wine steward. Now his wages were twelve pounds a month. He was one of a small group of waiters who excelled in their work, perhaps because they neither drank nor smoked and had expert knowledge of the brands of wine, cognac and whisky and continental cuisine. In their appearance they were neat, well-dressed and easy going. Peter had a great rapport with customers. Soon he was being sought after by owners of other hotels and restaurants.

It was while he was working as a waiter that Peter became politically active, as did some other waiters. The TIC and the CP became his political home. He became part of a hard core of political activists.

Peter and I looked alike except he was a few inches taller, better looking, neater and rather exceptionally quiet. Quite often the police would be trailing him instead of me. The first time I got banned the security police were baffled. When they wanted to serve the banning order, Peter said he was not Paul. When they came to me I said I was Peter. If the banning order was served on the wrong person, then the order would be invalid.

Eventually I decided to accept the order and suggested they came home. They arrived one Saturday morning to find both of us on the pavement. They looked astonished and still could not decide who the order should be served on. After a long silence I identified myself and accepted the banning order.

When we were working for the 1 May strike of 1950 – the first industrial strike of its kind in the history of South Africa, although the action was confined to the Transvaal – Peter gave all his spare time to bill-posting, chalking slogans, leafleting and canvassing. Late one night he and David Jack did not report back after the area work. They were the only two activists missing.

We searched the suburbs, phoned the hospitals and police stations. No sign and no clues. Maulvi Cachalia was convinced that the police had picked them up. He phoned the Marshall Square police station and asked, 'Those two Indian boys you got there, are they still with you?' Naively, the desk sergeant said 'Why, yes.' So Maulvi got on to Jack Levitan, one of our very able lawyers. When we arrived at the police station, Jack said, 'These boys you've got, I want them released.' Jack had a charming way of disarming authority. He was very fluent in Afrikaans and displaying his legal knowledge with such flair that the police immediately agreed to release them without bail, but said that they would have to appear that morning in court.

Whilst this exchange was taking place, Peter indicated to me that he had given the police my name. I immediately realized why. First, we looked alike; and second, he had to be on duty the next morning. It was now about 1 a.m. and Peter had to be on duty at seven. He looked tired and ruffled. Naturally I would have to be the one to go to court.

The police decided on a ploy. They would release Peter and David at their respective homes in the presence of their parents. When we arrived at home, now well past midnight, I walked ahead of the police. I told my mother in the best Tamil I could muster that Peter had given my name. The police asked her, 'Is this your son?' She replied 'Yes'. 'And what is his name?' She replied, 'His name is Paul.' And what is his date of birth?' She said, '1 June 1930.' The police turned to Peter and said, 'Right, Paul, we will see you in court at nine this morning' and left. That morning I turned up at court with David Jack, only to find that the charges were withdrawn. Peter meanwhile was on duty at 7 a.m. at the hotel.

My poor brother's harassment was not only confined to experiences with the police. Quite often mothers or acquaintances would confront him and enquire about his relationship with young women in the neighbourhood. 'How come you have walked past me. Last night you were chatty and danced with me. Now you seem so shy.' When he pleaded ignorance, it became clear that I was the guilty party.

One Saturday afternoon Mosie Moola and I had finished our rounds of selling New Age in the suburbs. We were fairly exhausted and enjoying a cup of tea with Mac Maharaj, when there was a knock at the door. It was a man from the Jehovah's Witnesses. He wanted to tell us about his church. We were in a jovial mood and engaged the man in a bit of chat. We were in a cynical spirit and put some questions to the man about the Jehovah's Witnesses operating segregated services and not coming out against apartheid. He fielded many questions until it got to the stage when the man was actually sweating. He finally gave up and left.

Soon after, Peter came in to ask what we had done to the man. It seems he had continued his rounds and gone to Peter's house. When Peter answered the door he looked shocked and said, 'Not you again', and fled.

Peter married Doreen. Doreen was previously married and had three children, and with Peter went on to have four – Kalie, Tony, Roshnee and Subhartri. Peter took responsibility for all the children. He evidently realized that, since he was now the breadwinner of two families, it was better to keep a low profile about his political involvement.

Peter was not only helpful in paying half our rent for a number of years, he also gave us other forms of help, as well as helping our aged mother. By chance I learnt he was also paying the meat and vegetable bill for the family of one of our comrades, Reggie Vandeyar, who was sent off to Robben Island. Peter never disclosed this to anyone.

In the centre of Johannesburg there was the Grand National Hotel. Presumably because of its name the National Party leadership would select this hotel for their meetings. MPs and cabinet ministers were frequent visitors.

Peter worked there for a while, as did several of my friends and acquaintances. At one luncheon a White man seated away from the distinguished Nationalist diners called a waiter and asked him how he could serve men like that, pointing to Dr Dönges and Robberts 'Blaggie' Swart, ministers respectively of Interior and Justice, 'who have introduced laws to harm your people'. The waiter meekly replied, 'Sir, what can I do? I have to work.' The customer nodded his head in agreement.

After one waiter served the distinguished visitors he went to clear the table. He asked the cabinet ministers whether they enjoyed the pudding. They chorused, 'Oh yes. Very good, thank you.' The waiter shuffled backwards saying 'Thank you, Sir' with a degree of self-satisfaction. He had cleared his throat and nose into the pudding. He said his only regret was not sprinkling *jamal koteh*.

At one of the high-class restaurants and dance halls in Northcliffe, an affluent area of Johannesburg, I would do work as an extra. An extra was a waiter employed only for specific functions. This was generally on a Friday or Saturday, the popular dance nights. A lot of the patrons were actually workers hitting the expensive night spots. They came in ill-fitting dress suits and gowns. From under the cape of a woman or from the side pocket of a man a bottle of whisky or brandy would appear, as the drinks from the bar were expensive. Whilst they were dancing (comically, totally unrelated to the music), some of the waiters would snatch the bottle off the table, which was sold to other customers as drinks from the bar. We would watch from a distance the puzzled and annoyed looks of the men when they returned to their tables.

When Peter worked in coffee bars and hotels, over a period of time he cultivated friendships with certain customers. He was careful and cautious. At the Gaggia Coffee Bar he got to know a Portuguese intellectual who was a frequent visitor. Gradually they exchanged political views and found they had shared views on racism and colonialism. This friendship went on for some time. Then there was a gap. The man had not turned up at the coffee bar. A note reached Peter. His friend had been picked up by Major Spengler, head of the Johannesburg security police.

Peter immediately got in touch with Ruth First, who was the Johannesburg editor of *New Age*. She managed to find out that the man was an oppositionist from Portugal working against Salazar and that he was in liaison with an opposition group in Mozambique. Major Spengler had taken the kidnapped victim and handed him over to PIDE, the Portuguese secret police, at the Mozambique border with South Africa. Ruth also found out that the prisoner died 'whilst trying to escape at the border point'. In fact he was killed by PIDE. *New Age* was the only paper to cover the story.

Peter got to know some Israelis at the coffee bar. They became very friendly and always engaged in polite and humorous banter. One evening they disclosed they were agents from the Israeli government who were in search of former Nazi members whom they believed were in South Africa. They showed Peter pictures of the wanted men, and asked him to contact them if he were to spot any of these men. Peter relished the request. He energetically looked for the Nazi criminals without success.

Quite often White members of our fraternity would visit the Gaggia Coffee Bar. They would also have a friendly chat with Peter. One evening, Beata and Alan Lipman came in for coffee. They gave him a two-shilling tip. He gave it back to them, suggesting they should give it to *New Age*. He resented tips from friends.

Amongst the many people Peter got to know whilst working at the Gaggia Coffee Bar was a Mr Alan Kallenbach, an architect, a nephew of old Mr Hermann Kallenbach, also an architect, who was involved very closely with M.K. Gandhi and Tolstoy Farm,[17] the first passive resistance movement.

The young Kallenbach and Peter had shared views on race discrimination and the history of the SAIC. He got to know more about Peter and his family. He learnt about a vacant plot of ground that Peter had acquired and the reason for it lying idle. Over the years, whilst still living in Charles Lane, Fordsburg, Peter had saved enough money to acquire the plot in the new township in Lenz. But for some years the plot lay bare for lack of funds. Mr Kallenbach said he would help, and soon enough he did a survey and set about drawing up a plan for the house. The house in Sparrow Road was designed by Mr Kallenbach free of charge.

One night after Peter left work he noticed he was being followed by the security police. When he got to President Street they stopped him and searched his car. They then asked him to drive home with them following. When they arrived at the house they carried out a search. They found nothing. After they left Peter came around the back to tell me about the raid. At that time I was under house arrest and whilst the raid was being carried out I was reading a copy of the banned *Daily Worker*, the paper of the British CP.

10

Harassment

My working experience in hotels and restaurants as bellboy and waiter gave me an insight into White people in their class and social positions. What was abundantly clear was that, whatever their background, on the whole they reflected their sense of White racial superiority, sometimes politely but mainly brazenly.

One day several friends and I went for a long hike into the country. It was a beautiful sunny day. We were heading for a stream and a pool we knew, walking in single file. Suddenly I saw this huge car heading towards us. There was a group of White men in it. I shouted to the rest of the lads to jump into the grass. The car missed us, but one of the White men hit me with a thick pole from the car window. They drove off laughing. There was no doubt they had made a deliberate attempt to kill or injure us.

We walked for some miles before we came to the stream, where we freshened ourselves. I washed my wound. We felt so angry. It was an experience which added to a lifetime of bitterness against White people. Some thirty years later I met one of my friends who was out on that hike. He had also not forgotten that incident. Some of his family had become very involved in the political movement. A number of lads on that hike also became politically active. One spent ten years on Robben Island. A few escaped into exile.

Years before my actual political involvement we were a gang of youngsters who would hang out after school at the corner shop. We would exchange stories or talk about the latest movies we saw. One afternoon two tall and well-built White men passed us and made some derogatory remarks to us. We looked up in amazement and someone asked, 'Hey chaps, are we going to let those Whites get away with that in our territory?' So we followed them and ambushed them. We left them in pain and bleeding, and disappeared. The police vans scoured the area in search of us. Somehow we felt we had released our hatred on White people.

For many years thereafter I felt remorse for my participation in what

I realized was a senseless attack. I could never erase the image of those frightened men.

From the catering trade I got a job in a leather factory and was fortunate in getting an apprenticeship as a clicker (the old term for a cutter). The factory made women's handbags and shopping bags. Most of the skilled jobs were held by Whites and Coloureds in the leather and furniture industries, a sector which I was to work in some years later as a clerical worker. I became a shop steward and took up the problems workers had. These were discussed by the shop committee. I was unaware that there was someone on the committee passing on information to the management. The management knew that the shop committee had the support of most of the workers including many of the African workers. Although the trade unions excluded the African workers, in my stewardship I took on the responsibilities of acting on behalf of the African workers. I was able in many instances to convince the Coloured workers of the need to include the African workers.

One day I left my worktable to visit the cloakroom. When I got back I found a dozen African women crying. On enquiring what had happened I was informed by a Coloured worker that one of the bosses decided on the spot to dismiss the African women machinists. One of the machinists had made some errors in the stitching and in his rage the boss dismissed a whole group of them.

After a short while the boss, who was a tall, imposing man, appeared on the shop floor. I left my worktable and approached him. I asked him on what basis he had sacked an entire group of workers. He mumbled and grumbled about the poor quality of work. I appealed to him on compassionate grounds, pointing out they were the lowest paid in the industry and all had families to provide for.

Little did I realize that all eyes of the workers were focused on me and the boss. Never had there been a situation where the boss was confronted on the floor of the factory. Much to my astonishment he agreed with me and said he would not fire the workers. I went up to the distressed women to tell them that they still had their jobs. There was an exclamation of relief, then handshakes and cheers.

In time I was retrenched. The reason given was that there was a downturn in the industry. I suspected it was an excuse to get me out.

In the same factory where I worked the workers were entitled to an annual three weeks' leave towards Christmas time. But the owners decided to add two more weeks leave without payment. To back their decision they got a petition circulating for each worker to sign saying that the worker had requested an extra two weeks without pay. This was untrue. If we did not sign we would lose our jobs. All the workers signed except me and a fellow worker, who was the son of the general foreman. We were sacked.

The lesson I drew from that experience was to sign the petition, as our sacking left the workers isolated and vulnerable. I realized that the next time I got a factory job, the aim would be to set up a firm base to wage any kind of struggle.

In the building in which I worked in the leather factory, there were a number of clothing factories above and below our floor. I got to know most of the workers during the lunch breaks. Quite a number lived in Fordsburg and surrounding areas. Others came from the East Rand. Many became avid readers of our weekly radical paper *New Age*. It was one of the few newspapers that carried stories of the plight of workers, shanty town and slum dwellers, the trade unions and the militancy of the ANC and the TIC. We developed a rapport with these workers by writing up some of their stories of hardship and victimization. Periodically they would make contributions from their low pay. Some fundraising events were held, to which the workers came to share an enjoyable evening in mixed company. Our social events were most unusual in that we had all nationalities mixing freely, easily and developing new kinds of friendship across national and colour lines.

New Age found its way into the homes of people in virtually all the black suburbs. We developed a team of weekly sellers to scour the area. The team was largely made of members of the TIYC. They did their work with a high degree of discipline. They were able to engage people in political discussions, from which they acquired greater and deeper understanding of the complexities of class, colour, cultural and gender issues.

Apart from these kinds of discussions, our activists would take up many of the problems of tenants who were being ripped off by landlords for higher rents, or faced notices of eviction, police intimidation and arrests. We would often intervene in what we believed to be unlawful arrests of Africans following a beating for failing to produce a pass.

One evening a group of us were walking near the Red Square where there was a low-quality funfair in operation. Suddenly there was a bit of a scuffle. A pair of White policemen were dragging a young African on the ground with his hands cuffed. I approached the policemen to ask why the African was being assaulted and dragged by the handcuffs. I was told that he did not have a pass and that in any event it was not my business. I insisted it was and that the actions were illegal. The young African was released and then the White policemen set about beating me up. I was bundled into the squad car and driven off to Fordsburg Police Station.

When we arrived there a crowd of people had gathered in front of the police station demanding my release. The numbers were increased by women who had been meeting at the Partidar Hall. The meeting was a women's section of the TIC and it was being chaired by my sister Darley. Word had reached them about my arrest and they descended on the police station with my sister and Amina Cachalia in the forefront.

The astonished policemen released the cuffs and one of them said to me, 'Why did you not tell me that you were a member of Congress?' I replied, 'You were beating me so fast that I did not have a chance to say more to you.'

The policeman was later involved in another assault in which three prominent members of the TIC were beaten up, charged with assaulting the police, disturbing the peace and resisting arrest. After a few court appearances the charges were withdrawn and the victims sued for damages.

One evening Constable Visser was doing his rounds in Fordsburg, calling in at various *shebeens* for his bribe money. He called on the Mazkowitz family, who were running a thriving *shebeen*. There he found Solly Jooma, one of the three SAIC leaders who had filed a suit against the state for damages. The other two were 'Aggie' Ahmed Patel, who was the TIC secretary, and Dr Hassen Moosa, an executive member of the TIC.

Constable Visser by now had established a notorious reputation for his ruthless violence on Indian, African and Coloured people in the area. He came into prominence when he forcibly entered the flat of Aggie Patel through the fanlight. Visser came in search of White women whom he was told were consorting with Indian men.

Earlier that night there had been a wedding celebration of two TIC activists. The guests were a mixed crowd of Congress activists. Present in the house was a young Coloured man who was unknown and uninvited. Nobody seemed to be particularly bothered until he opened a packet of cigarettes of a brand on the Congress boycott list. A further provocation was him singing *The Stem*, the Afrikaaner national anthem, when the guests were singing the Congress songs of resistance. I immediately realized that this could spark off some strong disagreement. I approached the owner of the home to suggest that this man leave the party since he was not invited and his provocative behaviour could lead to trouble.

The gatecrasher left with much annoyance. A short while later the party was over and Aggie invited some of the guests to his flat to continue the party. Visser pushed his head through the fanlight, since Qatun, Aggie's wife, had refused him entry. He shouted in Afrikaans at Qatun, who was very fair-skinned, 'So you have a *koolie* for a husband.' Then he viciously set about assaulting Aggie, regardless of Qatun's screams.

The commotion woke up Solly Jooma, who was sleeping in the next room. Solly, a humble and exceptionally mild-mannered man, asked Visser why was he assaulting Aggie. Visser turned on Solly and delivered a few blows. The shouts, screams and breaking of furniture drew the attention of one of the activists walking on the opposite side of the road. He also saw the squad cars.

He got to the nearest telephone to inform Hassen, who arrived within minutes. He walked in to see Aggie in agony and being handcuffed. When he asked what the problem was Visser assaulted him. Now Visser had handcuffed Aggie, Solly and Hassen, who were bundled into the squad car and driven to the police station less than two hundred yards from the flat. The men were charged with assaulting the police, resisting arrest and disturbing the peace. They were let out on bail. Aggie was taken to hospital and was treated for a broken jaw, damaged shoulder and injuries to his body.

There were a few court appearances. The accused engaged the most distinguished cross-examiner in the country, Vernon Berrange, who demolished the State's entire case, and Visser and their star witness, the agent provocateur, came out completely humiliated and angry. The freed men immediately filed for damages, assault and wrongful arrest. It was when their case was still going through the court's red tape that Visser found Solly Jooma in the *shebeen*. He dragged him out and shoved him into the squad car. He took him to a lonely spot and kicked him to death.

On the Sunday morning I called on Mrs Karolia, a woman running a boarding-house and one of our *New Age* readers. She was the one who told me that Solly Jooma was found murdered. She gave me the location of the incident but did not know who the assailant was. The location turned out to be a few streets away from where I was living. I went to the spot and picked up a tuft of Solly's ginger hair.

A few weeks later Visser was arrested and charged with Solly Jooma's murder. Visser came before Justice Rumpff. He got eight years and ten lashes. The judge said if he had tried the accused without the assessors, he would have sentenced Visser to death. Visser was quietly let out after a year or so. He was spotted in a street in Cape Town by Barney Desai, who alerted the press. Visser was put back into jail. We were not surprised when he was released well before the completion of his term.

One Sunday morning when I was doing my *New Age* rounds I called on the house of 'Aunty'. 'Aunty' was running a *shebeen* next to the Maskowitzes.

There I was given a graphic description of how members of the Bekker Street gang had come to the *shebeen* only to discover Visser was there. There was a confrontation and Visser was left spouting blood like a fountain.

I was ecstatic with joy when I heard this. At last Visser had got his comeuppance. I left 'Aunty's' house and crossed over to the house of another reader, who was a warm and friendly person. Aiysha Docrat, like Qatun, was exceptionally fair and could have passed easily for White. So could her children. With some excitement I told Aiysha what happened to Visser. There was a stony silence. Somewhat perplexed, I asked her why she was not pleased about what happened to Visser. Aiysha looked at me deadpan and said, 'Visser is my daughter's boyfriend', nodding in the direction of the daughter. I left Aiysha's house completely stunned. Without regret I lost a reader.

A few days later Aiysha's daughter and Visser fled South Africa for fear of the Immorality Act. They fled to Swaziland.

11

Resisting

For many of us, being active in the TIYC or SAIC was a learning process. But the learning process had to be translated into action, which in turn was another lesson.

People often came to the offices of the SAIC to seek help. Not only were they workers but small traders and vendors, who, like the flower-sellers, were being harassed daily by the police and traffic wardens citing breaches of the municipal bye-laws. The flower-sellers set up a body to fight the authorities and blatantly refused to be summoned to court. They found a loophole in the law. They also managed to solicit public support, including White people.

The government decided to ban Indian men from marrying women from India. Most of these marriages were arranged by the respective couples' families in South Africa and India. There was an important principle at stake: the right to choose one's bride or groom. The restriction was another attempt to inflict a racist measure against Indians. Soon we had a flood of young Indian men calling on the SAIC for legal advice. We managed to secure the entry of the women into the country in most cases.

Black people rarely had libraries in their suburbs, apart from the library at the Jubilee Social Centre, which was miles away from the black townships.[18] We launched a campaign for entry into the Whites-only library in the city centre. A group of activists daubed the walls of the city library with heavy-duty paint, 'We black folks want to read.' Some weeks later the walls were sandblasted. The next daubing read, 'Let us black folks in.' In time this was also sandblasted. Finally the new daubing read, 'We black folks ain't in yet.' This unit of the TIYC became known as 'The Picasso Club'.

The campaign caused quite a sensation. White readers discovered when they opened a book there would be a sticker reading, 'We black folks want to read.' This, we discovered, was the work of a couple of White friends, particularly Arnold Selby. Later we made formal representation to the city council for a library in Fordsburg. The council conceded.

It was not unusual when I got home from work or at weekends, either to meet someone or hear from my family that some person had come seeking my assistance. Quite often the person or their relation had been arrested, not necessarily for political reasons, and was in need of help. For example, families were evicted for being behind with their rent. Rents were hiked or houses were demolished at short notice and families left stranded. The TIYC's machinery would come into operation, one group dealing with the legal aspects, whilst another looked after the belongings of people who were left homeless. In one case several families had their belongings dumped on the pavement for days. A group of us set up a rota system to stand guard over the belongings.

There were some bizarre requests for help. A woman came to report the case of her little boy who was told by his teacher to drink caustic soda. After school the boy went home to look for caustic soda. When he did not find any he asked a neighbour. The neighbour was curious as to what the lad wanted it for. When told that the teacher had suggested it, she became alarmed and informed the boy's parents. The mother wanted some action taken against the teacher. The TIYC leafleted outside the school and informed the school head. The teacher was not fired but was taken aback at the degree of protest.

One evening a man came to see me. He was a supporter and a regular reader of *New Age*. He said he was in trouble with the authorities. He said he was helping Africans escape from prosecution and expulsion from Johannesburg under the pass laws. The way he helped them was to show that they were in his employ. The authorities arrested him. He was out on bail.

Having been a loyal supporter of the movement he felt he was entitled to help from the Congress Movement. He asked me to secure for his defence the services of Joe Slovo. I took down his details and said I would get back to him. I made some enquiries, only to learn our 'loyal supporter' had run a flourishing business helping Africans for a fee. The police had got wind of his scam. He got seven years' imprisonment.

A similar attempt was made by a TIC activist whose brother was running a cut, make and trim shop in the garment industry. The brother was paying the women exceptionally low wages but he inflated the figures for the record. The Industrial Council for the Clothing Industry, whose secretary was Helen Joseph, a prominent woman in the Congress Movement, was informed of the fraud. Helen was a good friend and we had worked together on many campaigns. The older of the two brothers approached me to ask her to go easy on his brother. I refused. The owner of the factory was made to pay back the money he stole from the workers.

Another evening I got home from work to find an elderly lady who was a family friend waiting for me. She was a well-known member of the Indian Catholic community. She was tearful and distressed. Her niece Agnes had been arrested by the Immigration Department. Agnes had come from Pietermaritzburg in Natal to live and work in the Transvaal without a permit.

Agnes was locked up in prison awaiting deportation. Her aunt thought that I would be able to rescue her niece by a marriage of convenience and thereby secure her return to Johannesburg. The plight of Agnes was not particularly new to me. We had waiters, labourers, and clerks seeking help and refuge. At times whole families were uprooted and deported. Quite often we were successful in providing help. But in the case of Agnes I had a dilemma. Agnes was attractive, friendly and one of our regular readers.

I decided that I would put Agnes at greater risk if I were to marry her. I explained to her aunt that the security police knew a great deal about me and my family, and marrying Agnes under such circumstances would also create further obstacles in my political work, and could create complications if I decided at some stage to marry for real. The aunt was crestfallen and disappointed that I could not help.

Some years later, when I visited Pietermaritzburg I called on Agnes. She was unemployed and dejected, though pleasant to me. We did not talk about her trauma of imprisonment and deportation. Not long after I heard she had died. Somehow I felt that her experience in the hands of the authorities shortened her life. I often agonized over whether I could have done something to make her life better.

One Sunday afternoon I was at home catching up on some reading when word reached me via Yusuf Cachalia, who was the banned secretary of the SAIC and was under house arrest, that the entire Indian audience at the Lyric Cinema in Fordsburg had been arrested and were locked up in cells at the Fordsburg police station for breaking the Sunday Observance Law.

I was asked to go to the police station to find out what were the charges and to get some legal representation for their release. I arrived at the police station to find the entrance blocked by the police with guard dogs. They at first refused me entry. I used some legal jargon about obstructing the course of justice and said that the legal firm had sent me with instructions to act on behalf of the arrestees. They appeared not to be concerned. Then I said that I would return with an advocate from the High Court if they did not allow me to enter the police station.

That did the trick. I was allowed in and saw the sergeant at the desk. I saw many faces of people I recognized from the neighbourhood and adjoining suburbs. There was relief that someone from Congress had come. Locked up were men, women and children. Some of the younger ones smiled and put their hands through the grille in acknowledgement.

I asked the sergeant what were the charges. He said it was the violation of the Sunday Observance Law. I asked whether it was not possible that the management of the cinema had acted incorrectly, rather than the men, women and children held in custody. When the sergeant did not question my credentials I suggested that the people be let out on bail and the children freed immediately. I said I would be returning with Advocate Vernon Berrange, the mere mention of whose name struck terror in the police.

I saw some of the people I knew and enquired what had transpired. They told me that a crowd of people had been standing outside the cinema when a police van drew up. The police got out to ask why the people were standing in a group. They told the police they were waiting for the cinema to open. The police decided it was illegal and promptly arrested the hundred or more people and escorted them to the police station, about a five-minute walk from the cinema.

I left the police station to phone Yusuf Cachalia to give him an account of the situation. Within an hour all were released without charge. I later found out that the cinema management was also not prosecuted. They could not have been. There was no audience in the cinema.

The SAIC was having its conference in Durban.[19] I was elected by the TIC as one of its delegates. To enter Natal required a visitor's permit. I applied for one at the Asiatic registration office and was promptly turned down, as were a couple of other delegates. One of my comrades took my details and set off to the little town of Roodepoort, outside Johannesburg, where he obtained a local address for a visitor's permit. With our visitors' permits we made our way to the conference. The conference was opened by Chief Luthuli and presided over by Dr 'Monty' Naicker.

There was a militant atmosphere, which was suddenly punctured by the security police bursting in. The police were led by a Coloured security man called Isaac Sharp. He knew all the Transvaal delegates. The police asked to see our visitors' permits. They checked and found them in order. We expressed outrage and got a rare apology. Later that afternoon the police made another raid. This time they scrutinized my visitor's permit and again left with an apology.

After a couple of days I was arrested in Johannesburg. I was charged with perjury. It turned out that the local address was that of a Chinese shopkeeper in Roodepoort who had never seen or heard of me. I was convicted of perjury and paid a fine of fifteen pounds. Thereafter I decided to visit the provinces without a permit. I never got caught.

One weekend I went to Durban with my wife Adelaide. We were enjoying ourselves on the Indian and Coloured section of the beach in the midst of a large number of people, when I had an awful feeling that I was being watched. I saw through the throng a set of eyes focused on me. It was Sergeant Nayagar of the Durban security police. I told Adelaide whom I had seen and that we should prepare to lose the police. We got away and found refuge with one of Adelaide's relatives in the city.

Some weeks later my brother-in-law in Durban told me that Sergeant Nayagar had visited him. He told him that in future if I wanted to visit Natal he should get in touch with him and there would be no problem. Sergeant Nayagar knew my brother-in-law sold pickles and spices. My brother-in-law sent him off with a couple of bottles of pickles and spices. I had no use for Sergeant Nayagar's corrupt practices.

12

Indians under apartheid

Indians in South Africa were the next most discriminated against people after the Africans. The Indian population in the Transvaal, Cape and Natal were confined and restricted to certain forms of work, occupations and travel. Indians were barred from living or working in the province of the Orange Free State. The Minister of Interior who introduced the law was the grandfather of Bram Fischer, who spent his life fighting unjust laws, both in the courts and in the political terrain.

Indian people suffered a range of racial persecution for many years before their actual arrival in South Africa. They were snatched off the coast of Malabar and the Bay of Bengal by the Dutch and brought as slaves to South Africa in the mid-seventeenth century. The Dutch found they could scoop up large numbers of slaves from Indonesia and ship them off to the Cape and Dutch Guyana (now Suriname).

When the slave system collapsed, the indentured labour system was introduced in 1834 and Mauritius[20] became one of the landing posts for the sugar plantations. The French and later the British authorities in Mauritius were quite ruthless with the labourers. Any Indian who fell foul of the laws faced severe penalties, including the punishment of being transported to Robben Island.

It was in October of 1860 when the first consignment of indentured labourers arrived on the SS Truro into Durban Bay. For more than a hundred years they were subjected to a maze of restrictions and were liable to deportation. Much of the labour control was by violence and abuse. It was only in 1960 the South African government granted the status of citizenship, though without the right to vote.

Their history, which has been well documented, also catalogues periods of resistance, from the passive resistance days of M.K. Gandhi, through the 1950s in alliance with the ANC and through the armed struggle, until the collapse of the apartheid regime.

It was in the context of discriminatory laws going back to 1885 that many of us joined in the liberation movement. For a long time I lived with great anger, which I soon learned would be better channelled through political organization. Quite often when in a complex situation I reacted impulsively, sometimes sailing close to disaster like being beaten or arrested, or hot-footing it out of an incident where I would intervene when Africans were arrested under the Pass Laws.

A number of times I would board a bus or a tramcar and sit in a section set aside for White people. The conductor would ask me to move to the section set aside for blacks. I would offer my fare and refuse to shift.

On one such trip the conductor raised his voice and in a temper stopped the bus. Other White people came glaring at me and demanding my removal. I quoted some obscure legal phrases on the question of public transport and the definition of public regardless of nationality. I displayed no sign of nervousness. There was a stony silence. I arrived at my destination without harm.

The next time I had this urge to defy the segregation laws on public transport, the conductor was at first annoyed at my stubbornness. I calmly explained my indignation. He listened, by which time the bus was virtually empty and heading for the garage, which was a couple of blocks away from my house.

He finally conceded my point of view, and refused to take my fare. He said his anger was more for my safety as he was sure that the White passengers would have assaulted me. As I set off he said, 'Please don't do it again. These White people will kill you.'

I had no doubt he was right. My protest as a loner would have no effect. Thereafter I decided that, unless it was essential, I would avoid public transport. My friends in the movement called me the 'One Man Boycotter'. I walked for some years until I got a job several miles away from Fordsburg, which necessitated the use of segregated public transport. But I quite often walked there and back.

In 1954 two very attractive women from Durban came for a holiday in Johannesburg. A holiday for black people meant leaving an overcrowded house only to stay in another overcrowded house in another part of the country. There were no hotels, motels or guest houses for black people.

The two women, who had never before left the city of Durban, duly acquired their visitor's permits and came up by train to Johannesburg. Had they travelled by car and passed through the Orange Free State they would have had to have a permit in transit and only drive on the road to Johannesburg.

They came to stay in our crowded house. My friends in the youth movement made great efforts in entertaining and showing them around the permissible parts of Johannesburg. One afternoon Babla Saloojee, a 'veteran' youth activist, borrowed a car and we set off on a jaunt in the direction of Vereeniging, the border town of the Orange Free State and Transvaal (where the African location of Sharpeville lies).

The reputation of the Orange Free State was on a par with the Deep South in America when it came to the treatment of non-Whites. We could drive across the Vaal Bridge but only halfway; going beyond meant going to prison.[21]

We sat in the car and talked about the various experiences we had had with the Orange Free State authorities. Babla quickly ran out of expletives and angrily suggested we cross over to the Orange Free State. Furiously, he opened the car door and we got out. The women freaked and cried from fear of possible arrests.

We left the women in the car and crossed the bridge. When we got to the Orange Free State end we unzipped our trousers and relieved ourselves, Babla defiantly saying, 'This is what we think of the fucking Orange Free State.'

My sister Darley and my young brother Daso set off on a trip to Kimberley by train from Johannesburg. That meant having to change trains at Bloomfontein. Waiting for the connecting train in Bloomfontein, the Judicial Centre for the High Court of Appeal, there was only a waiting room, no washing or toilet facilities or any refreshment service. Daso was desperate to get to a toilet, so Darley and he walked over the footbridge in search of one. They were stopped by a policeman, since no Indians were allowed in the Orange Free State. He found partial relief in some bushes. By the time the connecting train arrived my young school-aged brother was quite distressed.

In the Transvaal there were some sixty so-called 'Asiatic Bazaars' or Indian settlements.[22] Whites did not seem to know that the term 'bazaar' means an oriental market place, similar to arcades or shopping parades. These Asiatic Bazaars were some of the worst features of ghetto existence.

Traders anywhere near African or Indian localities had to display notices above their shops which read something like 'In terms of the Transvaal Ordinance Act this is a native shop.' A visitor from abroad who saw the notice said to me, 'It seems like they sell natives at this shop.'

Apart from the Orange Free State, Indians were barred from parts of Zululand, the Transkei, parts of the south coast of Natal and what is now Namibia. In the coastal resort of Margate in Natal, Indians were only allowed in the town when off-duty from hotel and restaurant service, and were confined to their sleeping quarters at the back of their work premises.

One of the most depressing cases that came to my attention was the plight of an orphaned family. They were orphaned in a Transvaal town and were sent to an orphanage in Durban. As they reached adulthood they were allowed to seek employment. One of the young men decided to join the police. When the police discovered they were born in the Transvaal, all the brothers and sisters were rounded up, shoved on to a train to Johannesburg and left stranded without food and accommodation. Relief came from the militant Anglican priest Reverend B.L. Sigamoney. The only space available was in the robing room of his church in Vrededorp. The only paper to write up the story of this distressed family was *New Age*.

The family were born in the Asiatic Bazaar of Germiston, perhaps the next most appalling locality after the Asian locality of Boksburg on the East Rand. The social and living conditions of the bazaars were primitive, without waterborne systems or electricity. Human waste was emptied from the shit-bucket into an open trough just a few yards from the ramshackle houses and from there on to the pavement, from where, usually on Sundays, it was scooped up into a horse-drawn cart.

A few miles away lived the White people. They had all the municipal facilities of tarred roads, street lights and a modern sewage system. The only Whites who knew, but were untouched by the conditions of the black inhabitants, were the municipal police authorities.

Over the years the apartheid government targeted black people with further laws, like the Group Areas Act,[23] which led to the uprooting of tens of thousands of people from the 'black spots' in Johannesburg, in which Sophiatown was a central feature. Similar removals were taking place in many parts of the country.

Whilst the SAIC tried to oppose them through legal means, it was an uphill fight. Although there was provision for a hearing to allow representation when a Group Area was declared, the only advantage we had was the chance to expose the evils of apartheid through the hearings. In many instances the authorities by-passed a hearing and summarily declared a Group Area.

The inhuman consequences were vast and appalling. The Congress movement tried to cope with the fallout. There were daily instances of racial persecution, accompanied by violent White authority. Victims often turned up at our offices or at advice bureaux set up by sympathetic White people. Neither was it unusual for people to turn up on our doorsteps seeking help. Over the years of my involvement in Congress I had got to know a very large number of people in Johannesburg, the Reef and Pretoria.

There was a Malay family in Vrededorp who I got to know through selling *New Age* to them. They were a humble, kind and pleasant family. The father was a butcher who worked many miles away. There were several children. Whenever I called with the paper there was some excitement from the children and the teenagers. Quite often I was given tea and spent time chatting with the family.

One Sunday, after a visit to the family, I was a block away from the house when I felt a gentle tug at my jacket. It was one of the little girls from the family. She sweetly said to me, 'Uncle, my mother would like you to come and have lunch with us after you have finished with your papers.' I thanked her and asked her to tell her mother I would join them.

I returned to join the family in having a most pleasant lunch. I had come to know the teenagers over some time. The second eldest daughter was called 'Julie' (not her real name). Like her siblings she was very beautiful and with a striking personality. As it turned out the family had some relatives living opposite our house in Fordsburg. The two cousins I knew were Samira and Dana.

I often dropped in at the Congress offices after work, either for a meeting or to meet members of the Congress fraternity. One afternoon I called at the offices and Babla Saloojee told me that a very attractive young woman had called specifically asking for me. She appeared stressed and had been crying. Babla asked if he could help. She again specifically asked for me. She asked that I get an urgent message to see her. She left giving only her first name, Julie. When Babla gave me the message he asked me quizzically, 'Jose, what have you done?'

Later that evening I made my way to the family's house. The atmosphere was rather subdued compared to my previous visits. The mother called Julie and sent the young ones to the back rooms. She followed them.

Julie looked downcast, far from the bubbly person I knew. We exchanged greetings. It took a little while before we talked. She said that she was in great trouble, which had caused her, her parents and the siblings a great deal of unhappiness. I asked what brought this about.

She told me that she and a friend were arrested a few nights ago in the vicinity of the zoo lake. Her friend Pascal was a White man from Belgium, who came to work as a skilled technician at the mines. Whilst they were lounging on the banks of the zoo lake the police suddenly placed them under arrest under the Immorality Act.

They were taken to the police station and thoroughly searched. They took Pascal's belt away. The two were charged. In the case of Pascal, there was an additional charge of being in possession of an unlicensed firearm. They were bailed to appear in court in several days' time. She thought that the one person who might be able to help would be me.

I agreed to do whatever was possible. The first thing was to get a lawyer, seek a postponement and whatever other help was needed. I contacted Joe Slovo, whose reputation as a fearless lawyer was widespread. Julie and Pascal got a formal notice for the court appearance. They went for consultations to Slovo's chambers.

At the trial Slovo cross-examined the police. The only exhibit they produced was Pascal's belt. Slovo saw a chink in the two police officers' evidence and successfully got them contradicting each other. The prosecution case collapsed and Julie and Pascal were acquitted. On the charge of being in possession of an unlicensed firearm Pascal was convicted and only fined.

Outside the courtroom a jubilant Julie and Pascal thanked us. Pascal asked Slovo whether it would still be possible to see Julie. Slovo advised that he could, but he would have to be very careful, as the police who lost their case would pursue them relentlessly.

For some time I did not see Julie. Eventually I made careful enquiries and was told both had disappeared. They did not disappear too far. Pascal had found a job with a mining company in Roodesport, some twenty-odd miles from Johannesburg. He rented rooms from the mining company and Julie lived with Pascal and tried to pass as White. They lived a very quiet life.

The police eventually tracked down Pascal. They came one night banging at his door. After a while he opened the door. They demanded why he took so long to answer. He said he was asleep. They barged past him. Pascal, who was a tall and well-built man, went back to lie on his bed. The police searched the kitchen, the cupboards and under the bed for Julie. They left annoyed, assuring Pascal they would get him and his woman.

After they left, Pascal turned off the lights. Julie appeared quietly from under the mattress. She was a few months pregnant. That night they fled Roodesport and made their way to the Belgian Congo.

Within a few weeks Julie died. It would appear that the stress and strain of being on the run had taken its toll.

Julie's two cousins, Samira and Dana (not real names), who lived opposite to us, were pleasant and sociable. Samira asked me to teach her to ride a bicycle. They had a slightly better lifestyle than average since both had a reasonable wage and lived in a flat. Dana's husband, Khan, was a teacher.

I was unaware that Dana and Samira sometimes slipped into White cinemas. They knew I was politically involved but avoided talking about anything political. Some years later they moved away. We lost contact.

I was still working in the leather factory in Fordsburg. Below was the garment factory, where I knew most of the workers. One day I was returning from my lunch break when I saw Dana standing on the corner of the pavement. I was delighted at seeing her, and greeted her. She looked away. I made another attempt. This was a clear snub. It was evident that Dana was working as a White, as her fellow White workers and she started chatting.

What puzzled me was that in the garment industry, Coloured, Indian and White workers were on equal wages, to the exclusion of the African workers. The only dispensation White workers had was separate toilet and restroom facilities. The only other possible factor would have been a better house in a White suburb. But then her husband Kara would not have been able to live there. Later I learnt that their marriage had broken up.

A couple of years later we were having a fundraising social for *New Age* at the home of Bram and Molly Fischer. At this party was Dana, who looked a little embarrassed. I merely acknowledged her appearance with a slight nod.

I noticed after a while that not many men danced with her, presumably because she kept aloof. I thought, since she had come to a non-racial social, she must have realized the futility of her lifestyle. I went up to her and asked her for a dance. As we danced she asked me why I ignored her. I reminded her of what she did when I last saw her. We made up and she felt more relaxed.

Some years later Dana turned up in London. She became an active member of the ANC. Later she married a Nigerian and they made their way to Papua New Guinea. Samira's life took a different turn. She lived the life of a middle-class White woman.

Once I was a guest at an Indian family's wedding celebration. Some Indians would ingratiate themselves by inviting their bosses and their families to such functions. They would set aside special tables with tablecloths, cutlery and plates, whereas we would eat with our fingers from banana leaves, which was thoroughly enjoyable.

A group of White guests walked in between the aisles and headed for the specially set-aside tables. Someone slightly brushed past me. It was Samira. I asked one of our hosts who she was. He said that she was a rich lady married into a Jewish family. He did not know that that the woman was born and brought up in Vrededorp.

In time I heard Samira had taken to heavy drinking. This I could not verify. I never heard what eventually became of her. I hoped she was all right and well.

A couple of years later a brother of Julie's was in a relationship with a young student called 'Margery' (not her real name), who lived at the back of another slum property adjacent to our house. She had come from a place called Schoenamara in Buysdorp. The bulk of the community were the descendants of a *Voortrekker* leader called Coenraad Buys. The reputation of Buys was that he had 'gone native'. He openly entered into several relationships with African women. He was the main character in a novel by Sarah Gertrude Millin called *King of the Bastards.*[24]

Many of the descendants varied in shade. Some looked African, some Coloured, some White. Some of the White-looking offspring managed to slip into the Afrikaaner community. Some integrated into the Coloured community. But the ones who got caught into a vice-like existence were the ones who looked African. They were often the target of police repression under the Pass Laws and were recruited for cheap labour. They were also sneered at and marginalized by the other Coloured people. The Africans did not accept them as Africans nor did they want to be Africans, since there was a cultural gap; their language was mainly Afrikaans, as were their social customs and their names.

The kind of house that Margery lived in with her poor relatives was a slum property infinitely worse than the one we lived in. Ours did not leak as much as theirs. We eventually got electricity put in at a joint cost with our neighbours. Margery and their neighbours still had candlelight. One of her cousins once described his room as seeing the sky by day and the stars at night. Rainy nights were a nightmare. Margery often told me that the lives of her people were wretched and they were disintegrating into drink and violence.

It was my brother Daso who first came across Margery. He felt she needed some help and some comfort. So he spoke to our mother for Margery to spend time in our front room to study and join in bites and teas. She would turn up some afternoons to study. She enrolled at the Euro-African Teacher Training Centre. Barely midway through the course she met a young chap from Vrededorp and bore a child. That ended her studies.

She managed to find a decent room in Fordsburg. With the help of some friends she got some support and also did some work. Over a period of time she became one of our activists and her social circle widened.

A brother of Margery, some six years younger, arrived from Buysdorp. He was Sidney Stevens, who had the potential of a promising artist and was keen to study. He lived with the relatives with whom Margery first stayed when she arrived. Sidney Stevens was a very pleasant and charming fellow. He fell into that category of looking like an African though he was Coloured. By now Sidney was familiar with the social ostracism towards people like him.

The machinery of the Population Registration Act reached him. To get an identity card he had to go through the process of an interview and tests by White officials. This was humiliating. Then came the dreaded news. He was classified African. This meant leaving college, carrying a Pass and moving to an African area.

Sidney's life was on a cliff-edge. Margery sent for her parents in Buysdorp. They rushed down and made desperate pleas to the White authorities. The bureaucratic process was going to be a long-drawn-out affair. Sidney's confidence collapsed. He took to heavy drinking and his life was clearly falling apart.

As for his sister Margery, she was getting demoralised, even though she continued with some political activity. Life was hard as a single parent. She met a photo-journalist by the name of Joshua Goldberg and quietly she and Goldberg got out of the country and made their way to London. They acquired a flat in Marylebone and set about organizing their lives. With the kids placed in school she got work and studied, gaining a BA Hons in history. The children, one in Canada, another in Spain and the third in West London, have become successful in their careers.

For years she kept in touch with Sidney. He never recovered from the damage of re-classification. He lived in Polokwane in the Northern Province on a small pension. In his seventies Sidney Stevens died alone of poor health and drink.[25]

Margery for some years was active in the ANC and worked for a welfare fund to provide assistance to the victims of apartheid. When the evil system of apartheid ended, she visited South Africa. She found very few of her relatives. Most had died of poverty or drink and some were scattered in remote parts of the country through the maze of laws of race discrimination that destroyed or damaged so many millions of people.

Whilst she cherished the new-won freedom, she returned to London, and still carries a great deal of pain. What happened to her and Steven, her relatives and friends she will never forget.

13

First journey out of Africa

Sometime in early 1953, the TIYC proposed that I be appointed as a delegate to the Fourth World Youth and Student Festival in Bucharest, Romania. This was to be held in August of that year.The biennial Festival for Peace and Friendship was initiated by the World Federation of Democratic Youth (WFDY).

There were several organizations that had emerged after the dreadful wars and devastation of countries and people in Europe and Asia. The first was the United Nations in 1945. Soon after there followed international federations for workers, women and youth. The WFDY was one such non-governmental body of which the TIYC (and for a while the YCL until it was proscribed in 1950) was a member.These groups campaigned vigorously against colonialism and racism, and on behalf of workers', women's and youth rights.

A great deal of support came from the Soviet Union, the emerging peoples' democracies in Eastern Europe, and from national liberation movements in Africa and Asia. Equally, there was strong support from working-class and professional organizations, as well as from communist and socialist groups in Europe and the Americas.

The WFDY was launched in 1947 at the Albert Hall in London. The two South African delegates invited were Ruth First and Harold Wolpe. A similar invitation was quietly sent to the youth section of the ANC. Equally unknown was a guest-of-honour invitation to Walter Sisulu, the Secretary-General of the ANC.

Since there was no public knowledge of our invitations, largely for security reasons, at an appropriate time only the delegates and their immediate families were informed. I had an especially difficult task in telling my mother that I might have to go abroad for Congress work. I knew she would be apprehensive, particularly following the death of our eldest brother, Ramsamy. To put her at ease and assure her that all would be well, I asked Roy Naran Naidoo, a dear and long-time family friend, to have a chat with her. His charm and sincerity won her over.

I dared not disclose that my trip abroad would be without a passport. All of us in the delegation were already on police files and there did not seem to be a possibility of getting a passport. The only documents I had were my birth certificate and my Asiatic Registration Certificate, which prohibited me from travelling freely to the other provinces. For the first leg of our departure we were to travel by train from Johannesburg to Cape Town. I did not have a visitor's permit to enter Cape Province.

My brother Peter accompanied me to the mainline station and there, to my surprise, were Alfred Hutchinson, Henry Makgothi and Lindiwe Ngakane,[26] who came with her father to see her off. The four of us were active in the Defiance Campaign against unjust laws. We courted imprisonment.

We journeyed into Cape Town. There we were to be met by some people. Nobody turned up. Apart from Alf, the rest of us had never set foot in Cape Town. Eventually we located the house of the Ali family. The front of the house was their little shop. The Ali family were well known through their twin daughters Rahima and Fatima. Both were married, Fatima to Dawood Seedat, a former communist and NIC leader, and Rahima to 'Ike' Moosa, a medical doctor in Johannesburg.

We found some of their younger siblings, one of whom, Farida, was of some help. We explained who we were but not the purpose of our being in Cape Town, only that we were stranded. Farida tracked down the telephone numbers of some of the known political people. I tried one. He was most unhelpful. As we were stranded, Alf left us for a while to take Lindiwe to someone he knew in Langa for an overnight stay.

After a while the rest of us were directed to a hotel for black people, called The Tafelberg. We stayed there overnight and the next day went in search of people who might help us. Eventually we were tracked down by Mary Butcher (later Turok). She seemed embarrassed and upset at what was a breakdown in communications that had left us in a risky situation. Mary quickly got us accommodated in safe places and set off to sort out the mess and get a set of affidavits for each of us.

We were taken to Sam Kahn's office. Sam was a prominent MP and lawyer. He arranged for the documentation, using Alf's and Henry's passes and my Asiatic Registration Certificate. My certificate also had my thumbprint, and words like 'born of British Indian parents'. What was quite perplexing was that I had number of Indian names but nothing like Paul Joseph. My document had my father's and his father's and my name, which read something like Navarajh Veersamy Moonsamy Veeraswamy; even the last two names were incorrectly spelled by the immigration department.

When Sam Kahn finished with us, he sent us to another office below. It was the office of Benjamin Kies, a prominent member of the Unity Movement, a high-school teacher and now a lawyer. He co-signed our affidavits. These were the documents to be presented to the immigration officials in Southampton.

Our passages were booked in the names of White members of the movement. There were three names I knew, Beata and Alan Lipmann, and Sidney Shell. I did not know in whose name Lindiwe's passage was booked. Together with them we got on the boat, one of the Union Castle Line. We were posing as labourers and domestic servants, carrying the madams' and masters' bags.

The booked passengers showed their passports and baggage tickets to the immigration officers. A steward led them to their cabins and we followed, depositing their baggage. We were left in the cabins and they calmly got off the boats. The boat was set to sail at 4 pm. We were to stay in our cabins for several hours and only emerge later.

After a considerable time I came out of my cabin. I went to check Alfred. He was in his striped pyjamas, completely relaxed and reading. I left him to check Henry. He was rolling from side to side and puking from seasickness. I could be of no help. I walked down the corridor to see Lindiwe. She looked calm and settled. As I left her cabin a stewardess came rushing out of Henry's cabin. She mumbled in annoyance, 'I thought there was to be a woman in that cabin, instead it is a man.' I told her there must be some mistake. I cooked up a name and told her that it was actually 'Beatam', which is a man's name. She got more annoyed. I did not go back to Henry's cabin.

Later I heard some movement in another cabin. Someone emerged from there. It was a well-dressed African in a three-piece suit. We greeted each other. He was Greenwood Ngotyana. He too was heading for Southampton. He told me he got on dressed in labourer's overalls and apron and also carrying someone's luggage. Once in the cabin he changed into a three-piece suit, rolled up his overalls and threw them together with his boots out through the porthole.

By the next morning we ventured out and were directed to the dining room. There was another shock in store for us. We were never told that we had first-class tickets and that we would be entitled to all the first-class facilities. Our presence sent the catering staff into a tizz and the fellow first-class passengers were startled. There were a couple of quick confabs. Later the captain arrived. He had already twigged what had happened. He could do nothing, since we were not stowaways. Our passage – first class at that – was paid for.

ANC & TIC volunteers gather at The Garments Workers' trade union hall in Johannesburg, prior to their first acts of defiance, 26 June 1952. Paul is in the front row second from left. OWLS000151-2

The first day of The Defiance Campaign 26 June 1952 Boksburg.
Left to right: Nana Sita (President of the TIC), Abu Dadoo, Ahmed Tirhy, Henry Naude, 'Babla' Salojee, Ibrahim Moola, Paul, Frank Kandiar and Sulieman Esakjee. OWLS000151-1

The Fort, Johannesburg where Paul was held in solitary confinement.

A dock worker was being banished to a remote part of the Transvaal. The Indian Youth Congress turned up at Park Station, Johannesburg, to offer their solidarity and give him a food parcel. c. 1958. *Left to right*: The dock worker, Mohamed Bhana, Kista Moonsamy, Adelaide and Daso Iyer (Paul's brother). OWLS000151-4

Winnie Mandela dressed in a saree after opening of conference of Transvaal Indian Youth Congress, alongside her is Adelaide, 1963. OWLS000151-3

Adelaide and Winnie Mandela outside the court of the Rivonia Trial, 1964. OWLS000151-5

At home 74 Avenue Road, Fordsburg. *Left to right:* Paul holding the family dog Druzba, Amah (Paul's mother) holding Zoya, Adelaide holding Anand. c. 1960.

At home 74 Avenue Road, Fordsburg. *Left to right:* Zoya, Adelaide holding Tanya and Paul holding Anand. c. 1964.

We were placed near the swing doors of the kitchens. Except for a few, most of the passengers made polite conversation. In time the crew became pleasant. Whenever Lindiwe wanted a bath, the steward would prepare it for her and in turn she gave him a tip.

We had in mind that, when we arrived in Southampton, we would tip the catering staff. One morning we were having our tea. I poured mine into a saucer and slurped from it. The waiter came along, expressed shock and commented, 'Sir, not even the lowest of the working class would drink tea like that.' I thought, well, there goes his tip. Fortunately the rest of passengers in the dining room did not hear or see what happened.

The rest of the trip was relaxing, and some of the passengers and crew were friendly. One of the passengers actually conversed with us. He wanted to know what we were going to do in England. We said we were going to study. Greenwood and Lindiwe were smartly dressed, and travelling first class perhaps created an impression of a kind of middle-class black. Alf, Henry and Lindiwe were already university graduates.

The passenger who spoke to Greenwood wanted to know what he was going to study. He said science. The man asked what branch of science. Greenwood was a bit stumped when the man also asked how he did in science at matric level. Greenwood replied that it was a little complicated, and he might decide to study law. The man looked bewildered and walked away. Greenwood had very little education and was of peasant stock. He came to Cape Town and found work at the docks. He eventually became a leader of the African dockworkers' union.

As we went for our regular walks on the deck we strolled past a French couple lounging in the deckchairs. They were most friendly. They had been in South Africa for academic research on race and politics. One of the organizations they had visited was the South African Institute of Race Relations. There, amongst the many people they met, was a Mr Ngakane. Lindiwe looked startled and held her breath.

After the brief chat we walked away. Lindiwe recovered. She said, 'Oh, my God! My father gave me the name and address of that couple just in case I got to Paris.' She asked what she should do. We chatted a bit and we agreed she should tell them that she was Ngakane's daughter, since we were already some days away from Cape Town.

The next time she met the couple she showed them their names and addresses that her father had given her. They were astonished. The man said he had thought there was something odd about us and had an inkling that we were politically inclined. They said they would be most delighted to receive her in Paris. The man said he once came across some people on a ship and discovered they were off to a festival in Berlin.[27] We disclosed we were heading for a festival in Bucharest. We all broke into laughter.

On our arrival in Southampton, we were directed to a couple of men who sat at a desk on the ship. They were customs and immigration officers. We showed them our documents, which raised their eyebrows. We were told to stand aside. Within a short while a couple of stripe-suited men turned up. They were accompanied by Vella Pillay. It dawned on me that Vella only knew me as Paul Joseph and not by the string of Indian names on my affidavit. I walked up to Vella to embrace him, and whispered into his ear in Tamil that my name was not Paul Joseph. I rattled off my Indian names.

The two men who accompanied Vella were barristers who had come to seek political asylum for us. After a fairly long discussion we were granted asylum. When the documentation was completed we were each given ration cards. I put my hand out to thank the officer; he just gave me a cold look.

We arrived at Waterloo station and from there to East Finchley, where Vella and his wife Patsy lived and their beautiful little boy Anand, who gave us a warm welcome. Later in the evening a group of South Africans arrived. They were Dave Kitson, Ben Turok, Mike Feldman and Cynthia Zukas. We were each taken to the flats of other South Africans in the suburbs of Chalk Farm, Camden Town and Muswell Hill.

Over the next few days we managed to make short trips to the centre of London, whilst the rest of the plans were in preparation for the trip to Bucharest. Much to our delight and surprise Walter Sisulu and Duma Nokwe arrived. They came by plane via Israel.

For the next few days we walked around London to see the historic sights. What was strange was that we could enter any shop or café without any kind of restriction; the people were friendly and polite. We could get on the tube trains and buses and experience no discrimination. We had never experienced this sort of freedom in racist South Africa.

Meanwhile our South African comrades were engaged in the logistics of arranging our documents, flights, and transport to London airport. We flew to Prague, where we received a warm welcome from the Czech youth movement. They provided accommodation for the delegates arriving by plane. We met the American delegation. Some had come by plane and others by train. Several took circuitous routes to avoid detection by US intelligence.

From Prague we took the train to Bucharest. It was a thoroughly enjoyable journey travelling with a collection of people from many parts of the world. There was a babble of languages, song and the playing of traditional musical instruments. One of the many delegates I struck up a friendship with was a young White student from New York, Bianca Moorehead. She told me that her forebears were slave owners and she discovered a related descendant was the famous jazz musician, Dizzy Gillespie. Bianca also got to know Walter Sisulu and followed his career until after he was released from Robben Island.

From the day we arrived in Bucharest and for the next two weeks our programme was packed, with visits to concerts, theatre shows, exhibitions, sporting activities, schools, film shows, dances and being constantly stopped by visiting delegates and Romanian citizens wanting to know our country of origin, the languages we spoke, our religions and occupations. Many had never met African, Chinese, or Indian people. The whole festival was an exhilarating experience for all who attended.

Towards the end of the festival I was asked by our delegation's leader, Duma Nokwe, to go to Warsaw as an observer delegate to the Conference of the International Students Union. Whilst I was not a student, the TIYC had students amongst its membership. I arrived in Warsaw and was amazed that the scars of the war after eight years were so stark, unlike Prague or Bucharest. This was also evident from many of the older people, as well as young people who were orphaned, injured and distressed from having their families, relations, friends and neighbours killed either in the concentration camps or by the widespread bombing.

As I walked around Warsaw I noticed volunteers fixing the streets and pavements. One of the American delegates was helping to level the tarmac. Then I walked to see the reconstruction of the part of the city called Old Warsaw. The restoration I was told was exactly as it was before the war.

Later in the day I met some people who had survived the concentration camps. They invited me to their homes. Among them were artists who spoke English and gave me some of their drawings. The way they embraced me with warmth and respect actually gave me a lot of confidence.

When I got back to Prague, I received a message from the Transvaal Council of Non-European Trades (who were affiliated to the World Federation of Trade Unions [WFTU]) asking me to represent them at the forthcoming Third Worker's Conference of the WFTU in Vienna. That was to be in the next two weeks. The Czech trade union body invited our delegation to stay in Prague until the start of the conference.

Staying in Prague was indeed a special treat. One day I was on a tram ride through the city. Sitting opposite was a woman who politely greeted me. She spoke in English. Soon we were exchanging bits and pieces of information of our respective countries. Her name was Gusta Fucikova. I asked whether she was related to Julius Fucik. She nodded her head, 'He was my husband.'

Fucik was the courageous journalist who was killed by the Nazis in prison. He had smuggled out notes, later published as *Notes from the Gallows*.[28] Copies of the book found their way to South Africa.

Gusta was delighted that I knew about the book. She invited me to her flat, where she showed me the actual notes placed between glass sheets. She also invited me to an exhibition on Julius Fucik to be held in a few days' time. Gusta was happy to see me there and introduced me to several people, who were pleased to chat with me as a rare visitor from South Africa.

On another visit to Prague I was taken around by a group of Czech trade unionists. They were friendly and asked a lot of questions about South Africa. I asked about the Slansky trial. They seemed surprised that I had heard about the trial. I had read about similar trials in Bucharest and in Moscow. This was not long after Stalin's death in March of 1953. There was something strange about these trials. Many of the imprisoned and executed were people of Jewish origin.

At the time I was quite ignorant and vague about the actual details other than what we read in the left-wing publications and what our party had put out. Three years later the whole story of what had happened in the Soviet Union and Eastern Europe exploded at the twentieth party congress with Nikita Krushchev's revelations.

Much to my delight I was joined in Vienna by Greenwood Ngotyana and Frank Marquard, one representing dockworkers, the other, food and canning workers. Both unions had their main offices in Cape Town.

This gathering in Vienna was unlike the other two in Bucharest and Warsaw, where there was lots of fun, dancing and jollification. It was more serious and businesslike. We were hearing and reading of the plight of workers and peasants. There was a strong urge for international solidarity for jailed trade union activists and their denial of legal rights, and strong resolutions from the colonized countries, whose resources were stolen and their people heavily exploited.

Many delegates at this gathering received invitations to visit the eastern socialist countries. The South African delegates were invited to visit the Soviet Union. We travelled by train from Vienna to Moscow, via Ukraine. That was quite a fascinating journey. From Moscow we travelled to Leningrad, Stalingrad and Kislovosk in the Crimea. These visits evoked a powerful feeling, particularly the visit to Stalingrad. As a young boy I had followed the battle in Stalingrad. We were in awe of how the Russians defended their city and rolled back the Nazi army right into Berlin. The cost in lives and destruction was vast but the victory was celebrated around the world.

In Stalingrad we stayed in a hotel opposite a building in the basement of which a prize prisoner, German general Friedrich Paulus, was captured. We were invited to see some of their finest ballets and operas at the Bolshoi theatre, the Hermitage, the rest houses and hotels, spas for the workers. We were taken to visit universities and training centres.

One of the more spectacular visits was to the vast Leningrad Library. It contained the largest collection of books in the country, reputed to have several million volumes. I was enthused. I asked if I could be shown the collection of the works of Fyodor Mikhailovich Dostoevsky. There was silence. I thought they might not have heard me clearly, so I repeated the question, 'Comrade, would you please show me the collection of the works of Fyodor Dostoevsky?' The interpreter stuttered, 'Actually Dostoevsky is not published in the Soviet Union.' I gasped, 'What? You do not publish Dostoevsky? What is the reason?' 'He's a counter-revolutionary.' 'Are you sure?' I asked. He said 'Yes'.

I said I could not believe that. I went on to express my utter disappointment, that Dostoevsky, one of Russia's greatest writers, was banned in the Soviet Union. I then rattled off some of Dostoevsky's works, stressing his classic *Crime and Punishment*, widely regarded around the world. I then said in exasperation, 'Comrades, when I get back to South Africa, I actually come from the slums of Johannesburg, where I will meet my friends and have to tell them that Dostoevsky is banned in the Soviet Union! One of my friends is doing his degree on Dostoevsky, and I will have to break this news to him.'

There was only silence. Then I heard a whisper in my ear. It was the Indonesian/American in our group of visitors. 'Ask them where the works of Trotsky are.' I whispered back, 'Why don't you ask them? As it is, I'm in trouble for asking about Dostoevsky.'

Some days later, during a rest period, one of the interpreters sat with me for a casual chat. He was curious about the Indonesian/American. Did I think that our visitor was a Trotskyite? It occurred to me that the interpreter must have heard that whisper. I said 'Comrade, you should improve on your information. Our fellow visitor is actually a follower of Earl Browder (who was the former general secretary of the US Communist Party), and Browder actually believes that capitalism will make a peaceful transition into socialism. Our friend could not be a Trotskyite.'

By the following year Dostoevsky was widely published in the Soviet Union. He was hailed as one of Russia's greatest writers.

We were back in Moscow for the 36th anniversary of the October revolution, celebrated in Red Square on 7 November. We were loaned heavy overcoats and fur hats, but no boots. To ward off the cold, I folded copies of *Pravda* to put in my shoes and line my ankles. We were given flags to wave as the contingents of workers and soldiers passed us. We saw the huge tanks and gun carriers. Overhead was a massive fly-past.

As we cheered, we gave the thumbs-up Africa salute. We saw a group of Australian visitors chuckle. We responded with glee, showing them the thumbs up again. After the demonstration some of the Australians came up to us wanting to know why we did it. In Australia, they said, it means 'Get f...ed'.

We got back to London in early December. We still had roughly two weeks before our departure to Cape Town. The two weeks were well spent in attending meetings and demonstrations in support of the Kenyan liberation movement, and a meeting in support of the South African struggle at which Walter Sisulu spoke at Holborn Town Hall. Visits were made to Marx House, the Marx headstone in Highgate cemetery, the CP HQ, the *Daily Worker*, Central and Foyle's bookshops, the British Library, and a brief audience with Palme Dutt.

We attended a conference on racism in England. I managed as a last event to attend a piano concert at the Albert Hall.

We set sail for Cape Town and arrived a week before Christmas. We made our way to the *New Age* office, followed by the security police. We were back into the circuit of the apartheid machinery. Henry and I were a bit nervous, as neither of us had documents to validate our presence in the Cape Province.

Friends rented a house and we shared the accommodation for several days. One day the owners popped in to collect some items. They introduced themselves to us as I.B. Tabata and Jane Ghosh, who were leaders of the Unity Movement of South Africa. Theirs was a Fourth International brand of Trotskyism and ours was the CP of the Lenin/Stalin brand. It was an amusing and pleasant encounter.

We left Cape Town courtesy of Percy Cohen, who drove Aggie Patel, Henry and me. We drove through the Orange Free State, mindful of the fact that we could be stopped by the police. Aggie could get away with saying he was Malay, but not Henry, whose pass document showed he was a resident in Johannesburg, nor I without a visitor permit.

Our respective organizations arranged for a series of report-back meetings on our trip and some of our experiences in the countries we visited. Virtually all the meetings had a police presence taking notes of the speakers.

14

Julius First's Furniture Factory

One day in 1954 I went with a friend who had some business matter to discuss with Julius First. I was told he had been a member of the CP in the early days. He apparently left the party to engage in his furniture business. I had already met his daughter Ruth through my involvement in the YCL. I asked to speak to him with a view to enquiring about a vacancy of a clerical nature in his firm. There was none available.

Several days later Eli Weinberg, whom I already knew as a comrade, phoned me with a message to contact Julius First. He asked me to come over to see him at his factory, the Anglo-Union Furniture Manufacturers, in a locality called Industria, Johannesburg. The firm manufactured domestic and office furniture and at some stage made coffins for African undertakers. After a brief interview he offered me a position as production clerk in the cabinet workshop.

The factory was a vast complex. It had a large timber yard with a railway siding that carried imported timber. There was a big machine room, a cabinet shop, a polish and sanding shop and a large space for the finished products ready for dispatching.

The composition of the workforce was White, Coloured, Malay and Africans, who were in the majority and who worked as labourers, with a few doing semi-skilled jobs as machine sanders. The firm, as in all White places, had to adhere to the strict racist laws in providing separate toilets, washing facilities and restrooms for Whites, Coloureds and Africans.

The overall effect of racism quite often surfaced in paradoxical ways amongst two groups of the workers, the Coloured and the White workers. These two 'nationalities'[29] were allowed to be the cabinet-makers and machinists. This meant both groups got the same rate of pay and they were in the same union, which excluded the African workers.

The Transvaal law pertaining to certain industries only allowed Whites to do skilled work. In the case of the furniture industry Coloureds were also allowed to do skilled work. Indians and Africans were not allowed. However, some Indians were smuggled in as Coloureds. The African workers did mainly the manual and labouring work and in a few instances were allowed semi-skilled work like machine sanding.

Julius took on a young Coloured worker as an apprentice cabinet-maker. The Coloured cabinet workers rejected his apprenticeship, saying the young man was an African. When Julius refused to listen, the cabinet-makers threatened to strike. Julius still refused. They backed down. This was a year or so before I joined the firm. When the young man was qualified we celebrated with glasses of milk.

One Christmas break after we returned to work I had a chat with the newly qualified cabinet-maker. We were exchanging our Christmas break experiences. He told me that he had a good time. The 'good time' was going around with his brother, who was in the police force, arresting Africans for 'pass offences'.

We had a couple of Coloureds who passed for Whites. Since both groups got equal pay I worked out that the only possible advantage would have been getting a decent house in the White working-class area. Another who passed for a White cabinet-maker joined the firm. He asked me who that 'coon' was, directing his gaze at our newly qualified cabinet-maker. I said, 'He is a qualified cabinet-maker.' He was not impressed. He quit his job within an hour.

My job developed from being only a production clerk into a range of other tasks as well. These were to be in contact with suppliers of accessories for fittings (some being imported) and to maintain stock records.

The Africans always had trouble with the Pass Laws, because of which there was virtually daily harassment by the police. I was to ensure that the pass documents were correctly endorsed and signed on behalf of the firm. I often got off at the rail station near the factory. There it was quite common to see Africans handcuffed to the railway fences by the police.

The firm gave its African staff coffee and tea for the morning and afternoon breaks at a charge of a few pence. One day Julius called me in for a discussion about providing a free lunch. He wanted to know how best to go about it. There was already a kitchen and a restroom. What was required was a menu and a couple of people to do the cooking and serving.

I knew a mother and daughter running a coffee cart. It was actually a kitchen on wheels which could be seen sited in several industrial areas. These coffee carts, sometimes called 'café-de-move-on', which could be pulled like a handcart, offered them a better and regular income instead of working in all weathers for a meagre income. Sorting out the menu was quite straightforward and in any event the meat would be of quality. Now the workers had free tea, coffee and lunch, which was received with delight. Any non-African member of staff who wanted the lunch would have to pay. Their payments went into the women's kitty as a bonus.

In some ways my working in the factory was like a workshop, discussing issues on race, class and work issues that caught the attention of the workers. Many of the workforce were long-time workers at the firm. They had a high regard for Julius. Quite often some of these workers were in need of help. In the case of the Coloured workers they could purchase a house in a Coloured area. They would approach Julius for a loan, which he gave them without interest.

In the case of the Africans, they lived in matchbox houses which were controlled by the municipal authorities. There were no freehold rights in the 'native locations'. Some of the Africans asked for loans with regard to family matters, and some who had bits of land in their hometowns and needed farming implements would request a loan.

It was known that Julius had some old-time African staff who were involved in the CP before it was banned in 1950. There were also a few who were in the ANC. I met some of these workers who were involved from that period.

Pius Masisi was a CP member who had dropped out of active politics, but somehow he still retained confidence in socialism or, rather, in the catch phrases.[30] Sometimes Pius would go out on deliveries to furniture shops. Then a call would come in from a customer complaining that one of our workers was brazenly obstreperous with them. He would tell them about how they were exploiting the workers.

One day I was with Julius when the siren indicating a break went off as Pius was carrying a large piece of timber. Pius dropped the timber, shouting, 'Workers down tools'. Julius said to me angrily, 'That is the sort of worker Michael Harmel[31] recruited into the CP.' On another occasion we had to get out an urgent consignment of sewing-machine cabinets destined for Ghana, so it was all available hands on deck. The general manager, a Mr Hymie Rostovsky, rolled up his sleeves and joined us. When Pius saw him working he said to him, 'Ah, I see you are working for a change.' Rostovsky was furious and shouted 'fuck off!' at Pius.

I had heard from some of the older workers that Julius had sacked Pius a couple of times. Pius would dash off to Ruth to plead with her to get him reinstated. Ruth would phone her father and Pius was back in work. I soon discovered why Pius wanted to be in the firm. He had a lucrative business on the side. Pius was a moneylender. His interest rate was 25 per cent on a pound a week. In time Pius's non-political activity was no safety valve.

When the State of Emergency was declared in 1960 after the Sharpeville massacre, Pius was amongst those detained.

John Khebubetsi, who was an old-time employee working in the sandpapering department, had been taken on more or less at the same time as Pius Masisi. John was also an old Party member until it was banned in 1950. Like Masisi he ceased to be active in political involvement. However, he retained an interest in socialism and was an admirer of the Soviet Union and in particular of Stalin.

When Khrushchev delivered the famous revelations at the Twentieth Party Congress in 1956, especially about the crimes committed by Stalin, I had a chat with John. At the time John was busy preparing the shellac for filling and covering the knots in the cabinets and making the French polish. He had a knife in his hand for cutting the shellac.

I asked him what he thought about Khrushchev's account of Stalin. John ranted and fulminated that, 'Khrushchev is a Trotskyite, Titoite and counter-revolutionary bastard. It is all lies, lies, lies.' He half raised himself, making a sort of swipe at me, saying, 'If Stalin was alive he would cut all their fucking throats.' I withdrew my face in time and wiped some of the spittle off my hand.

When I was arrested in 1956, charged with 155 other people with high treason, and then again after Sharpeville, Julius ensured that first my family, then my wife Adelaide got my monthly salary. For my part I made sure that whenever the court was in recess I would turn up for work.

There was a time when I was asked to go to a conference in Durban. I asked Julius if I could have the Monday off on the understanding that I would have a day's pay deducted. At the end of the month I noticed no deductions. I went to see Julius to enquire why I got my full pay. He angrily sent me away.

One of the firm's employees was Alpheus Maliba, a former member of the CP. He could not find a job. Someone had asked if Julius could help. Alpheus was taken on as a security night guard, a job specially created for him by Julius. One evening Alpheus did not report for duty. We later learned that he was arrested by the security police and placed in solitary confinement. He died in prison. The police claimed he committed suicide.

Julius and his wife Tilly First were of Lithuanian Jewish parentage. Both were born in South Africa. Most South African Jews came from the same Lithuanian origins or the other Baltic states, Russia and Poland. Czarist Russia was notorious for its pogroms and blatant anti-semitism, and many Jews left to make their way to South Africa.

Within that segment of people were Bundists, communists, supporters of

Trotsky and people of no political persuasion. Some of the immigrants were involved in the 1905 and 1917 revolutions. It was known that there were some relatives of Trotsky in South Africa. One of them now lives in London and is not a Trotskyist but was jailed in South Africa as a communist.

The South African state was, as a consequence of the Dutch and British brands of colonialism, the first racially instituted state in which White people of any class had complete domination over black people, who were kept in servitude as workers, labourers and domestic servants.

The European immigrants realized the advantages of being White and were easily seduced into supporting the system of racial discrimination against Africans, Coloureds and Indians. They soon made the quantum leap from the persecuted to the persecutors.

In time many of the Jews became amongst the wealthiest of White people. As the Jewish community prospered they moved slightly north of the city to Doornfontein. As prosperity increased the richer members of the community moved to the posher parts of the northern suburbs like Park Town, Rosebank, Melrose and Emmarentia Park. Tilly and Julius moved to Emmarentia.

Tilly was brought up in Fordsburg. At that time there was a fair-sized Jewish community in Fordsburg, which had the second synagogue in Johannesburg. She lived in a house with a corner shop on which 'Levitan's Building' appeared embossed above the building. Levitan was Tilly's maiden name.

Levitan's building was situated on the corner of Lillian and Avenue Roads. We lived at the bottom end of Avenue Road. Many years later it was acquired by an Indian, which would have been done through a White nominee as Indians were restricted in ownership and occupation under the Gold Law of 1885 of the Transvaal Republic. The premises became a gambling den.

Tilly, as a young radical socialist, was outraged by the actions of some of the Jewish owners of furniture shops, who repossessed the furniture of White striking miners who were defaulting on their payments. She was incensed that Jews who had come from a persecuted background could not show compassion to the families of White miners who came out in a general strike in 1922.[32]

Tilly was known to have been active in the CP in the early days. Her admission to the party was not straightforward. Some of the puritans in the party created obstacles, the main one being that she was the wife of a capitalist. Julius was becoming a successful furniture manufacturer. In his time Julius was on the central committee of the party.

It often made me wonder who these doctrinaire communists were, so puritanical that they could block people like Tilly. They evidently forgot that Friedrich Engels was the son of a prosperous manufacturer in whose firm Engels was manager. Besides, some of the leading socialists in the world came from the rich and middle class.

In time Tilly gained admission to the party, and in the mid 1930s visited the Soviet Union, an account of which appears in her granddaughter Gillian Slovo's book *Every Secret Thing*.[33]

In her own quiet way Tilly and her friends, Annie Goldberg and Annie Kotkin made a formidable trio, visiting businessmen of progressive sympathies for donations. These women were not only attractive but were strong personalities who knew just how to shake down the men for money. Like many of our womenfolk whose sons, daughters, husbands or relatives faced intimidation, restrictions and imprisonment, they became the backbone of support.

This was the role Tilly took on when her daughter Ruth worked for *New Age*, appeared as a Treason Trialist in 1956, evaded detention during the State of Emergency in 1960 and was detained in solitary confinement for 117 days. On every occasion Tilly stepped in to care for the granddaughters, Shawn, Gillian and Robyn, eventually taking them over to London.

Joe Slovo

Joe's father was a van driver and Joe was brought up in the sizeable semi-working-class Jewish community of Doornfontein. He had won a scholarship as an ex-soldier to do law at Wits. After qualifying he occupied chambers in the famous 'His Majesty's Building'[34] within walking distance of the magistrates' court and the supreme court in the city.

He soon became a barrister in demand by a cross-section of the community and was much talked about in the black communities as on a par with celebrated lawyers like Vernon Berrange, Rowley Arenstein, Bram Fischer and George Bizos. Such lawyers were held in high esteem and were much feared and respected by the police and magistrates.

At one of the tea breaks during the Treason Trial hearings in the Drill Hall, a White Security Branch officer by the name of Pampendorf, whom I knew by sight, walked towards Joe, with whom I was in conversation. He asked to be excused and wanted to take the opportunity to thank Joe for successfully handling his complaint against the police authorities, who had denied him his right to promotion. All his departmental appeals had failed so he decided to go to court. He got Joe as his brief. Joe won the case based on a form of discrimination because Pampendorf came from South-West Africa (now Namibia).

Joe and Duma Nokwe defended themselves in the Treason Trial. One of the witnesses brought to testify against Joe was an African policeman. The prosecutor asked the witness whether he knew the accused. He said, 'Yes, he is well known because he fights for the rights of the African people.' The prosecutor immediately stopped the questioning. After some months Joe told me that he had received a report that the policeman had been taken to a prison farm and killed there.

On a personal level Joe, who was striking in his attire, was very pleasant and easy-going. It was a pleasure to be with him. He was a good listener and never talked down to us. He was a comrade we could freely relate to. We always liked to visit him and his family and attend the lovely parties in their house.

One party was to celebrate the quashing of the first indictment on the treason charge. Amongst the guests were virtually the entire battery of the defence team, including Issy Maisels, Bram Fischer, and Vernon Berrange. Having mixed parties was very much frowned on by the apartheid authorities and, in the case of Joe, to serve alcohol to Africans and Indians was a deportable offence, since Joe was born in Lithuania.[35] When a raid took place, the black guests simply poured their drinks into the plant pots.

Some of us noticed the security police crawling around the outside of the house, while others were gawking from trees. I saw a chap hovering outside the kitchen door, which was open. I shut the door. Suddenly the police barged in and carried me out. My wife Adelaide saw this and shouted to some of the guests about what was happening. Alfred Hutchinson and another comrade dashed out, grabbed me from the police and carried me indoors.

When the Communist Party revived in 1953 Joe invited me to join, and when MK was formed in 1961, he recruited me.

Ruth First

I was walking down Market Street, carrying bunches of flowers for sale to passing pedestrians, when I saw a beautiful young woman in the vicinity of the Johannesburg White library. She gave me a friendly smile. I had never been smiled at by a White woman before. I noticed she was of a slightly darker complexion and smartly dressed. The next time I saw her was again in Market Street in the Indian trading quarter. She was about to enter a building called Kholvad House.

Sometime in 1948 I went along with Barney Desai, who was one of my closest friends. We attended the same school and lived a few doors away from each other. We went to the offices of the Young Communist League (YCL) to enrol as members. Our membership was processed by Barney

Feller, the organising secretary. Joining the YCL was quite an event and certainly a turning-point in my young life.

There at the YCL office I saw the young woman again. I learned that she was working on a newspaper called *Challenge*, the YCL journal, as the editor. Her name was Ruth First. As I got more involved in the activities of the YCL and later the TIYC we became friends.

It was in the YCL circles that I got to meet Mike Feldman, Bessie Blecher, Harold Wolpe, Maropeng Seperepere, Vella Pillay, Lenny Fonn, the Levy twins and Sadie Forman. I met many more at the Jewish Workers' Club in Upper Rose Street in Doornfontein. Later I met two of Ruth's flatmates, Patsy Gilbert and Winnie Kramer. I saw a lot of Patsy, who was very active in the YCL. There were not many Indians, Coloureds or Africans in the YCL.

In June 1946 the TIC was making its presence felt. It launched a passive resistance campaign against segregation. This campaign brought many people into prominence who came from our neighbourhood and surrounding areas. They included two very impressive law students, who lived in a flat in Kholvad House. They were Ismail Meer and J.N. Singh. Later it was known that Meer and Ruth were dating. Now I understood why Ruth was visiting Kholvad House. There was even talk of marriage.

The ability of the TIYC was very much recognized by the Johannesburg staff of *New Age*, especially Ivan Schermbrucker. The TIYC played a major part in boosting the sales of *New Age* and was also very involved in fundraising. They would bring guests to the multiracial socials which, if not raided, were snooped on from the outside by the security police. The police would take down the car numberplates and later call on the owners to inquire why their cars were parked at a party for *New Age*. Ruth, who was also editor of *Fighting Talk,* was also involved in the fundraising events for both publications. When the publications reached dire straits because of insufficient funds, her father Julius First would quickly step in to the rescue.

Apart from having to sort out the logistics for the events, she and several White friends would have to transport some of us home to the black areas on account of the poor transport after dark and the prospect of being held up because of the Pass Laws.

Not long after *Challenge* folded, Ruth was giving *The Guardian* much more attention. *The Guardian* had a national circulation and carried reports of most of the events. She was submitting reports to them for publication. The Johannesburg editor was Michael Harmel, who held the position for several years. Ruth was also involved in the Progressive Youth Council (PYC). She tried to get the PYC to affiliate to the ANC Youth League. She wrote to Nelson Mandela as its head, but he turned down her proposal.

Soon Ruth's ability and talent were noticed. She had a sharp nose for news. Many of her reports were groundbreaking. She ventured into uncharted territory, like uncovering the prison farm labour scandals, taking the Reverend Michael Scott and Henry Nxumalo, accompanied by a remarkable countryside leader, Gert Sibande, to meet the slave labourers, who were living in terror and appalling conditions.[36]

A distinguishing feature about Ruth was that she never hogged her work as a journalist. She encouraged and brought in several people to contribute to *New Age*, for example, Henry Nxumalo, Robert Govender (under the name of Bert Williams), Robert Resha and Beata Lipman. On several occasions she got me to send in reports of the numerous stories of people being evicted from their houses, workers intimidated and assaulted, and deportations that I came across.

Other distinguishing features of Ruth were her ability to cultivate friends, and her skill in getting through government bureaucracy to make her reports factually correct. She was always thorough, with friends, contacts, and political and trade union leaders. She was a prolific journalist and kept a tight schedule: work, the courts, the family and some socialising. She was highly regarded by several White journalists and academics. Some gave her help and wrote articles under pen-names. She also caught the attentions of European correspondents, who also assisted her.

Ruth went on a trip to China in 1954 and on her return wrote a very interesting account of her visit. She edited a pamphlet about a number of South Africans who visited the Soviet Union, including Walter Sisulu, Duma Nokwe, Sam Kahn and me. These pamphlets were widely read in Congress Movement circles and were subjected to police confiscation, even though not banned.

In the early 1950s we were able to get English editions of Soviet and Chinese publications. We received stacks of publications, largely because there were loopholes in the law and a degree of clumsiness on the part of the customs department.

One that was particularly popular was *China Today*, a monthly pictorial. I found a ready-made clientele in the local Chinese community who had no access to any literature on China. Once a month I went to the Chinese quarters selling pamphlets. I often came back empty-handed. This proved a lucrative source of income for *Fighting Talk*.

Another boost for our meagre income was the arrival of a can of film, smuggled in by a progressive English seaman. It contained *The White Haired Girl*.[37] This film and a staged version had caused a sensation in communist

China and Europe. The Chinese community lapped it up. One Chinese businessman paid for the exclusive screening of the film for his family.

Fighting Talk was a progressive journal started by a group of men in the Springbok Legion. By the early 1950s the journal had gone into decline, as had the Springbok Legion. A handful of people revived the journal as it seemed there was a need for such a publication in view of a potentially wider audience in and around the Congress Movement. Ruth was asked to edit the journal, with her an editorial board made up of Cecil Williams, Rusty Bernstein, Norman Levy, José Podbrey and, on occasion, Nelson Mandela and Dennis Brutus. Ruth invited me to join the board. Whilst my main function was to deal with circulation, she encouraged me to write for the journal.

Since I lived out of bounds of the northern White suburbs, one of my comrades would arrange to pick me up in Fordsburg to attend board meetings. Late one night, as we were returning to Fordsburg, Ruth and I noticed we were being tailed. A black male sitting alongside a White woman could easily be interpreted as suspicious. Ruth decided to step on the gas and we sped through the Indian business quarters into Fordsburg. Our pursuers also accelerated. Ruth was an excellent driver. I directed a route and, as we arrived in a road with two cinemas diagonally opposite each other, the crowds were pouring out. Ruth drove carefully through the crowds. As she stopped for a moment I jumped out and told her to move on. I got lost in the crowds and so did the police. I did not think they were security police but rather zealots from the Immorality Squad.

The journal became a channel for promising short-story writers like Alex La Guma, Richard Rive and Alfred Hutchinson. Some academics were contributors, as was a highly respected parliamentary correspondent who wrote fascinating and incisive articles on the apartheid government, based on his close connections in government circles. That was Stanley Uys. Many articles appeared under pen names.

Once a month the traders in the Indian business quarters around Kholvad House readily bought *Fighting Talk,* and in the suburbs of Fordsburg and Vrededorp it was sold alongside *New Age*. In the city on the pavement outside the main Post Office we had African newspaper sellers who sold *New Age* and *Fighting Talk*. I noticed some White people buying them. Since they did not look like people I saw at any gatherings of a political nature elsewhere, I felt confident that our efforts were meeting a need.

I often had copies of *Fighting Talk* during the Treason Trial. One day I approached Oswald Pirow, who was the chief prosecutor, to ask him whether he would like to buy a copy. To my surprise he responded, 'Oh,

Fighting Talk .Yes, of course!' and rapidly brought out a shilling. He sat down and read the journal in full view of the Court. A bemused Duma Nokwe quipped to me, 'So you have provided him with further evidence!' He was referring to Pirow's statement in court, 'Your Worship, I am waiting for further evidence.'

One person who was a tower of strength as manager of *New Age* was Ivan Schermbrucker, who also gave much of his time in distributing *Fighting Talk*. Others who gave their unstinting support for the journal were members of the TIYC. Not only did they sell the publications but helped and contributed towards fundraising events. There was a similar core of people in the COD.

At one of our fundraising socials there was a loud shattering of glass. When we looked out we saw the Secretary of the TIC. He was lying on his backside, feet up and a cigarette between his fingers. He had fallen through the plate glass of the lounge, having had more than his share of a tipple. When I asked what had happened, he said, 'Some fucking Trotskyist pushed me through the window.' We picked him up unscathed.

Norman Levy and I went around collecting second-hand clothes for our jumble sales. Joe Podbrey arranged card games to raise money. Norman once told me how his mother would contact her friends asking for clothes. The ploy she used was, 'It is for poor Africans.' What she got was handed over to Norman.

Ruth told me how one day she arrived at the theatre director Cecil Williams' flat to collect some clothes. Cecil was noted for his stylish suits, shirts and shoes. When she got there, Cecil had a neat pile of clothes. As she was lifting the pile Cecil asked her to wait whilst he started peeling of the clothes he had on except for his underpants.

Ruth would arrange for her father to bring the clothes to his factory where I worked, where I would arrange a lunchtime sale.

The government's attempts to stifle our publications through banning orders, arrests, intimidation and raids of our homes and workplaces succeeded. There was still a legal gap where we could breathe some opposition through a publication. It was a newspaper, *The Forward*, the organ of the old Labour Party which had become dormant, as had the Labour Party. The last leader of the Labour Party was Alex Hepple, a former prominent MP. *The Forward* had not lost its registration. He allowed us to use the paper.

Once again Ruth became the editor alongside a small team – Ivan Schermbrucker, Eli Weinberg and some members of the TIYC. This time we also had the help of Mac Maharaj. We all saw this as a challenge. Ivan asked what quantity we could handle. I talked with members of the TIYC. We agreed we would take 300 copies since it was a special attempt. We scoured all the local areas in our suburbs and also made a special attempt in the Asiatic Bazaar in Pretoria. We sold our quota.

A few issues followed but then came Ruth's arrest and detention for 117 days. Just about everyone connected with *New Age* and *Fighting Talk* was a victim of the apartheid government.

15

Adelaide

I was sitting in our front room in our house in Avenue Road, Fordsburg, having a chat with Sophie Williams, an activist from the Coloured section of the Congress Alliance. It was 1957. There was a knock on the door. I got up to open it to a slender woman with impressive features, beautiful eyes, lovely teeth and a Grecian nose. Her hair was tied in a bun.

Adelaide had come to give a message to my sister Violet from some friends in the eastern town of Barberton in Mpumalanga. She was living with an aunt and uncle who moved to Ferreirastown from Barberton. She was most friendly and in the short time my sister chatted with her I secured her name and the locality she came from, which was about a mile or so away. I casually mentioned that it would be nice to see her again.

Within days I was around at her house in Ferreirastown where she was living with her aunt Dhano and uncle Harry Masher. They were part of the well-known Masher/Sebastian clan. Most of the family were members of the Seventh Day Adventist Church and living in Barberton.

The clan were originally Hindus, whose forebears came to South Africa as indentured labourers to work on the sugar plantations in Natal. Members of the clan who were at the end of the indenture period of their contract left by ox-wagon to make their way to the Transvaal Republic and settled first in Heidelberg, Pietersburg, then in Nelspruit and Barberton.

Some converted to Christianity, mainly as Anglicans. Later on others became Seventh Day Adventists. Their defection to the Adventist Church shook the Anglican Headquarters and the Reverend Bernard Sigamoney was hastily despatched to Barberton to avert the defection. All his eloquence could not dissuade the switchover.

My meeting with Adelaide was my introduction to this section of the community. Up to then I only knew of Indian Christians being members of the Catholic, Anglican and Methodist churches and, in Durban, the Bethesda Temple. I knew that Catholics had a strong code of conduct but I found the Adventists even tougher and stricter on diet, hygiene, dress code, dancing, cinema and certain kinds of social gatherings.

They strictly observed the sabbath, which started at sunset on Friday and ended at sunset on Saturday. They did not, on their interpretation of the Bible, observe Christmas Day or Easter, apparently because there are no given dates for these events. The consumption of alcohol, tobacco or any drink near to alcohol like vinegar was taboo, as were pork, beef and duck. The only beverage allowed was Rooibosch tea, which I found to be an awful drink.

Regardless of their religious affiliations all the black communities were racially discriminated against and the mindset was deeply rooted in that framework. The Adventist Church quietly upheld racial segregation in their churches. The Coloured and Indian Adventists had their own churches. In Natal they were mainly Indian only. The Africans had theirs, as did the Whites. None of their members ever got involved in any form of opposition to apartheid.

When I started dating Adelaide, I found all kinds of complexities that governed the members of their church. One of the many factors was not to get involved in politics. Adelaide's family had heard of my political involvement. It was the first time they were meeting someone involved in the Congress Movement. They also heard that I was something of a communist, a concept which they did not know anything about. I was mindful that this community, like the rest of the different nationalities, were trapped in their cultural and racial stratification. I had to tread very carefully. I exercized care in the way I conducted my relationship with Adelaide and her family and relatives and their friends. But in no way was I going to keep quiet if a political issue arose that needed a response. Instead, my responses would have to be carefully crafted, concise and respectful with no intention of bruising any of the religious people.

Some years before I met Adelaide, the mother of a young woman I was dating asked to see me. She told me that as a member of the Catholic church she could not allow her daughter to see me, as I was a communist. I did not engage in a debate but agreed to break my relationship with her daughter. We remained friends.

I naively believed Adelaide was in the same category and that it would be a matter of time before I was given the push. I soon discovered I was rather presumptuous in assuming that Adelaide was non-political.

Adelaide's experience as a trainee nurse in Barberton involved her in a racial dispute. Black nurses were generally lowly paid and experienced shabby and inferior treatment and bullying by the senior White nurses. A White matron was intimidating the black staff. This led to an outburst of anger among the black nurses. They went on strike and submitted letters of resignation, and went on a deputation to the superintendent, much to the astonishment of the authorities.

Adelaide emerged as the ringleader and was called a communist. This was the first time she had heard the word 'communist'. She did not know what a communist was. The superintendent agreed to look into their problems with the matron. They found the matron at fault. She was reprimanded, the intimidation stopped, and the White racist nurse was removed. I only got to know about this incident from Adelaide some time after our meeting.

Adelaide already had some grounding in relationships with people across the race lines whilst working in the Barberton hospital. She developed a close relationship with a White doctor but had to keep a low profile because of the Immorality Act. She also developed a relationship with an African teacher. This, too, was a quiet relationship because of the prejudice of the Indian community. Moving to Johannesburg some years later she found employment in a garment factory which brought her into contact with Coloured, Indian and African workers.

I was not the first political person she met. Living in Doornfontein in Beacon's Road, a street dubbed '*Hondesbeck*' (dog's mouth), amongst her new friends, was Maurice Hommel, a Coloured teacher who was a member of the Non-European Unity Movement. Though friendly, he never really discussed politics with her.

I found Adelaide was fairly well read in the English classics, largely through her mother's influence. Through me and her political friends, she was introduced to a wider selection on English, South African, American, Russian, and Indian literature. She delighted in reading John Steinbeck, Upton Sinclair, Mulk Raj Anand, Jack London, Oscar Wilde and Bernard Shaw. She did not take to Marxist literature. She was introduced to Robert Tressell's *The Ragged Trousered Philanthropist*, which she found most fascinating and that seemed to have done the trick in introducing her to the concept of socialism. She became a regular reader of *New Age*, *Fighting Talk*, *The New Statesman* and *The Observer*. Her aunt and uncle, as ardent Adventists, did not take kindly to Adelaide's choice of books and newspapers. They clearly believed I was poisoning her mind.

Of her own volition Adelaide's attendance at the sabbath weekly service was irregular. She was beginning to show a sense of independence. This was also towards me. I was slowly to discover I was on a trial period. I was not the only person interested in her. She told me she was keeping her options open. There were a couple of proposals for marriage.

Adelaide evidently discovered that I, too, had a number of women friends

– but no offers of marriage on my part. I thought the only way I could convince her of my credentials was to introduce her to my women friends. She realized after meeting most of them that they were fellow-workers, friends, dancing partners, political colleagues and a few ex-girlfriends. I told her that I was not keen to avoid or disown any of my ex-girlfriends. The net effect of this was that Adelaide developed a friendship with these women, who over the years came to help us in our difficult times in the movement and our family.

When we met it was during the Treason Trial. I was one of the accused. She came to some of the hearings and she got to know a lot of the accused, with whom she developed warm and lasting friendships. Many of the new-found friends would come to play an important part in our lives.

It was at the Drill Hall[38] that she met Zainab Asvat, who had a remarkable capacity to organize a daily lunch for the accused. Zainab had drawn on the support of Indian women and shopkeepers to help and supply vegetables, spices, etc., to prepare the food and arrange for delivery. It was an arduous task. Adelaide was drawn to help in a rota system.

The Treason Trial hearings were the central and effective forum for meeting such a wide range of personalities from various parts of the country. Adelaide got to know scores of political leaders and activists and their families, including the Fischers, the Mandelas, the Naidoos, Mosie Moola, Ahmed 'Kathy' Kathrada, Babla Salojee, the Asvats, J.B. Marks and Moses Kotane, as well as a crop of leaders from Natal and the Cape.

We often talked about the kind of people she met in the Congress Movement. She would be quite candid. She had a degree of shyness and sometimes felt intimidated by people like the Bernsteins and the Cachalias, especially Yusuf, who could come across as abrupt and conceited. It was only after she became active that she began to find people like Ruth First, Winnie Mandela and Helen Joseph much easier to get on with. Her confidence increased as she met Blanche La Guma, Mary Moodley, Ruth Mompati, and Lilian Ngoyi in the course of many activities. She found Amina Cachalia, who some people thought showed airs and graces, to be easy and pleasant.

I made a specific point of taking Adelaide to the homes of the Fischers, the Barsels, the Haymans, and the Naidoo family. I wanted her to meet the kind of people who were in the liberation movement. She adored Bram and Molly and described them as a rare couple. The other family that made a particular impact on her were Amah Naidoo and her children.

I also took her to meet Maulvi Cachalia and his family. There we had tea and samosas and a hearty chat. I had not noticed Maulvi taking her aside to engage in a one-to-one chat. A couple of days later I met Maulvi.

He said to me, 'That woman you brought to us, she is very nice, but don't marry her. She is too clever for you.' When I next saw Adelaide I mentioned Maulvi's advice to me about her. She retorted, 'Bloody hell. No wonder he questioned me so closely.' She then asked me, 'What kind of leaders have you got in the Indian Congress?'

By the time the preparatory hearings for the Treason Trial took off the South African Treason Trial Defence Fund had been formed, on the initiative of Bishop Ambrose Reeves, Alan Paton and a band of very distinguished progressive citizens. Their concern was that the accused be given the best possible defence and that the welfare of the accused and their families was assisted.

In December 1957 Adelaide and I set off on a trip to Barberton, mainly to meet most of the rest of her family, relatives and friends. Barberton, named after the Barber brothers, was where gold was first discovered in 1884, two years before it was found in Johannesburg. The remains of the first Stock Exchange are still partially preserved. The town is set in a valley, surrounded by a spectacular series of mountains which straddle parts of Swaziland, Natal, the Free State, into Mozambique and rising in Tanzania. I love the climate, which is sub-tropical, sprouting the most exotic summer and winter fruits.

One of the only two English-speaking towns in that province, at that time Barberton had a population of about ten thousand, the bulk being Africans and confined to their locations. A short distance away were the Indians in their Asiatic bazaars, and not far from them were the Coloureds in their localities. The Whites, of course, had the best parts in and around the town.

The non-White communities seemed docile and went about their lives in work, church and social gatherings calmly compared to life on the Reef. The African area was bustling with animation and laughter. Most of the inhabitants were farmhands, domestic workers or doing menial tasks in building and construction. The Coloured people in their area (which some years later was dubbed Katanga) looked despondent and spiritless and were noted for their heavy drinking. The area looked quite desolate. The small Indian community lived in better built houses, all being zinc, wood and brick, with little gardens. Adelaide's Uncle Sam was the first to have a solid brick-built house with attractive porthole windows. Local Whites would drive by to see the construction of this, the only beautiful brick house in the racially segregated area.

Barberton was one of only two areas in the Transvaal (now Mpumalanga and Gauteng) where Indians were granted freehold rights. The other was Nigel. The rest of the sixty-odd Indian areas were recorded as Asiatic bazaars, where no freehold rights were allowed. Two hours' drive away was the game reserve. The facilities there were for Whites only; blacks could only drive in but by sunset had to be out.

Adelaide and I got up well before sunrise to go for walks along the streams and pick fruit still glazed with dew.

One of my bail conditions was that I report once a week to the local police station. Being in Barberton meant reporting to the police there. On my first report the officer in charge was rude, abrupt and showed contempt. I realized that he had never met a person from the Congress Movement. His reaction was a consequence of the hysteria the government had created about us. I remained calm but merely mentioned I would be talking to my lawyers about the visit to the police station. On my next visit the officer was most polite, called me 'Mr Joseph' and was helpful in the way he recorded my visit. I had never talked to any lawyer.

One evening as Adelaide and I walked to the town we saw a policeman on a bike. Some yards behind him was an African, handcuffed and trotting with a rope from the cuffs to the saddle.

Adelaide's family and relatives received me with warmth and kindness. Her grandmother was clearly the village elder and Adelaide, being her eldest granddaughter, was much fussed over. Apparently her uncle, Sam Sebastian,[39] had me checked out and was satisfied that I was suitable, but was quite concerned that I did not have a religious faith. Since they never approached me on the matter, there was an amicable relationship.

Meeting the families and Adelaide's relatives resulted in numerous invitations. The families in Barberton had a tradition and a reputation for a very high standard of Indian cuisine, most of which was passed on to the offspring.

After Adelaide and I had been dating for almost a year, we decided to get married. I still had a job, and Adelaide was working in a garment factory. We both lived in small and overcrowded conditions. She lived with her aunt and uncle and I lived with my mother, sisters and brothers. I was confident I would find some accommodation. I searched for a long time and began to despair. We thought of putting off our intention of marriage.

I talked to one of my friends. He advised that we should go ahead and get married and some kind of accommodation would come about. I took his advice and came across a man whom I knew through my political work. He had a house with three bedrooms, a lounge, bathroom and kitchen. He had a wife and two young children and was in need of extra income so he was willing to let out a room. We took the room as a temporary measure.

We arranged to be married by the Reverend D.C. Thompson at his manse in the town of Springs. Thompson was a fellow Treason Trialist and was chuffed to officiate since we were the first political couple he had registered.

A week later we had our celebration party in the house of Hilda and Rusty Bernstein, long-time political comrades. In 1946 Hilda Watts, as she was then, was the elected communist councillor for the White voters from the suburb of Yeoville. Rusty was a fellow Trialist. In fact most of the guests were Treason Trialists as well as other political activists.

Adelaide wore a simple attractive two-piece costume. My sartorial outfit caused a bit of a stir. The guests had never seen me dressed up. Little did they know the only items that were mine were my briefs and socks. The rest was borrowed from my brothers.

We lived in the room of our friend and, although we had the use of their kitchen, we decided to prepare our food in the room. Our friends were vegetarians and followed the Hindu scriptures. Maganbhai sometimes left his bedroom door slightly ajar so that we could hear him chanting in front of some kind of shrine, and the beautiful smell of *agarbathi* made its way into our room. One evening as he was mumbling aloud, his little son emerged from the room calling 'Uncle Paul! Uncle Paul! See what my father brought,' and he lifted a litre bottle of whisky, at which point Maganbhai's eyes widened, his ears pricked and he dived to secure the bottle, speechless and out of breath.

Adelaide and I made the room as comfortable and attractive as possible. We had a Primus stove. Adelaide was able to make a selection of curries and rice which were piping hot when served. Quite often we had a guest or two for meals. It always baffled me how Adelaide managed in such a confined space to cook, wash and iron. We slept on a single bed. I held her so that she did not roll off.

We lived there for several months. Then Adelaide got pregnant, so the search for a bigger place became urgent. Adelaide's grandmother was concerned, and arranged for her to come over to Barberton to enjoy the comfort and care available there whilst I spent time looking for suitable accommodation. The situation became quite acute as the exciting news reached me that Adelaide was going to have twins.

My brother Peter was able to secure some rooms next door to the family house in Avenue Road in Fordsburg. The rooms had been used as a shop, first for a herbalist and later as a tailor's business, which was actually a front for a *shebeen*. The rooms were in a very shabby state but within days I was able to turn the place into suitable accommodation and had electricity connected.

The landlord charged us business premises rent and would not budge to lower it. As usual my brother Peter came to our aid. He paid half our rent, which was £10 per month; my wage was £30 per month.

Both Adelaide and I were confident we would have a boy and a girl. We tossed around several names and, as tradition would have it, we consulted our respective elders in the families. In the end, Adelaide and I decided to call the children Zoya Tamara and Anand Shura, after a young sister and brother who died fighting in the partisan movement against the German invasion of the Soviet Union. Zoya Kosmodemyansky, having sabotaged the German advance, was captured, tortured and hanged in 1941, aged nineteen. Shura, a senior lieutenant, commanded a battery of self-propelled guns. He was killed in April 1945 at the age of eighteen, during the bombardment of Königsberg.

My mother requested that Indirani be added to Zoya's name but was happy with the choice of Anand. I chose Anand because it was from the name of the house in which Jawaharlal Nehru was born, which I had discovered when I read Nehru's autobiography in my teens. Anand Bhavan – House of Happiness –was handed over by Motilal Nehru, Jawaharlal's father, to the Indian National Congress in the freedom struggle.

Adelaide's grandmother was keen for Adelaide to stay with her for the birth. She knew that we lived in cramped conditions, and her house in Barberton was spacious, with all the facilities, and surrounded by a beautiful garden. The hospital was only a few minutes' walk from the house.

The twins were born on 14 February 1959, to great excitement in the neighbourhood as they were the first set of twins to be born there, and at my work, where I received the telephone call with the news and shared it with my workmates. Adelaide's Uncle Sam and his wife Auntie Maisie, together with Grandma Elizabeth and her grandsons Devine and Wilson, provided all the help and attention that Adelaide and the twins needed.

A few days later I received another telephone call at work telling me that the twin boy was not well and that I should come over. That evening I made my way to Barberton, some 250 miles away. Adelaide was happy, and I was delighted with our beautiful children.

Adelaide explained that Anand was not suckling so she realized there was something wrong. He was delivered with forceps and was injured in the process. In other words, his brain had been damaged. The hospital staff were ill equipped. Adelaide trained in that hospital and she believed the doctor was negligent. Apart from the doctor, the rest of the team were black, and the hospital, as in all segregated hospitals, lacked facilities. Some of the nurses were Adelaide's friends.

It was a most distressing experience. The twins were beautiful. Zoya was bubbly and alert, Anand chubby with a growth of wavy hair. But he was quiet and seemed to be in agony. We had no idea how severe was his cerebral damage. No further checks were carried out. The doctor never came to see me to explain. Adelaide stayed in the hospital for a few days before being taken to her grandmother's house. I discovered that Zoya and Anand were given another set of names by the African nurses. Zoya was named *Sibongile* ('Thankful') and Anand *Busisiwe* ('Blessed').

Given the condition of Anand, it was decided by the family in Barberton that we should not take the twins to Johannesburg just yet, we should wait for a more suitable time. My mother and sisters were informed about Anand's condition. This was most upsetting. Some weeks later my mother went to Barberton to see her twin grandchildren.

Meanwhile I took the opportunity to carry out more work in fixing the two rooms and getting the cots and other necessities for the twins. Our quarters had an outside toilet and a standpipe shared with two other families. That not being enough, passers-by would make use of the meagre facilities, thus adding to the already unhygienic conditions.

After a couple of months the twins came home. Their arrival caused quite a stir in the neighbourhood. Many of our comrades turned up with gifts for the twins and some put us in touch with some medical friends and a chemist, whose pharmacy was about two miles away. The chemist was Max Schlaghter, who was not only kind but reliable and only accepted payment for medicine and baby food when we were in a position to pay. Doctors such as Zainab Asvat, Aziz Kazi, Hazra Ismail and Essop Jassat also gave their service not only for the twins but also for Adelaide. We were introduced to a child specialist, Dr Boetie Gordon. These people were a tremendous asset to us.

Since Anand was not suckling on his mother, Adelaide was rich in milk. The retention of the milk, in spite of her expressing frequently, led to her become quite ill. Eventually Dr Gordon decided Adelaide be sent to hospital. He phoned me at work and asked that I come over immediately to accompany her to the Coronationville Hospital. He stressed she should be taken by ambulance. I got home and made the arrangements, sorting out the care for the twins with my mother and sister. The ambulance arrived to transport Adelaide and me to the hospital.

At the hospital she was placed on a trolley and pushed to the reception desk, where I handed in the doctor's letter. We waited for a considerable time for a doctor to turn up. He made what appeared to be a superficial examination and said he would return later. The examination was carried out in the reception area. I saw him disappear into the common room. I knew this room, which is where the doctors took their tea break.

After an hour or so he returned again to check Adelaide. He squeezed her breasts a couple of times and decided there was no need for admission. She should be returned home. He clearly ignored the letter from Dr Gordon.

I asked the reception staff if they could arrange for an ambulance. The response was to ask for payment for bringing Adelaide to the hospital. The fee was ten shillings. I told them that I had left my jacket at home and had no money on me. If they would oblige I would pay them for the round trip. They refused to accept my request.

We were left abandoned. I left Adelaide alone and wandered off to the neighbourhood of Newclare where I knew a few people. I had no joy, as most were at work. I then phoned a friend in Fordsburg, Hassim, the owner of the Lyric Cinema. He immediately obliged and sent his driver around to collect us from the hospital.

After I took Adelaide to her bed I phoned Dr Gordon and told him of our experience. When I got back in the house, I found Adelaide had fallen out of bed with a high fever. Dr Gordon arrived, angry and outraged at the way she had been treated. He treated her to relieve most of the fever, and advised me to write a letter of complaint to the superintendent of the hospital. Then the ambulance turned up at our house. They had come for the ten shillings I owed. Several days later I got a reply that the doctor who saw Adelaide was correct in his assessment. But no apology.

Anand was prone to infection and was periodically taken to hospital. One evening I turned up in the children's ward. I found another toddler lying at the other end of the cot. The child was brought for treatment of diarrhoea. I called for the doctor and he advised we take Anand home. Soon after he was brought home he showed signs of being infected with diarrhoea. For Adelaide and me Anand's condition was highly stressful. We had what was called 'surface sleep'. So we took turns sitting up with Anand. Fortunately, with my mother next door, we could send Zoya there, which helped relieve the stress for us.

Before the children were born we had decided we would not take on any domestic help. We thought we could manage. But after their birth we changed our minds. So we got the occasional help. This was clearly not enough. Adelaide's aunt sent us a woman, Rosie, who was desperate for work. We explained the situation. We also explained we lacked suitable accommodation.

Rosie's African name was Matselane. She looked frail, but showed a sense of commitment and had an air of gentleness. We agreed to take her on. I got a fold-up bed which she used in the kitchen. She was delighted, since the coal stove provided warmth in the evening. In time Rosie proved to be a gem. She loved the twins and would go for walks with them, taking Anand in a pram with Zoya along her side, followed by the children's pet dog, Drushba. They became familiar characters in the neighbourhood.

Soon our two-roomed house became a meeting point for political activists, friends and relatives. Rosie clearly understood that the people frequenting our house were people involved in the Congress Movement. She got to know Winnie and Nelson Mandela, Mosie Moola, Issy Dinat, Reggie Vandeyar, Ramnie and Shanti Naidoo and their brother Indres, Wolfie Kodesh, the Turoks and the Asvats among the many. When there was to be an important hard-core meeting, Rosie would sit outside with Anand, keeping a lookout.

When our place or that of my mother's was raided by the police, Rosie was ignored and never questioned. When we were not in, Rosie would monitor everyone who popped in and those who knew her well enough would leave a message.

Whenever we went on an outing, we took the children, sometimes to the swimming pool at the Fischers or the Bernsteins, or to the zoo lake and, if we could manage, we would invite Rosie. Since we called her Rosie or Matselane, we asked her to call us by our names. Instead she called Adelaide Mama and me Papa and sometimes *Buti*. Actually Rosie and we were about the same age and we had a mutual regard and respect and affection.

Some weekends and some nights she would prefer to spend time with her companion Jacob. Jacob was the caretaker at the school which Zoya was attending. He stayed at the back of the school grounds where his zinc rooms were his quarters. One night there was a knock on the door. When I opened it there was an African asking to speak to Rosie. I called her. As I turned back there was a howl from Rosie. Adelaide came dashing from the kitchen. Through her sobs Rosie said the police had killed Jacob. She decided to go with Jacob's friend to the school. We told the family next door and we told six-year-old Zoya. She was shocked, and cried.

By the next morning we got a full account of Jacob's death. Prior to the killing the police often called around to get their kickbacks so that Jacob could have a visitor or two as 'lodgers' – that was the police term for men without passes. So it would mean any African found on the premises was a lodger without a permit or without a pass. The police station was no more than a hundred yards from the school. This time the police had gone to the school and banged on the side gate demanding to see Jacob. Jacob emerged with an old overcoat slung over his bare shoulders. They demanded to know why he took so long to open the gate. Before he could explain he was shot in the chest, killed instantly.

I made more enquiries and was informed that the school principal was dealing with the matter. The principal had agreed to arrange for Jacob's funeral and burial. There were no further inquiries into the circumstances of the killing.

I wrote a letter to Helen Suzman, the only decent MP left. I set out the details of the death and requested the matter be raised in Parliament. I got a reply from a Margaret Roberts,[40] who was Helen Suzman's secretary. The Minister of Justice at the time was John Vorster. Vorster's reply was that the police shot Jacob in self-defence and the matter ended there.

Rosie, my mother and sisters next door and Adelaide's aunt and her daughters a couple of blocks away provided us with a great deal of help and would take turns in caring for Anand and Zoya. Unknown to us, my eldest sister Chella would carry Anand when visiting friends in the neighbourhood. One summer's evening she took Anand to the Red Square where a group of faith healers were offering their prayers and blessings. When we heard about it we did not take a critical view. We realized that Chella was hoping that the faith healers would help Anand.

In spite of the help and support we got, the main burden of care was on Adelaide. This was physically arduous and emotionally stressful for both of us. As Zoya was fast growing up, she too became unhappy as she had no siblings to play and interact with. She was clearly affected by having a disabled brother. We often talked about the need to have another child, but uppermost in our minds was the question whether the next child would be physically fit. How much we could cope with was the recurring question.

We decided to talk to some of our friends who were in the medical profession. They were confident it would be quite safe; besides, Zoya would do well in having a brother or sister. With that assurance we decided to allow a reasonable time, particularly for Zoya, who was becoming quite independent in caring for herself and doing some chores in the house.

Zoya was also beginning to understand about the kind of people who frequented our house. On occasion she was taken to public meetings. She also understood why her mother had to go to certain types of meetings dealing with matters concerning the women and their suffering. Our house was subject to periodic police raids, which were generally in the evening or the mornings.

Her first real distress came when I was taken by the security police after the Sharpeville shootings and the declaration of the State of Emergency.

By now Adelaide was already familiar with the events concerning the Treason Trial and the shootings in Sharpeville followed by the declaration of the State of Emergency in 1960. The State pounced on some two thousand activists and leaders of a range of organizations such as the ANC, the Pan-Africanist Congress (PAC),[41] the Pan African Freedom Party, the banned CP and Liberal Party and some members of various Fourth International components.

Some leaders and activists managed to evade arrest. A segment of detainees in Natal was released due to a technicality. Within a day or two the police came looking for them without success. Those who got away skipped either to Swaziland or to Botswana and some accepted a directive to make their way to Zambia or England to garner support.

A hard core of communists stayed in Johannesburg, finding shelter in safe houses. They set up structures and in time were able to announced the existence of the CP, which had been relaunched in 1953 but without any public announcement. The leading figure who initiated the announcement of the party's existence during the State of Emergency was Moses Kotane.

It was only after my release at the end of the State of Emergency that I discovered to my astonishment that Adelaide was a key courier for Moses Kotane. Apart from carrying out assignments for Kotane, she kept in touch with the womenfolk whose husbands, sons and relatives were in detention.

She again came to play an active part before and after the Rivonia Trial as well as in lesser trials. She got her strength and courage from the wives, mothers and sisters of detainees. She worked with a band of women to provide welfare needs and arrange visits to prisons, and had running arguments with security police and prison authorities about prisoners' safety and their visiting rights.

In one instance when she suspected physical ill-treatment she took it up with Zainab Asvat and a lawyer. This resulted in an application for habeas corpus. The lawyer who made the application was Joel Joffe. This attempt failed, even though the police paid the costs. The government had removed the right of habeas corpus. Nevertheless, it did make the police back down on some of us.

She did all these tasks in spite of having the responsibilities of Zoya and our ailing child.

Once again my mother, sisters and brothers were helping out with the twins, especially when Adelaide had to move around at night with messages and arrangements for meetings. Rosie was a solid support. She was friendly but barely spoke and when she did it was in Afrikaans to me and in an African vernacular to Adelaide. She was on nodding acquaintance with some of the activists.

The situation in the country returned to a relative calm. I returned to full-time work and got back into the swing of things, doing my *New Age* rounds, picking up the pieces and regrouping of Party cells.

A new crop of young people emerged. Reggie Vandeyar did some sterling work in drawing in people like Isu Chiba.[42] I heard from Adelaide, Reggie and Wolfie Kodesh of the new-found talent of some of these people. We drew some of these people into the Party structures. Others we retained to activate them in the TIYC. Effectively they did almost what Party members were doing, i.e. working in the community, selling *New Age* and carrying out work related to the SAIC and the ANC (the ANC was carried on underground). We took a considered view not to draw this new crop of young people willynilly into the Party.

For example, Adelaide and some of her women friends were not drawn into the CP, largely for their security. We saw the kind of damage families experienced when husbands and brothers were imprisoned, leaving the women to fend for the families. Besides, the police did not hesitate to intimidate the women. Inadvertently, the police methods actually strengthened the women.

I saw the transformation in Adelaide from someone seemingly quiet and shy to her taking on the police. By now she had become 'that cheeky Indian woman'. Our lawyer, Joel Joffe, was told by a senior security officer to 'tell that cheeky Indian woman to keep quiet and not be rude to my men'. Prison warders complained to the security police about Adelaide's demands for the rights of prisoners.

The police threats did not deter her. On one occasion they sent a message through our lawyers complaining about Adelaide's persistence in her demands, otherwise they would take some action against her. One of the lawyers conveyed this to her with a bit of a smile on his face. He knew she was not frightened.

By now Adelaide was active in the Transvaal Women's Federation. When the ANC was still legal she attended some of the Congress Alliance meetings. When the ANC was banned there was still some form of structure. Unknown to the police, some of the meetings took place in our house to which Nelson Mandela, J.B. Marks, Mosie Moola and Ben Turok would turn up.

Sometimes Nelson turned up early and handed some money to Adelaide to buy meat from the butcher across our road so as to prepare some curry. The representatives would arrive either from the backyard or through my mother's house, or they would slip in through the front door. The meetings never got raided. The venues frequently changed.

When we were again detained in 1964, Adelaide was visiting prisoners. This time the visits were much more risky. We smuggled out messages to warn other comrades to evade arrests. But perhaps the most crucial assignment was to arrange the removal of arms and documents. Since this could not be entrusted so easily, Comrade Bram requested that Adelaide, together with Issy Dinat, shift the goods. The first time they were helped by an African comrade whose identity was not revealed. Another time she and Issy had the help of my brother Daso and some African comrades.

16

The Asvats

Amina – or Minky as I knew her by her pet name – and I were friends, comrades and neighbours from the time we were teenagers. The Asvat family lived opposite to us in Avenue Road and Park Lane in Fordsburg. They were a large family of seven brothers and four sisters. Amina was the youngest and Zainab the second oldest sister. Dawood was the youngest of the siblings.

Zainab completed her education at the Euro-African Training Centre (ETC) in Vrededorp. She went on to do medicine at Wits. Amongst Zainab's contemporaries were my sister Darley and Swami Thandray. They went on to become teachers. Swami was the sister of Mervin Thandray, who later became the secretary of the TIC. Peter Abrahams was another contemporary. He was later involved in the Non-European Union front and went on to be an internationally famous writer.

During the 1946-48 Passive Resistance Campaign Zainab and Abdul Haque (who was also at ETC the same time) suspended their medical studies to join the campaign. Abdul Haque became the secretary of the Passive Resistance Council. He and Zainab later married.

Zainab courted imprisonment with a batch of volunteers led by the Reverend Michael Scott, for breaching a couple of racist laws by entering Natal without permits and squatting in an area set aside for Whites. One night a band of White thugs pulled down their tent and assaulted the passive resisters, much to the outrage of the Reverend. He remonstrated with the thugs not to assault the defiers. Zainab said to Scott, 'Leave them alone, Father, for they know not what they do.' After their release from prison the resisters arrived to a packed meeting at the Gandhi Hall where Scott related the violent attack and what Zainab said to him. This story was later told to the delegates at the United Nations and around the world.

Saleh, one of Amina's older brothers, was a member of the CP. He was often seen around the CP meetings on the Red Square on Sunday mornings. On Sunday evenings he would be on the Johannesburg City Hall steps protecting the CP platform from the attacks by the fascists.

One Sunday evening the fascists attacked the platform. Saleh grabbed one of the attackers, who managed to get away. Saleh went in hot pursuit of the thug. He brought his man down and gave him a hell of a kicking accompanied by a flurry of expletives which I doubted the man could hear while holding his badly bruised head. Just as well Saleh was not a passive resister.

Then there was Freddy Rangan. He did not seem to have a full set of teeth, and was a bit long-winded. What he said was quite difficult to follow but he would invariably say, 'Mr Chairman, on the point of the Constitution…' and mumble on, emerging with the phrase 'on the point of the Constitution'. We never knew what the point was, and none of us had a constitution on hand.

Goolam Pahad would speak at meetings and would often say 'Indian Com' when he spoke in Gujarati. I asked him was he saying, 'Are the Indians called comrades?' I was told 'Indian Com means the Indian community.'

Amina and I, together with a body of teenagers, were organized into the Transvaal Indian Volunteer Corps. We did the leaflet distributions, bill posting, stewarding of meetings and all sorts of help that was required. Later Amina, Saleh and I served on the working committee of the TIC. I always enjoyed sitting next to Saleh at these meetings. He had quite a sense of humour and would make comic remarks about some of the speakers. One of the regular speakers was D.U. Mistry, a barrister who had a shrill voice and often punctuated his remarks with 'Mr Chairman, this "haspect" or that "haspect"'. Saleh mumbled to me, 'You'd think his arse got specs.'

Amina was pleasant, patient and non-confrontational. Once she and I called at a house in a backyard in Vrededorp. The people were poor and the children ill clad. The eldest daughter received us in a polite and friendly way. They had never actually met political activists before. Amina established an immediate rapport and engaged the mother and the daughter. We heard their demands. On several visits we invited the daughter to events and activities. Initially she was shy but in time she became confident and involved in the women's section.

We were now busy building the unity of the Africans, Indian and Coloureds against racial oppression. Many of us stayed in the TIYC, which was engaged in myriad activities. One night we went out bill-posting. The posters called on the workers to stay at home on 1 May. We could not call it a strike as that would have openly breached the law. The protest was against the banning of gatherings and certain political leaders at public meetings. There was also going to be a series of savage laws on liberties and race classifications, etc.

We were in the vicinity of the bus garage in Fordsburg when we noticed what appeared to be an off-duty staff member armed with an iron bar. Evidently he had seen our freshly put-up poster, so he set out looking for us. We had not prepared ourselves for physical confrontation. We hid against a wall in the dark, holding our breath. We agreed that if attacked we would defend ourselves. Fortunately the man with the iron bar walked past us. We quietly walked away.

The 1 May 1950 industrial action led to the death of eighteen African workers who were shot by the police. June 26 became an annual day of mourning.

In June 1952 the Defiance Campaign against Unjust Laws was announced. Among the eight thousand people who courted imprisonment was Amina. Several of her comrades as well were involved, including me. We were active in all the major campaigns launched by the Congress Alliance. The ANC, SAIC, South African Congress of Trade Unions (SACTU) and the COD supported a proposal for a Congress of the People, where the people could set out a list of demands for a free and democratic South Africa.

The idea was that people from all kinds of social backgrounds, working people in farms and factories, peasants, teachers and any professionals, unemployed and partly employed people should write down their demands. Those who could not read and write would be asked what they wanted, their replies recorded in their own words and then read out to them. If they were satisfied they would put down their name or make a cross.

It was the function of the activist 'to call in their demands'. That meant tramping from house to house, from workplace to workplace, from church to church, in villages, towns and cities. We spent entire weekends and after working hours and school gathering the demands, written on scraps of notepaper and cardboard sheets. There were all sorts of encounters. One of our activists was locked up in prison. There he got prisoners to send in their demands on toilet paper. There were instances when we were chased out by people who were pro-government, and some were distinctly anti-Congress and anti-communist.

Many people were won over by discussion, overcoming their reluctance and in that way also gaining clarity. These discussions actually helped us in understanding issues that we ourselves did not know or understand. All the demands were checked and sifted and then couched in the Freedom Charter.

One of the major activities that Amina undertook was helping to set up the Federation of South African Women (FEDSAW). It became a major component of the Congress Alliance, shaking the country in its mobilization of women.

The members of the TIYC and the young members of the COD assisted a great deal at the founding conference of the FEDSAW. The male members undertook to do the catering, seek accommodation, assist with transport and even entertain the delegates. We were mindful not to take centre stage. We were dealing with a band of women warriors.

The march of the twenty thousand women in 1956, led by Helen Joseph, Lilian Ngoyi, Sophie Williams and Rahima Ally, to Union Buildings to present a petition against the introduction of the Pass Laws for African women has become a major historical event in the struggle for liberation.

Whilst we were very much involved in the movement, there was still something lacking – political theory. Around 1954-55 we decided to set up political study classes. In our class we had Amina, Mosie Moola, Percy Cohen and me.

We studied Marxism, which in turn led us to the fascinating subject of historical and social dialectical materialism. This opened a new vista in understanding socialism and nationalism and the scholars who wrote about the subject as pertaining to China, India and Europe. But we did have one advantage, we had knowledge of practice. Now, trying to understand theory was to enable practice to dovetail with political understanding.

Our study class met once a week for fifteen months. Soon there were several classes in progress in various parts of Johannesburg. These classes, in one case a women's only group, were conducted on the quiet and with care.

One of the colourful figures involved in the TIYC was Barney Desai. After a stay in London for studies, he arrived back in South Africa several months before the launching of the Defiance Campaign. Tall and handsome, he had a fine sense of humour. He was well liked and popular with the youth and he fired their imagination. He was elected as Secretary of the TIYC.

In January of 1952 we started recruiting for volunteers for the Defiance Campaign. The recruits had to be inducted in discipline in all aspects of how to conduct ourselves and especially in the event of provocation. We were asked to assemble at some place. Barney was the team leader, which surprised us since we were not consulted. But being disciplined we raised no objections.

On the first occasion we were put through the drill. Amina was the only female in the team. When the drill was nearly over Barney, over our heads, appointed Amina as deputy team leader. To the surprise of Barney and the team, I objected. I suggested we nominate first and then vote on the name. Barney accepted the suggestion and asked for nominations. I proposed

Amina and it was accepted by the team. The team saw this as an exercise in collective procedure.

One evening Amina, Shanti Naidoo, Fatima Nagdee and I were going to a Party cell meeting. The four of us arrived in Fatima's car, then headed for Amina's house. When we pulled up in front of the house, Amina noticed the front door slightly ajar. As we entered the house a couple of chaps stampeded past us. They ran into the arms of two policemen strolling on the beat. One chap had three suits on. They were charged and pleaded guilty. So ended our cell meeting.

One of the issues that occupied our attention was the lack of Indian women's participation in the movement. The only time women seemed to be involved was in actual periods of resistance, for example, during the first passive resistance movement in Gandhi's time, and then in 1946 (of the two thousand who volunteered for imprisonment, two hundred were women). But during the Defiance Campaign the numbers had dropped considerably.

We noticed where the problem was. It was with the menfolk in the leadership. The women were brought out of the kitchens as volunteers who cooked, catered for and accommodated delegates and visitors. Only a few served on the executive of the TIC and the NIC. The women were never brought in to make policy decisions or to exercise their leadership and executive ability.

This was clearly a reflection of a male-dominated society.With that in mind, Amina and a small band of women decided to set up a mechanism to activate the women and sustain their involvement in the organization. So she and some of her comrades arranged a meeting for the women at the Partidar Hall. It was well attended.

One evening after we finished an executive meeting of the TIYC, Amina and Ismail Bhoula, the secretary, boarded a tram heading for Fordsburg. A couple of us were down the road and we saw the two of them upstairs in the tram as it was passing.

Within a few moments we heard a huge crash. The tram had gone off its rails and veered to the right in the direction of the tramshed. It toppled sideways to lean on a couple of buildings. There was no pointsman to adjust the lines in the direction of Fordsburg. Fortunately nobody was injured, though everyone was quite shocked. Ismail crawled out and said heroically, 'I made sure I held on to the file of the TIYC minutes.'

Another encounter the women had was with a group of Indian collaborators. Word had reached the TIC office that these collaborators were scheduled to meet government officials in Pretoria to set up Indian Management Committees as a sop, for the Indians to have a say on the administration of their apartheid policies. A group of women led by Amina burst into the conference room. They angrily berated the band of astonished stooges. This was Adelaide's first act of militancy in the Congress Movement.

Whilst this was taking place, someone phoned the TIC office and gave the names of the collaborators. Bundles of leaflets exposing them were prepared and distributed in the Indian business quarters. This caused a sensation, as some of the stooges came from there.

At the time of the Treason Trials Amina and Zainab responded to the needs of the accused by arranging a cooked curry meal for them in the Drill Hall in Johannesburg. When the accused appeared before a judge in the old synagogue in Pretoria, Mrs T Pillay (the daughter of T.N. Naidoo) and some of the women supporters undertook to continue to supply lunches.

In July 1955 Amina married Yusuf Cachalia. The marriage appears to have been the cause of deep dissension between Yusuf and his older brother Maulvi. It seemed that Maulvi resented Amina. Initially we did not pay much attention to the rift, assuming it to be a personal family feud. Over time, however, the effects of the rift made their impact on the TIC. Maulvi had intrigued to win over the support of several people who together went on to conduct a sinister campaign. This led to a faction within the TIC. It was no longer a family feud. Numerous attempts were made on our part to heal the difference. The one regrettable failure was on the part of Yusuf Dadoo as President of the TIC. He failed or, rather, made only feeble attempts to resolve the dispute.[43]

For some unexplained reason, Maulvi targeted his attack not on Amina but on her sister Zainab. It was already known that Maulvi held some conservative views, one of which was his opposition to a brother-in-law of his who married a Tamil Christian woman. Maulvi ran a sustained campaign against Zainab. This created such tensions that Zainab was forced to resign from the executive of the TIC. But Maulvi and his supporters failed to gain the leadership of the TIC. The TIC was quite damaged, as Maulvi and his supporters then resigned from the TIC.

When the State of Emergency broke out following the Sharpeville shootings in 1960, amongst those scooped up were Maulvi and his supporters. Some of them appealed to the security police that they were no longer members of the TIC. The police said they knew, 'But all the same we are still taking you.'

That feud between the Cachalia brothers was never really healed.

Amina and Yusuf had two lovely bubbly children, Coco and Galieb. Their parents doted on them. One Sunday Amina took the kids to the zoo lake. The land where the lake was had been given to the council by a philanthropist for use by all its citizens, according to the terms of the bequest. But the rowing boats were controlled by the city council, who determined that they were to be used only by Indians. No Coloured or Africans were allowed, and no Indian was allowed with Whites.

The park facilities, especially the playing equipment like slides and swings, could not be used by any non-White kids, nor could they use the benches and playing pools. Coco and her brother Galieb so much wanted to play on the swings and slides and could not understand why their mother stopped them. She then explained the facilities were only for White children. The crestfallen faces of her two children upset Amina. The next day she wrote a letter to the *Johannesburg Star* setting out her experience and disappointment at the zoo lake. This led to a flurry of letters for and against from readers. The correspondence went on for a considerable time.

The government slapped a series of severe restrictions, including banning orders, on Amina and Yusuf. To complicate matters, similar orders were placed on Zainab and her husband Aziz. Although the two families had attached houses and a shared backyard, they had to make representation even to be allowed to talk to each other.

Aziz and Zainab were relatively fortunate in that, as doctors, they could still get about and visit people's homes, which was a means of effectively networking and keeping in touch with political people. This was most useful when Nelson Mandela and Walter Sisulu were hiding in safe Indian homes.

Yusuf, with the help of Amina, continued to run his clothing shop. In spite of the restrictions he was able to build up his business. But the success of the business earned the wrath of a friend, Ahmad Laher, who had invested some capital into the business. Laher wanted more and quicker returns. Laher's reputation was on a par with Mafia-like operators. He had bankrolled a notorious gangster by the name of Sheriff Khan. Khan had spent several years in jail for theft. He had hired a gang of thugs to intimidate the small shopkeepers, demanding protection money from them.

When Yusuf was reluctant to respond to Laher's demands, Laher sent his thugs around. They duffed up Yusuf and had Yusuf and Amina trussed up. Amina told me when I phoned her, 'We were naïve and underestimated Laher.'

When UN Secretary General Dag Hammarskjöld visited South Africa in 1961 he was received at the airport by senior government officials and an audience of influential White people. No invitation was extended to the Congress Alliance. Some of the Congress people did put in an appearance, however, and Amina was allowed to present a bouquet of flowers to

Hammarskjöld. In the bouquet was a letter from the Congress Movement, briefly setting out their position under the apartheid government.

Eventually Zainab and Aziz went into exile on exit permits. The strain and stress of the restrictions and imprisonment had taken its toll. They left for London with their two young daughters, Zenobia and Dilnaz.

Several years later the government lifted the bans on Yusuf and Amina. Galieb and Coco were sent to Atlantic College in Wales. The government allowed the Cachalias passports and they visited London several more times thereafter. We still exercized caution because the ANC, PAC and CP were still banned organizations, and South African Intelligence was active in London.

Amina had a lifelong commitment to work for the freedom struggle, as did Yusuf, Zainab and Aziz. On a personal level Zainab and Aziz gave much of their medical time to our disabled son Anand and to Adelaide, refusing to accept payment. This they did for many families in need.

17

The liberation struggle

As we entered the 1960s and for some considerable time afterwards, the repression increased towards the political activists. Now my brother Peter became much more careful. He always made sure he had nothing incriminating on him whenever he was searched. Nor did he engage in arguments with the police. He was always calm and polite. He was no longer mistaken for me. He kept a low profile and to some extent that gave him scope to quietly carry on his political work.

However, in a liberation struggle one cannot be too careful. There is always a possibility something would go wrong. One Sunday some of us went on some political fieldwork in the Asian quarter of Pretoria. The group travelled in a couple of cars. I went by train since I was banned from attending gatherings and from leaving or entering certain parts of the city of Johannesburg. (Kathrada and I were amongst a handful of people who never really observed the banning orders.)

The group who set off were in their Sunday gladrags. I was the only one who was not. I wore a short-sleeved shirt and a pair of khaki pants (trousers). The group canvassed in pairs. I worked alone and kept a watchful eye.

Soon enough the security police arrived and I saw an Indian chap directing the police to all those dressed in suits and ties, who were then arrested. I stood casually leaning against a shop window and gradually melted into the local crowd watching the arrests. The police passed me several times but presumed me to be a local. All of our activists including Peter were taken to the Pretoria police station and later locked up in Blue Skies, the Boksburg prison, and held under the twelve-day detention law which later became the 90-day and then the 180-day detention law.

When the request came to us in our CP cell to join the newly created MK, the armed wing of the ANC, though expected it was received with great excitement. It was only the second body to be non-racial after the formation of the CP in 1921. The formation of MK was in response to the apartheid government's (and its predecessor, the United Party of General Smuts) years of violent suppression of peaceful protests by the African, Coloured and Indian people.

The massacre of peaceful protesters in Sharpeville in 1960, followed by the banning of the ANC and the PAC (the CP had already been banned ten years previously) immediately followed by the declaration of the State of Emergency, placed the major liberation movements on a collision course which was to change the political scene for all time.

We had an inkling several months before 16 December 1961, the day MK announced its existence by launching its first acts of sabotage, that the leadership of the ANC and CP were involved in high-level discussions to work out a new strategy to meet the challenge. The change to armed struggle was a decision not arrived at lightly. It took several months of discussions at various levels. It required the highest tact, care, and consideration amidst tight security. The situation was complex, what with the security police and their agents throughout the country as well as the intelligence agencies of the British and Portuguese bordering in and around South Africa.

Politically there were other complex and sensitive situations within the segments of African leaders long associated with the ANC and in the Congress Alliance. For example, Chief Albert Luthuli, a devout Christian and a recipient of the Nobel Peace Prize, was still regarded as the president of the ANC. The new strategists and the chief proponents of armed struggle, like Nelson Mandela and Walter Sisulu, were also highly esteemed leaders. They took every care not to offend the top leaders of Chief Luthuli's calibre. They did not want to embarrass or place them in an invidious position. Besides, they could not afford to earn their wrath and endanger the whole ANC. Nevertheless, it was vital that Chief Luthuli and others be informed of the most profound decision that the banned ANC was going to embark on.

The situation had further problems. The ANC was a banned organization, unlike the SAIC, the South African Coloured People's Organization (SACPO) and SACTU. They had been part of the Congress Alliance and their leaders too had to be informed. SAIC was a pioneer organization in non-violent struggle from the days of M.K. Gandhi. There had been two further non-violent campaigns, one in 1946, and the other in 1952 in alliance with the ANC. The Indian struggles threw up a crop of leaders like Dr G.M. Naicker, Ismail Meer, J.N. Singh, Nana Sita, Yusuf and Maulvi Cachalia, Dr Yusuf Dadoo,[44] Dr Goonam Naidoo and Manilal Gandhi, son of M.K. Gandhi.

Nelson Mandela spent considerable time in discussions with the main leaders of the Natal and Transvaal Indian Congresses. Several of the senior leaders had strong doubts and reservations as to whether the Indian people would take to armed struggle. J.N. Singh was quoted as saying, 'Non-violence has not failed us; we have failed non-violence.'

That these discussions were held without any setback was itself an achievement. Whilst people like Chief Luthuli and Dr Naicker may have had reservations about armed struggle, they did not lose their vision for freedom in South Africa. Their silence was very helpful.

There were, however, some strong criticisms from two people, Yusuf Cachalia and Ismail Meer. Yusuf Cachalia sensed that members of the TIYC favoured armed struggle. He was anxious to address the youth. The youth body arranged an activist meeting to hear him out. He believed he would command their attention because of his standing in the liberation movement (his father Ahmed Cachalia was a contemporary of M.K. Gandhi).

That evening he expounded on the history of passive resistance movement campaigns, as well as the struggles in India, and their deep impact on the Indian people. He firmly believed the Indian people were wedded to non-violent struggle.

Very few of the young activists responded to his argument. Whilst they had some respect for him, they knew he was a weak leader. This had been shown in his lack of effort to fight the Group Areas Act. Cachalia had lived in Doornfontein, which the authorities designated for White occupation. He did not challenge the order, in contrast to the non-violent resistance of Nana Sita, who was ordered out of his home in a White area, and another young activist, Mohammed Bhava, both of whom were arrested. In anger a couple of the young people daubed the slogan 'Defy Group Areas' on the wall of the house Cachalia moved into in Fordsburg.

This perception about Yusuf Cachalia was conveyed to me over a period of time by some of the young activists. What it reflected was that, whilst MK would lead the armed struggle, it did not necessarily prevent people from engaging in other forms of protest, including non-violence. During the 1970s and 1980s there was a huge upsurge of non-violent protest.

Now back to the activist meeting. The young audience was made up of the sons of shopkeepers, merchants, hawkers, traders, tailors, waiters, factory workers, teachers, students and a couple of doctors. Their overwhelming quietness clearly frustrated Yusuf Cachalia, and in anger he took a box of matches out of his pocket and threw it on the table saying, 'If you want to start sabotage use this!' Cachalia's perception that some of the young Indians favoured armed struggle was right, except he had no idea how many present were already in MK.

In the audience were two chaps who were to play a prominent part in MK. One was Indres Naidoo, the grandson of Thumbi Narainsamy Naidoo, a contemporary of Gandhi in South Africa. Indres was one of several members of his distinguished family, who were in their fourth generation of freedom fighters. The other was Shirish Nanabhai, who was the son of a senior TIC leader and related to Nana Sita.

By now we had set up several MK units in and around Johannesburg. For security reasons we were not actually informed how many other units were set up. The unit which I was in consisted of Wolfie Kodesh, Isu Chiba and Reggie Vandeyar. Our liaison man with regional command was Wolfie Kodesh. He was only in contact with one person from the regional command. It was part of the security arrangements that we do not reveal ourselves to other activists in MK. But human nature being such, it was at times unavoidable. Many of us were engaged in a number of organizations of a public nature, so we were known as political activists.

We went through short periods of exercises and experiments. For example, we learnt how to make Molotov cocktails and how to lob them. We went to isolated spots to saw off pylons and cut telephone cables and damage electric installations. We read manuals on explosives and bombs, learnt about ballistics and guns, read books on guerrilla warfare in Vietnam and the Philippines and partisan struggles in Europe during the Second World War .

We worked in a democratic way, with the proviso that when there was a disagreement we could refer to the regional command, provided it did not hold up progress. There were, however, some serious disagreements and lapses which originated from the regional command.

Our first disagreement was on the question of recruitment. The directive we got was we 'could recruit anybody as long as the person was opposed to apartheid. The person need not belong to any political body.' This we rejected as absurd and risky. We argued that the person must have a political record, and that we needed to know their social and work background and any family and friends.

We were ordered to adhere to the original directive. We decided to ignore it and not engage in polemics with the regional command. We would recruit with the criteria we had set out. In the event we were proved correct as disaster took a heavy toll in one of the units.

In another instance we rejected a directive from the regional command to locate some of the cars belonging to the security police in the areas where they lived and pour sand into the petrol tanks, as this would cause 'inconvenience and disruption'. We threw this out as infantile behaviour fraught with senseless risk.

Later there were some minor disagreements or criticisms. I noticed a degree of uneasiness on the part of Wolfie Kodesh which surfaced at a meeting of our unit. Wolfie said he was severely criticized by the regional command for influencing us in our decisions, and for not being firm enough with us. We listened to him carefully, then sent back a message to the regional command that 'we are quite capable of thinking for ourselves' and that Wolfie was in no way responsible for our decisions.

In the meantime we had other tasks to deal with. We were in search of arms, explosives, police and army storage places and firearms magazines. We looked out for possible recruits, safe houses, reliable people who could act as couriers, drivers, people with specialist skills. We also looked for people who could forge documents such as identity and registration papers.

An important sector of our backup was our womenfolk. Our mothers, sisters, wives, nieces and other women were supportive of the movement. Many were garment workers and union members. They helped in providing protection, cover and food and in carrying messages between political contacts. They also set up a rota to take food and changes of clothes to those in detention. Sometimes the authorities would limit visits or simply cancel them. The women demanded their rights and quite often succeeded. They became quite militant when stories seeped out about torture.

The women were led by Adelaide. She became a familiar figure outside prisons in various parts of Johannesburg and Pretoria. In one instance she secured a contact visit with Nelson Mandela at the Fort. When the warder asked what she was to Nelson Mandela, she replied 'I am his wife. Did you not know that he has an Indian wife?' The warder asked her to wait. He went to Mandela to tell him that there was an Indian woman claiming to be his wife and wanting a contact visit. Nelson swiftly responded, 'Yes, that is my Indian wife.' On meeting they warmly embraced each other in the presence of a bemused warder.

The next time Adelaide called was to bring food for Ben Turok. The warden said, 'Don't tell me Turok is your husband.' Adelaide responded, 'No he is not. Your laws don't allow black and White to marry.' The warder took the food but did not allow a visit. That 'cheeky Coolie woman' had a series of spats at various prisons about the visiting rights of spouses, mothers or sisters to prisoners.

Quite often when restrictions reached beyond endurance point, she would consult Bram Fischer or Joel Joffe. On one occasion Joel reported to Adelaide that the police told him, 'That Indian woman Adelaide Joseph should control herself, otherwise we will lock her up.'

Adelaide became a most important contact. She instinctively knew to search for messages in the clothes sent for washing or food dishes containing leftovers. When the warders asked why she was taking food back home, she said it was 'for his dog he loves very much. Besides we are poor people and we cannot waste food.'

The messages smuggled out were to alert those whom we were being questioned about. At other times it was about equipment for use in our underground work, the most important being arms. Adelaide reported to Bram Fischer about the cache of arms concealed at a place only known to a few people. Bram asked her to spirit the arms away. This was done in the dead of the night.

Several comrades on receiving the messages from Adelaide managed to get out of the way. Some got to the Botswana border and decided to turn back. They felt they could not uproot and leave their families. As it turned out they managed to avert arrest and were able to continue to keep employment and quietly carry on political work.

Adelaide also became one of the central figures in keeping up the morale of the prisoners' wives and sharing whatever money and support they received for welfare. The other person she worked with was Winnie Mandela. She also worked with Nelson Mandela, Moses Kotane, J.B. Marks, Mac Maharaj and the Naidoo family. Some of the work was open; at other times she was asked to carry out tasks by some of the leaders and activists in the underground.

Her visits to the police stations or prisons were often traumatic. She would come back with coded messages of the police brutality. She took a decision that, when confronted by the security police or prison warders, she would not cry in their presence. She would come home and have a cry but never in the presence of other wives or mothers.

In one encounter with the head of the Johannesburg security police, Major Spengler, he asked her, 'What is a beautiful woman like you doing with an ugly man like Paul Joseph?' Spengler was astonished at the sharp and swift response from Adelaide. He was quite embarrassed and apologized to her. She reported her account with Major Spengler to her lawyer.

We started getting ready for the countdown to 16 December. Traditionally the White governments celebrated 16 December countrywide as Dingaan's Day. This was the day in 1834 when the Boers lured the Zulu king Dingaan to his death and immediately unleashed a violent attack on his warriors and the Zulu people. The massacre was on such a scale that the river turned red with blood. The battle was henceforth called 'The Blood River' and at times 'The Battle of Blood River' by the Boers.

Generally, the Whites marked the day in festivity as a reminder of their victory. It was a form of humiliation that had rankled in the minds of not only the Zulu people but all Africans in South Africa. So when MK chose that date to launch its existence, it was sending out a message to all the racially oppressed people in the country that it would shake off the shackles of oppression and make a determined and united bid for freedom.

We were to target certain symbolic sites. We chose the pass office in Bezuitenhout Street, off the corner of President Street; the 'Native' law courts in Newtown, a district between Fordsburg and Bramfontein; and the segregated post office in Central Road, Fordsburg.

The first two targets were premises that tens of thousands of African people had to visit to seek their pass documents in order to obtain employment. Those who failed or were caught in the dragnet were transported to the Native law courts to face fines or imprisonment. This humiliating experience was meted out on a daily basis.

The third target was the post office, with two distinct sections, one for White use only and the other for all Blacks only. As always, the facilities for the Blacks were inferior and the White staff rude, crude and racially insulting.

We soon learnt that, no matter how much planning goes into an assignment, things can go wrong. Our earlier reconnaissance missed the guards of a building opposite the pass office, while the lights of the post office and the street lights were quite strong. We could easily have been exposed. About three blocks away in Central Road was the Majestic Cinema. The cinema would finish at about 10 p.m. We had to ensure there would be no people passing the post office. We had little time to get things done.

In the case of the Native law courts, we found a couple of MK cadres in the vicinity. They were in a fretful state; their target was the same as ours. The other problem was that they believed one of the planted bombs had toppled over and caused possible leakage. We told our unit to move out fast. I volunteered to secure its position. When I got in, to my horror two of the three bombs had toppled over and there was some seepage. I spent a few nervous and sweaty moments putting the heavy bombs in position, each of which had timing devices.

We speedily departed, rather upset at the blunder of two units assigned to the same target. We arrived at the backyard of our house and had barely got out of the car, when there was one hell of a bang. The post office bomb had gone off.

I got into the house quietly. The children and Adelaide were asleep. Or so I thought. I soon realized that Adelaide was not asleep. She relaxed when I got into bed. Saturday was a night I stayed home or if I did go out it was for a short while. As I lay next to Adelaide my thoughts were racing about what we had just done. The effect was just beginning to surface. I had been involved in passive resistance campaigns in 1946 and 1952. I had never handled a gun, let alone a bomb before. We always prevailed on people to apply peaceful means of protest.

I lay awake unable to sleep. My thoughts were suddenly interrupted by two more explosions, the one at the law courts, the other at the pass office. The sounds of the explosions were as if they were only a block or two from our house.

Within minutes police cars were racing from various directions and coming to a screeching stop at our corner to make their turns. It sounded as if they were stopping in front of our house. I broke out into a sweat from fear and held on to Adelaide by the waist. After some moments I got up to drink some water. Adelaide asked me what was the matter. I said my throat was parched. By now she was aware that I had been involved in something but neither of us spoke about the explosions, the screeching cars or my nervous disposition. I went back to bed, still not able to sleep. Neither could Adelaide. We heard the gentle snores of our children.

The next morning I got ready to do my usual *New Age* paper rounds and gradually worked my way towards Central Road. There were people talking about the explosions. I carefully avoided joining in. There was no doubt there was a great deal of excitement at the damage and at the people who caused it.

The crowd was milling around the edge of the bombed site and was being kept at bay by the police. There were uniformed and security police mingling with the crowd. I stood a long way from the site. As people, passed me some were holding copies of the Sunday papers. I could spot part of the headline 'Sabotage breaks out in…' As I walked away to continue with the *New Age* round, I noticed posters announcing the existence of MK. These were evidently put up the night of our work.

The launch of MK had caused a sensation, as reports in the papers and radio gave accounts of events in Durban, Port Elizabeth and various parts of Johannesburg. There was also a report of the death of an MK member from a bomb that went off prematurely, injuring another as well. The reaction of the majority of the White people was not surprising: utter disgust, hatred and condemnation, and the backing of the state to take whatever action necessary against the 'terrorists'.

Within weeks more MK units were being formed. There were to be more acts of sabotage. As always, our instructions were specific. We were to ensure no loss of life or danger to the public. Our protests were against the apartheid government and not against White people as such. Knowing that police would raid the homes of known political people, we were to ensure that our houses, workplaces, and cars had nothing to incriminate anyone. After any acts of sabotage we would have a debriefing to ensure safety.

The house of Reggie Vandeyar was raided. The police found him reading a manual on explosives. They did not show any overt reaction. After a while they left, to return about an hour later. This time the house was given a thorough search. They found a broken pistol on top of the wardrobe. Reggie was led away to be charged for being in possession of an unlicensed firearm. He was remanded and imprisoned at the notorious No. 4 Fort jailhouse awaiting trial. He was fined and given a suspended sentence. His blatant and brazen breach of security led to his suspension from MK. This decision was endorsed by the Regional Command. Our MK units carried on with greater vigilance.

Up to then Reggie was virtually unknown as a political person. In the mid-1940s he was recruited into the YCL. He was not very active and his membership had lapsed. Early in 1950 he again showed political interest. This time he was recruited into the CP. In the early 1950s he would occasionally join us on a Sunday morning doing the suburbs with the paper. He was a waiter, so often worked late into a Saturday night, which did not give him a lot of free time.

One day Danie du Plessis, a former secretary of the Johannesburg District of the CP, approached me with a view to reviving the Party. He asked me to talk to some of our former members and said he would come over to speak to them. I put the proposal to our comrades and they were keen to hear what he had to say.

Danie came over to Reggie's house for the meeting. His talk clearly raised our hopes. He was enthusiastic and confident, even though critical of the proposed ANC–SAIC plans for a non-violent campaign, the Defiance Campaign of 1952. He was keen on revolutionary action rather than passive resistance. He was held in high esteem. He was one of a handful of Afrikaners who had joined the CP. He was of working-class stock and a bricklayer by profession. He attended, as a delegate from the SACP, the International Conference of the Communist Parties of the British Empire in 1949, held in London.

After Danie's talk we never heard from him again. Some months later Reggie got a letter from a government official, a Mr De Villiers Louw, who signed himself as the Liquidator of the CP. The letter stated that Reggie Vandeyar would be placed on a list of known communists and that if he had any objections he could write in and ask for the evidence.

Reggie brought the letter to me and we discussed what to do. I suggested we ask a friend for some legal advice. As a result Reggie wrote to the liquidator asking for reasons. The liquidator replied that he had information about a meeting held in Reggie's house with a number of people to discuss the CP. Reggie said he would like to know who were the people present and who actually raised the question of the CP. The liquidator's reply simply informed Reggie, without answering his questions, that his name would be taken off the list of communists.

In the meantime I was in touch with Dr Dadoo, who was the district chairman and was on the central committee of the Party before it was dissolved. The last letter to Reggie from the liquidator was shown to Dadoo. Dadoo by now was convinced that the informer was Danie du Plessis. Later it was reported that Danie had joined the Dutch Reformed Church and was dubbed 'The Red Elder' by the press.

When he was arrested it was clear Reggie was never taken off the list.

As most of our unit were members of legal bodies like the SAIC and the TIYC, there was still a lot of other work to do. People knew they could come to us for assistance and advice on police intimidation, false arrests, rent racketeering, illegal evictions or job dismissals. Neither was it unusual to intervene on behalf of Africans being physically abused and arrested under the maze of provisions under the pass laws.

The people knew that *New Age* articulated their problems under apartheid with an unmatched fearlessness. They contributed from their little income to support the paper. There were other aspects of our work when there would be an urgent need to find safe houses or a safe passage for activists on the run.

Apparently our activities had caught the attention of the Unity Movement in Cape Town. We had requests from them and we obliged.

At about this time Mac Maharaj arrived from London. I first met Mac at the Drill Hall during the preparatory hearing of the Treason Trial in 1957. At that time he was on his way out to London. Mac was trained in printing and communications, especially in coding, explosives and various mechanical skills. He was highly articulate and a skilled debater, well read, and versed in Marxism. Mac got his training in London and the former German Democratic Republic (GDR).

Kathy Kathrada brought him to me with certain specific requests. Mac was essentially a party man whose task was to assist the national high command. Initially he was not placed in an MK unit, though he got to know some of the activists in the units. This was permissible since Mac was to tap the potential of activists, which proved to be a boon to his work.

There were a number of immediate objectives to sustain Mac in his work.

The most immediate was to find accommodation for him and his wife Tim Omprakash Naidoo. We found them a room in the house of a family I had known for some time. Adelaide and I rented the same room soon after we got married.

Although the house was situated in a quiet area, it soon became clear that the room was inadequate for Mac's work. By now Mac had got to know the Naidoo family. It was Amah Naidoo who managed to find more suitable accommodation, secluded in the backyard of another house. It was designed as a granny flat in a part of Doornfontein which in the early 1920s was a Jewish locality. This was one of the few areas Blacks could walk around unhindered. Tim and Mac were delighted. They had the much-needed privacy, space and the luxury of a bathroom.

There were a few more hurdles to overcome. Since Mac and Tim were born in Natal they were not allowed to stay in the Transvaal. To be there they would have to show a visitor's permit. So what was clearly required now was a set of documents identifying Mac as a Coloured. Such a document would enable him to travel relatively freely throughout the country, as Coloureds did not have the same restrictions as Indians and Africans.

My younger brother, Daso, and I approached two Coloured people we knew. One was Nicolas, who worked with me in the furniture factory, and another was Mrs Kubie, whom Daso knew very well. They signed documents confirming the birth and the identity of one Solly Matthews. Mac was now officially Solly Matthews.

The next step was to get a driver's licence in the name of Solly Matthews. Daso had a contact in the little town of Germiston who ran a driving school. Mac passed his test (he was already a skilled driver) and got his licence in the name of Solly Matthews.

A network of activists was set up for Mac's work. The network covered a number of suburbs in Johannesburg. Mac set up a printing operation known only to a few people. He also got to know a man who ran a printworks called West End Printers. Mac managed to work there to get better quality and quantity print.

As the Rivonia trial was taking place, the propaganda work in defence of the trialists was most important. By then *New Age* was banned, as well as some smaller left-wing publications. Soon stickers appeared on the walls of Johannesburg calling for the release of our leaders. Police enquiries could not trace the source.

Mac was constantly on the look-out for premises. I introduced him to a fellow worker of mine, a young Coloured chap. He had come to seek a job at the factory one day, and turned out to be Harold Kingsman, my one-time playmate in Fordsburg. Harold was a survivor of a train disaster in which three of his brothers were killed on their way to school. We had lost contact when he moved to a peri-urban area for Coloured people called Grasmere, well beyond Soweto. So it was delightful meeting and renewing our old friendship.

Harold turned out to be a very highly skilled cabinet-maker and an accomplished antique furniture restorer. Besides his knowledge of carpentry, Harold also had knoweldge of building and plumbing as well as organisational ability. As a consequence I persuaded the general foreman and Julius that Harold should be promoted to foreman of the cabinet shop. Productivity and quality of work improved without added stress.

Socially we saw a lot of each other and Harold showed political interest. From him we built up a nucleus of people in Grasmere who showed an interest in the struggle against apartheid. This is where we found Nicolas. It was Harold who laid part of the groundwork for Mac's Coloured identity. I at no time indicated to Nicolas that I knew Mac. Harold and Mac developed close contact.

We visited Harold a couple of times in Grasmere. Mac had a mischievous look on his face. I could see he was coming up with an idea after looking over Harold's house and grounds. He asked Harold whether he would consider a printing works under the ground of his house. Harold was delighted at the idea. Mac never let a potential slip by.

Unfortunately that project did not come to fruition as Mac and several of us were detained in 1964. Harold was also picked up; his business card was found by the security police who raided Mac's house in Doornfontein. Harold managed to talk himself out by admitting he knew me as a workmate but that at no time did I engage him in anything political. He told them that he met Mac at our house and Mac had asked him if he wanted some business cards printed. Beyond that there was nothing incriminating. Harold was released.

Harold was aware not to make any contact with any of our activists, of whom he knew several. Some of the activists knew Harold by reputation only. To find a Coloured attracted to the liberation movement was like finding a gem.

Harold's house was the first and only house in Grasmere or nearby Kliptown where we organized a meeting for Coloured people to hear from SACPO. Much to our disappointment the secretary of SACPO failed to turn up or tender an apology. So as not to lose an opportunity we did the political presentation.

One Sunday morning early in 1964, Dr Essop Jassat, who was doing his housemanship at the Baragwanath Hospital, called on me. He told me that earlier he treated a woman, Rose Kingsman, who died of severe burns following an accident in her house in Grasmere. 'I believe she was the wife of one of your comrades.' Adelaide and I were distraught. After nearly 25 years in exile, Adelaide made a visit to South Africa after the ANC and the CP and PAC were unbanned. She located Harold Kingsman and visited him. They embraced and Harold broke down in tears. He thought we had forgotten him.

It may well be asked why such a long account of Harold. He was amongst the many unknown who made their contribution to the liberation struggle and it is important that some kind of record be kept. When I visited South Africa after exile, I made a visit to Harold's house. It was a wonderful experience. Harold told me the closest he got to a political organization was to join the African Christian Democratic Party. That was his prerogative. Harold was kind, honest and committed.

We need to remember other people who played their part in the liberation struggle, particularly between 1960 and 1965. Two brothers come to mind, the Padiachee brothers. They came from a family who had long been in the flower business. The brothers were Boya and Sonnyboy.

Sonnyboy was better known as 'Thunder', although he was quite a reserved person and nothing like thunder. He had started his career as a teacher in a countryside school. He was into his first term, when one day he got a private letter at the school address. When the school head handed him the letter he noticed it was opened. He asked the head whether he had opened and read the letter. The head answered abruptly, as if it was his entitlement to read the staff's private letters. Sonnyboy reacted so furiously that he punched the head, sending him sprawling. He was fired. He left having acquired the nickname of 'Thunder' from fellow staff.

The elder brother, Boya, was running the family flower business. With Thunder's teaching career gone, he was brought into the business.

These brothers became long-time supporters of the movement. They were not directly involved but moved with us as fellow-travellers, keeping a sensible distance. They often responded to my requests positively. The brothers seemed instinctively aware not to disclose any of the tasks that they undertook for any of us. This was only discovered many years later.[45]

The family business was having regular run-ins with the White-controlled city council, which seemed bent on ridding the city of Indian flower sellers. The council attempted to block them from setting up flower stalls in and around the city, serving hundreds of notices and summonses on them. They were threatened with prosecution. The brothers sought legal advice from a firm called James Kantor and Partners who assigned Harold Wolpe to deal with the matter. He found a loophole in the bylaw. The council could not prosecute. The brothers became more militant. They plastered their vans with all the summonses and defiantly drove around the city.[46]

The Padiachee brothers had a couple of rooms in an outhouse in their back garden in Ophirton. These rooms became a place of refuge for comrades on the run from the police. To cover the tracks of the brothers, we arranged with the comrades in hiding to offer rent for the use of the rooms. The comrades knew the owners only as landlords and nothing else. They would hand the rent to the landlord, who quietly handed it back to us. There was an occasion when I slipped out of house arrest and sought refuge in one of those back rooms. I spent a week there. Of course I did not pay any rent.

When Mac and Tim were detained, immediate measures had to be taken to clear the workplaces and storage rooms Mac had used. The brothers were called in to help. They turned up with a van they parked some distance away from the premises. My brother Peter kept a lookout, whilst my younger brother Daso and Issy Dinat entered the room. They carried the bags to the awaiting van and the brothers safely disposed of the collection.[47]

Daso got to know a young Dutch immigrant called Gill. He came to South Africa to take up employment. Most European immigrants did not find it easy to socialize with the local White people. There were cultural gaps and generally there was an apparent reluctance to mix with Dutch, German and Belgian workers. A lot of these workers got on well with the African, Coloured and Indian people. Many were invited around for parties, drinks and meals. The Dutchman met an attractive young Indian teacher. Her family were known to us and a couple of her brothers were good friends of Daso. So Gill would come around for visits and meals.

One Sunday afternoon he arrived and soon made himself comfortable. He removed his jacket and I took it from him. It felt quite weighty. I asked him whether he had a gun there. He had. I asked him whether he was aware how much we disapproved of the apartheid regime. He said he did and was quite keen to help. I told him I would take his gun and would like him to get us some more. He agreed.

A couple of weeks later Gill turned up with a Hungarian friend called Gustav. Gustav came to South Africa as a refugee following the Hungarian uprising in 1956. He was not keen on communists. He was very handsome, intelligent and friendly but like most young European immigrants not able to fraternize with the local White community. He came around a few times with Gill. I avoided talking any kind of politics with him. One day when he was at our place, Adelaide's cousin Ethel dropped in. She was a very pretty young woman. It was clear Gustav was taken with her. Ethel was friendly but kept a tactful distance. She was quite aware of the Immorality Act.

When Gustav showed this kind of attention, I drew him out on his reaction to the apartheid laws, especially the Immorality and Mixed Marriages Acts. He intensely disliked the laws and was amazed at the system of apartheid. I discovered Gustav would not miss making a quick buck by any underhand method. He once asked me to find him a buyer for some jewellery that came his way. The jewellery was worth £17,000. I said I would look out for a buyer. I informed Mac, who had a relative who was a wheeler-dealer. I suggested if I got him a buyer, in return I wanted some guns. He agreed.

Gustav got us a 303 rifle and we arranged a rendezvous. He wanted a sum of money, the amount of which I cannot remember. I had been keeping my unit informed. It was agreed that I make the deal. At certain points of the meeting place, Isu and Wolfie would keep observation and if necessary would make an intervention if things went wrong.

After waiting for some time in the flat in a White area, eventually Gustav turned up. He walked in as if his leg was in plaster. From the side of his hip he pulled out the 303 rifle. I had seen this type of rifle carried by the prison guards at No. 4 the Fort.

As I was making the payment, it was already dusk. Two men burst in. It was Isu and Wolfie. They thought I had been set up. Initially Gustav was shocked, and then he smiled. We left with the rifle. Isu and Wolfie said they saw this man walking as if crippled across the road and cars stopped for him. Then they saw him enter the building.

I did not see Gustav for some time. Neither did Gill. We discovered he had been arrested for being in possession of substantial amounts of stolen jewellery. He often said to me that when he left Johannesburg, it would be left empty.

When I was put in prison, I was concerned in case Gustav had made a deal with the police about supplying me with the 303 rifle. To his credit he did not. Maybe he thought about pretty Ethel. However, he did tell the police that he was working for Puskás, the world-famous Hungarian footballer. Gustav said Puskás was living in exile in Spain. The South African police arrived in Spain to take evidence from Puskás. Gustav's claim turned out to be a fabrication. He was sentenced to seven years' imprisonment to be served at the Pretoria Central Prison.

Some years later I met Lewis Baker in London. Lewis was a co-defendant in the Bram Fischer trial. He also served his time in Pretoria Central. We talked about the various White comrades in prison. I casually asked about a Hungarian who, it was reported, got a long stretch for stolen jewellery. Lewis remembered him as 'God, that mad Hungarian who ranted and raved against the police.' Gustav sees Gill occasionally in Holland. Gill and I still keep in touch.

Activists, informers, arrests

In the course of our propaganda work on the Rivonia Trial, one night we sent out pairs of activists to put up small posters. We made sure the pairs were not known to each other as they were drawn from different areas. Only one from each pair would send a report to a contact.

That night the security police were on the prowl. A pair of activists was apprehended. As they were being led away one of them slipped out a knife and slashed the police officer on the hand. The officer let go of the attacker, who immediately slipped away. The officer held on to the other activist, who was led away. He was very young and still at school. When questioned he could give no description of the other activist, since they were in dark streets. The police found no evidence of any material used. He was eventually allowed out but would have to visit the police. At each visit the youngster's account was consistent. After a number of visits he was not charged.

We soon discovered that the youngster was the nephew of Yusuf Cachalia's wife Amina. The activist that got away was Magan Narsee. He was known for his agility and was an MK member.

The date 17 April 1963 will always be remembered as a unique day in the annals of MK activity in Johannesburg. It was on that night that an MK unit which consisted of Shirish Nanabhai, Indres Naidoo, Gamal Jardine and Reggie Vandeyar, who was unit head, went out on an operation. They had planned to blow up a signal box near a railway line in Riverlea.

Everything had been prepared and all that had to be done was light the fuse. But the site was suddenly lit up by powerful lights, and the awaiting band of security police pounced on them. They were brutally beaten up. Indres was shot in the shoulder, Reggie's arm was damaged and Shirish sustained serious injuries over the eyes.

The missing person was Gamat Jardine. He was the police plant. The bomb he supplied was dud (he had provided dud bombs for some of the previous operations). The raiding police band was led by Captain Swanepoel, dubbed 'The Beast of Belsen'. The arrested men were taken to the police station and subjected to more assaults. Later that night they were taken to their respective homes, which were raided in the presence of their shocked families.

I got a frantic phone call from Ramnie, the younger sister of Indres, about the arrests, assaults and the raids. I was in a difficult situation. I had no transport and was reluctant to put in an appearance at the police station, if they were held there, or at the Gray's Building, which was where the security police operated from. I had a feeling that I was under surveillance. (I later discovered that each of the arrested men was put into a security car and driven around to point out the houses of their contacts. Reggie told me that he pointed out my house. This was already known to them but this time they were keen to link me with Reggie and his unit.)

Ramnie also contacted Kathy Kathrada, who was in a more complex situation as he was under house arrest. By the next morning the ever-resourceful Kathrada had contacted some people about the arrests.

The next day Isu Chiba and Abdulhay Jassat were arrested and tortured. Since neither Isu nor Abdulhay were involved in the actual operation at the Riverlea target, it was clear the police knew about their connection with MK. Also held in detention were 'Mosie' Moola and Wolfie Kodesh. Mosie was not connected with MK. He was with the TIC as a full-time functionary, and was a CP member. There were more arrests. This time Harold Wolpe and Arthur Goldreich were detained.

All the men were held at the Marshall Square Police Station. After some time they got friendly with a young prison warder, Johannes Greef. He was eighteen years old, naïve, easy-going and with a passion for cars that he could ill afford. When the time seemed opportune, the men worked out a plan, and an offer was made to the warder. If he let out four men he would be given a very generous sum of money to buy a car.

A communication system was already in operation and information was flowing both ways between the detainees and the political structures outside. Before the escape, Isu was released. He immediately went into hiding in the countryside. I was brought into the escape plans. Yusuf Cachalia approached me to see whether I would be prepared to make the agreed drop at a house to someone by the name of Johannes Greef. This was to be on Sunday morning, as the planned escape would be the night before. The house I was to go to was the house of Isu Chiba. I realized that was why Isu disappeared soon after his release.

The four to escape were Mosie Moola, Abdulhay Jassat, Arthur Goldreich and Harold Wolpe. Wolfie Kodesh was not considered, since he had accepted the police offer of an exit permit.[48] He opted for England as a place of exile. He was temporarily suspended from the party, but reinstated some time later.

I arrived at Isu's house at the agreed time of 10 a.m. I was received by Luxmi, Isu's wife. She told me that she had noticed the police sitting in a car at about 6 a.m. At 7 a.m. they suddenly burst in, to find only Luxmi and her three children. They searched around, found no money and left quite furious. The police raiding band was led by Captain Swanepoel. There was clearly some confusion about the agreed time. I nearly wet myself at the thought of falling into the clutches of Captain Swanepoel. I thanked Luxmi and made a quick exit. The money still tied in the handkerchief under my pants (trousers), I returned and gave it back to Yusuf. I went home, picked up my bundle of *New Age* and went about my rounds.

There was elation and joy about the escape, news of which the radio was regularly blasting out with the description of the escapees.[49]

Whilst Mosie Moola was not involved directly with MK, he did have knowledge that some of us were involved, but never broached the subject. Once Mosie had to attend an executive meeting of the SAIC in Durban. On his return he came to see me. He said he was only a messenger. Whilst he was at the meeting he was approached by Billy Nair, who suggested that he take a message to pass on to someone who might be connected with MK in Johannesburg. Mosie said he would not know where to pass on any MK messages. I told Mosie that I was the least likely person to transmit any messages.

I asked him the nature of the message. It was that the house the government had set aside for Nana Sita to be forcibly moved to in the Indian Group Area in Pretoria should be blown up. Nana Sita was resisting all attempts to quit his own house, where he had lived for over forty years, in what was considered a White area. Nana held on to his own non-violent decision not to move. He was arrested.

When Mosie told me this I showed no interest and shrugged my shoulders. Immediately after he had gone I contacted Isu Chiba and conveyed what Billy Nair had suggested. Isu gave no indication that he had taken the suggestion on board. Some weeks later the vacant house for Nana Sita was blown up.

I was getting mixed reports about the role of Yusuf Cachalia. One report was that he was getting closer to the CP. There was no way I could authenticate that. On the other hand there were reports that he was getting increasingly disenchanted with MK. We knew he was in contact with Ismail Meer and J.N. Singh, who also did not support MK. The reports came from reliable sources and our MK activists, whilst they accepted Yusuf had the right to disagree, thought he should behave like most of those in the ANC and SAIC who felt the same, and who kept quiet. By now the political situation had become tense, so any forum to discuss the problem was not quite the same as when we had the first activist meeting with Yusuf in 1960/61.

Yusuf was an important political figure in the country. He had played a major part in uniting the political actions of the ANC and the SAIC, which led to the epoch-making creation of the Defiance Campaign against unjust laws in 1952. He and his older brother Maulvi came from a political family going back to the days of Gandhi's passive resistance movement in South Africa. As for his wife Amina, she too came from a family with a distinguished political background, starting with Gandhi, whose other contemporaries were the grandfather of Indres Naidoo, Thambi Narainsamy Naidoo and the Pillay brothers. Between the 1946 and 1952 passive resistance campaigns, seventeen members of the Naidoo and Pillay families experienced imprisonment.

This was a dilemma which I had to handle very carefully. What if I got it wrong? So I contacted comrade Bram Fischer. I explained the situation. There were two sorts of problems the activists presented to me. In their view Cachalia had failed to make a stand over the Group Areas Act, and he was opposed to violent struggle.

I had a chat with Yusuf on the question of opposing the Group Areas. In the past our opposition had been primarily through court hearings. I told him the time had come for more active opposition, and said he should give a lead. Yusuf listened but was noncommittal. He despaired of violent struggle and honestly believed that Indian people were raised on passive resistance. He was partly right. However, Dr Monty Naicker and Nana Sita were lifelong passive resisters, yet neither came out against the formation of MK.[50]

Bram asked me whether I could suggest a way out without damage to Yusuf or the struggle. I suggested that he approach Yusuf, who at the time was under house arrest, to discuss the dire straits of the leadership and the increasing repression by the state, and to explain that as his contribution would be needed in the future, for the time being he should take a quieter position. Hopefully this would avoid him getting into any controversial position with any of the activists, as they were getting restless.

I knew Bram would not have hesitated to tell me if I was wrong. I also knew Yusuf had immense regard for Bram and he would value his point of view. Bram agreed to speak to Yusuf. This was done and Yusuf accepted the suggestion.

After some time Isu reappeared and went about normally. He was a remarkable person, completely controlled, calm and, when the need arose, swift and decisive. In his young days he was a tearaway kid on the block. As a teenager he got involved with the notorious Sheriff Khan gang. The gang intimidated small shopkeepers for protection money.[51] Isu's father was tearing his hair out on account of Isu's behaviour. He was getting involved in fights and avoiding work. The father's solution was to ship the lad out to India to live with the clan and cool his heels, and whilst living with the extended family, they would get him married.

Isu returned to South Africa with a pretty young and somewhat shy bride, Luxmi. He soon found employment in a dairy, quickly taking on management responsibility. His employer was very impressed with his discipline, organizing ability and cordial relationship with staff and customers. Isu worked seven days a week from 5 a.m. to 1 p.m. He accepted payment in lieu of annual holidays. His employer paid for the natal attention Luxmi had for each of her three children and other expenses Isu incurred.

I used to see Isu as a dashing-looking Casanova. I was actually acquainted with his younger brother Govan, who was a promising science student. When I was selling Soviet pamphlets on science, especially on rockets, Govan eagerly sought me out for some. Later he worked for Rolls Royce in England and joined the ANC in London.

After I was released from detention during the State of Emergency at the time of the Sharpeville massacre[52] Reggie Vandeyar told me that he had got to know a chap who was keen on being involved. It was Isu.

Moses Kotane, the CP's general secretary, who was not amongst those picked up in the swoop of some two thousand political activists, had kept the party machinery functioning with the help of a core of party comrades and supporters. Adelaide was not a party member, but she was the go-between for Moses, Kodesh, Bram Fischer and others. I talked with Adelaide about the sort of things that happened whilst we were in prison. She mentioned Isu, who was aware of the party members. A number of times during the Emergency he had come to our house to meet Adelaide.

I asked Reggie to bring Isu over to my place for a chat. Isu told me that, whilst he was aware of the political situation, he had never really bothered before. He knew there were people active in politics and had seen some of us around. But what happened at Sharpeville shocked him. In this context Isu seemed the sort of material we sorely needed. He was recruited into the Party. He joined a Marxist study class, did a lot of reading, and attended political meetings.When the Party directive came to us to support or join MK, Isu was amongst the first recruits. In time he was a key participant.

A salutary lesson I learnt from Isu was to keep good time. One day we arranged to meet. I turned up, but Isu was not there. When I next saw him I asked him what happened. He asked me what the exact time was when I arrived. I said, well, it may have been a few minutes after the agreed time. Isu replied, 'Exactly. You were not on time so I left. Comrade, remember lives are involved.'

When Isu reappeared from hiding after his release he was ever alert. He was back in the apparatus of MK. We were in need of new blood. Whilst the need was urgent we did not want to repeat the kind of disaster we had with the Gamat Jardine episode.

We carried on with our programme of action. There were several spectacular explosions. One was a huge transformer near the railway line of the south-western direction. The transformer was near a bridge between Fordsburg and Vrededorp. All the lines carried high-speed trains. We were asked to carry out a survey of this target. None of us had any knowledge of how the lines lay, or the switching of lines into different lines. We had to watch carefully or move fast so as not to get caught between the lines. The lights of the fast-moving trains fell on the gleaming lines and the glare blinded us each time for a few seconds. It was a risky and a nervous reconnaissance.

Much to our horror once again we stumbled on another unit who were on the same assignment. So as to avoid further identification of cadres, I pulled out our unit. The next day I complained to Isu about the dangers of the assignment and the serious blunder on the part of the regional command. Isu apologised profusely and said he would pass on our criticisms.

A week or so later the transformer was blown up, causing widespread damage with no loss of life. Isu led his unit for this assignment. He gave me an account of how they placed the explosives. After some time the device did not go off. He kept his unit members well away and went back to the site. He walked casually so as not to draw any attention from people in the street. He found that the fuse had died out about an inch or two from the device. The only way he could relight the fuse was with the stub of his cigarette – and then flee. As he got through the fence and a few yards away a massive explosion took place.

I asked him why he took such a risk. He said he had been told by the regional command contact that the explosion would be 'a lovely present for Nelson Mandela's birthday'. I said this was an absurd and dangerous task. We were not in this for celebrations. Isu agreed with me that it was, on reflection, a high risk and dangerous assignment. From the nature of the conversation it was evident that the long-distance adventurer in the regional command was Jack Hodgson.

Some days later I met a young woman who lived on the Fordsburg side of the railway lines. She told me about the massive explosion of the transformer that shook the whole locality. She said her elder sister (whom she did not know was a CP member) like the rest of the family was asleep. When the explosion took place the elder sister jumped up from her deep sleep, gave a clenched fist salute, shouted 'Long live MK!' and promptly slumped back on her bed fast asleep.

We were given a new directive that each of us was to take charge of our own units. Isu, now on the regional command, would be our contact man. Wolfie had already left for England. It was most practical and sensible, as Isu had a car. He also had the better part of the day off to do the running around, and in the evenings he could melt quite easily into the northern White suburbs for meetings.

I felt increasingly uneasy at the way signs were developing of breaches in security. We had no idea from where the high command was operating, neither did we want to know.

When MK was formed, amongst the many things it did was recruiting. Some recruits were selected for military training abroad. Some of the countries that accepted the recruits were the Soviet Union, China and Algeria. After a period of training they returned to South Africa. Some of these returnees thought they were keeping a low profile by wearing boiler suits. They would walk around in the vicinity of where the office of the ANC was situated before being outlawed. Now the only offices functioning there were those of the TIC. I saw some of these chaps, who actually acknowledged me. The impression I got, apart from cheap bravado, was the danger they had opened themselves to.

One chap in particular was Patrick Mtembu, who was the vice-president of the Transvaal ANC. At the time of the Rivonia Trial, Mtembu was brought before the accused as a state witness. A couple of years later Mtembu was assassinated by MK operatives, as was Bartholomew Hlapani, another MK man turned state witness.

During my interrogation by Captain Swanepoel, he let slip a bit of information about me which could have come only from Mtembu, who was by then on the regional command of MK. Bartholomew Hlapani and Piet Byleveld served on the Johannesburg district committee of the CP. I was on the same committee. I was always baffled why these two men were never brought against me when I was on trial.

Quite often on a Sunday afternoon Winnie Mandela would turn up at our house in Avenue Road in Nelson's car, driven by Brian Somana. Somana worked for *New Age* as a journalist and was in the ANC. He was appointed by Nelson to look after Winnie and the children.

Some Sundays Brian would bring Winnie and the two girls, Zenani and Zindzi, to us. The children liked to be with Zoya and Tanya, our younger daughter, who were about the same age. Winnie would bring a supply of fresh vegetables for us. Adelaide and I would notice that the car's wheels and mudguards were covered in red and brown soil, as if it had been driven over farmland. Winnie would then be driven to the giant Newtown market for the weekly shopping. It often occurred to us that if the police tailed Winnie they could have been led to the high command hideout at Lilliesleaf farm in Rivonia.[53]

For a considerable time I felt uneasy about Somana.[54] Several months later a report appeared in the papers that Somana's wife had filed for divorce and Winnie was cited as a co-respondent. Meanwhile, we learned that Winnie had gone to Joel Joffe's office with a request to apply for a court order placing Brian Somana under a peace order for having assaulted her.

I heard from a source in the ANC that the newspaper report of the divorce was cut out and slipped under Nelson's cell door. The ploy was clearly the work of the Security Branch. Somana disappeared from the scene.

On another occasion we were informed by two reliable comrades that they had seen one of our highly placed leaders at a local cinema in Orange Grove in the company of his girlfriend. Fortunately his disguise helped. When the leader came to speak to us, he was asked about his night out. He vehemently denied it.

Soon after the arrests of Reggie, Indres and Shirish, there appeared some kind of breakdown of our political structures. Up to the trial of the three MK comrades, nobody from MK, the party or the SAIC came to see me about the legal and welfare plight of the arrested and their families, particularly in the case of Reggie and Indres, who were the main breadwinners of their families. I was not aware whether anyone else may have taken up their problems. But equally important was the position of the MK unit I was involved in. Several of my key contacts had also been arrested or were in hiding.

During these difficult and stressful times, the one person some of us could go to for advice, help or a comforting embrace was comrade Bram Fischer. My main purpose in contacting comrade Bram was not to discuss party or MK structures. It was how best aid could be brought to the arrested comrades and their families. Bram assured me that he would give the matter urgent attention. Welfare aid soon arrived and Shirish's father assisted financially.

When the men were brought before the magistrate their lawyer made a powerful exposure of the torture they had endured at the hands of the security police. This was widely reported in the press. The men were committed to a trial and were represented by senior counsel, Dr George Lowen. Dr Lowen had had a distinguished legal career in Nazi Germany, where he appeared as junior counsel for the defence in the famous Reichstag fire trial in which Georgi Dimitrov[55] appeared in 1933. Dr Lowen had to leave Nazi Germany and he made his way to South Africa.

Issy Dinat was one of our activists who came to play a brave and daring part in those crucial years. I knew Issy's father and an uncle. The family was part of a community known as Kholvadians, whose forebears came from a village in Kholvad, India. Several of these families settled in the small town of Krugersdorp. Dr Yusuf Dadoo and a number of people from that sub-community played a very active part in the TIC, CP and the TIYC.

Issy, tall, trendy and very much a Casanova, easily made friends. As repression increased, he worked very closely with me. Socially he saw a lot of my family and my brothers and sisters. Since a lot of the work was confidential, not many people knew of our political relationship.

One night a group of activists asked me to meet them to discuss an urgent matter. I got to the house, where several activists were present, all of whom had several years of political involvement. They expressed doubts and reservations about Issy. They said he was keen to fraternize with some of the young women in well-known political families. They cited Ramnie, the sister of Indres Naidoo, the niece of Dr Kazi, who was treasurer of the TIC, and a niece of Amin Kajee, a veteran political leader. Then someone said they were informed that Issy was seen coming out of Gray's Building.[56] The view was that he was attempting to infiltrate by getting into one of the political families through their daughters or nieces.

But the astonishing objection from one of the activists was from someone whom I considered astute. He was a doctor. His objection was, 'I don't like his face.' The allegation about being attracted to the young women was frivolous and without substance. The only common factor about the three women was that they were beautiful. Any Casanova would have been attracted to them.

The allegation 'coming out of Gray's Building' needed more discussion. I asked for the source of the allegation. There was no source, but in unison they believed it was true. I pointed out that this was a serious allegation which could prove to be very damaging. I then made a suggestion. Issy should be tailed for a couple of days. I asked for volunteers. There were none. I suggested that the matter be dropped immediately.

Issy was not drawn into MK or the party. I thought it advisable that he continue his activities in the TIYC. Besides, he was popular with the younger generation in the TIYC. He was showing leadership qualities and initiative, and he was courageous. He had an idea of my involvement in MK and the Party but at no stage expressed a wish to be involved. [57]

By now Issy's relationship with Ramnie was going steady. Sometime later he expressed a wish to marry her. He enlisted the support of Mosie Moola. Issy and Mosie knew there could be some objections. One was that Issy was Muslim and Ramnie was Hindu. The objections, if any, would come from Issy's relatives in Krugersdorp and perhaps from Ramnie's in Pretoria rather than from her immediate family. The other was to have the matter raised with Ramnie's widowed mother. Issy and Mosie approached me to speak to her mother, who was affectionately known to all as Amah. I declined, saying it was a matter that should be raised by them with Amah directly.

Issy and Ramnie got married and set up home in two rooms at the back of a shop in Vrededorp. I never told Issy about the meeting or the allegations against him. I knew he had a short fuse.

Dennis Brutus was a teacher who helped set up the South African Non-Racial Olympic Committee (SAN-ROC) and and became its first president until a banning order was served on him in 1963. He made an attempt to leave South Africa by way of Mozambique, but, in spite of being in possession of a British passport (he was born in Rhodesia) he was arrested by the Portuguese police and handed over to the South African security police. This was a complete violation of international law.

Dennis was transported via Nelspruit police station to Johannesburg. As the security car was heading to Marshall Square police station through Fox Street, where the Anglo-American mining company headquarters were sited, Dennis leapt out of the car and made a run for it. He was shot in the back by warrant Officer Herbst from the political squad.

Dennis was left lying on the pavement until the ambulance arrived. When it came it was an ambulance for Whites, so there was a further delay until the ambulance for Blacks arrived. He was taken to Coronation Coloured/Indian hospital in Coronationville, several miles away. There he was operated on and placed in a ward on police guard.

Word of the shooting had got around. That evening a large group of activists mainly from the TIYC gathered outside the hospital in sympathy and protest at Dennis's plight. By the next afternoon John Harris,[58] a prominent radical Liberal, contacted me. He had an idea how we could spring Dennis out of the hospital. He outlined a plan and asked whether I could get some people to assist. I agreed to see what could be done. We arranged for a further meeting to discuss the principle, and then its application if there was an agreement. I asked Mac Maharaj, Issy Dinat, Joe Kajee and a couple of others to attend.

The plan would be to get some of our chaps to dress up as doctors with stethoscopes, some as orderlies or porters, and a couple to act as decoys to swiftly crisscross the ward in order to create diversions and confusion. In the process they would disarm the guard and smuggle Dennis as quickly as possible to an awaiting getaway car. We met a couple of times more to go over the plan. Finally we abandoned the attempt as there were far too many people involved. In the event Dennis got only two years' imprisonment. Had we been caught we would probably have got much more and possibly a good working over.

John Harris was a member of the African Resistance Movement (ARM). This was a group of radical members in the Liberal Party who secretly decided on violent action against the apartheid regime. John planted a bomb in the White section of Park Station, the mainline rail station in Johannesburg. ARM had phoned in a warning, which was ignored. The bomb killed a woman. John was arrested and tortured.[59] His injuries were put down as being sustained whilst trying to escape from a moving car. He was put on trial and sentenced to death. He went to his execution singing 'We shall overcome.'[60]

On the morning John's execution was announced over the radio, our daughter Zoya was lying next to me in bed. She said 'Dad, the bastards have killed him.' She was six years old at the time.

In that year Mac was jailed for twelve years, Issy had two separate terms of detention, and Joe Kajee managed to slip over the border and head for Zambia. Two others who were part of a planned escape team also got out for military training.

18

Banned and detained

Adelaide and I were having to cope with our family needs, particularly the health condition of our disabled son Anand. We were helped greatly by doctors, family members and friends. We also had an understanding pharmacist who allowed us long-term credit.

We were living in cramped and insanitary conditions. We shared an outside toilet and tap and a large rubbish bin. Quite often the toilet and the bin were overflowing. Our party comrades were very much concerned about our son's condition, which was beginning to affect us and my political work. At one stage I had to withdraw from MK, as Anand's health was going down. Mac made strenuous efforts to arrange for our party comrades in London to search for a sympathetic institution to treat Anand.

One day in 1964 the security police arrived at my workplace, the furniture factory, to serve a banning order on me. The restrictions were quite comprehensive. It banned me from work, from gatherings, from schools or any places of education. I was confined to house arrest. The ban was to last five years. The only dispensation allowed was that I could leave my house from 7 a.m. to 7 p.m. and on Saturdays from 7 a.m. to midday. I was confined from Saturday midday all weekend and on any public holiday days. I was to report to the local police station each Saturday before midday to sign a register.

After the banning orders were served I was told to leave the factory immediately. I asked if I could collect my jacket and lunch box. They agreed. When they did not follow me, I hurried to the mill to tip off a comrade about the presence of the security police. I was the only one who knew that Joseph Molefe had breached his banning order by continuing to work at the factory. I got back to the office, where the police were waiting for me. One of them spotted comrade Molefe in the timber yard and arrested him.

Several weeks later I met a woman who was a nurse at the Non-European General Hospital. The hospital was opposite the No. 4 Prison, The Fort. She turned out to be the daughter of Comrade Molefe. I enquired about her father. She told me that he had died a couple of weeks back. One morning she was on her way to work when she noticed a man bent over on the edge of the kerb in agony. She went over to help him. When she raised his head, she was horrified to see it was her father. He had taken ill in prison. He was given no medical treatment, instead he was sent out of the prison.

She got her father admitted to the hospital, where he was operated on. In his stomach was found undigested, hardened, virtually raw *mealies*, which was the diet he had been fed on in jail. The maize had lacerated his stomach. That is what killed him. I often agonized whether my tipping him off about the presence of the security police had caused his arrest.

I arrived home at about midday. Adelaide could tell something was not right. I showed her the banning order. It was typical of what a lot of political people were experiencing. Many were confined for 24 hours. I had to make sure that I did not breach any of the restrictions. Apart from having to report once a week to the police station, the police could drop in any time to check on me. I noticed their surveillance had increased, with more visits to our house and a more frequent presence in the neighbourhood. Not being able to work was a major factor.

During the day I could go around the city. One morning I dropped in to see a couple I had known for a long time. They had a problem with the city council about selling flowers in the manner of the Padiachee brothers. In fact, they were relatives. I gave them the number of a lawyer I knew to contact with a view to getting advice. As I was writing down the lawyer's details, a couple of security men rushed in. They questioned the couple, who told them of the nature of my visit. They grabbed the note from my clenched fist. They warned me and left. I apologized to the shaken couple.

I was quite upset. I contacted the lawyer Ronnie Michael, whom we had come to know when Reggie, Peter and I worked as pageboys at the Orange Grove Hotel. I explained to him what had happened. It was not the first time I referred people to him with problems. He assured me not to worry. He would deal with the matter should it arise.

The most important question was how I was going to fend for my family. Our son Anand's condition was a 24-hour matter. Zoya was aware of our situation. She met many of our political comrades at our house and could recognize some of the security police. One in particular was Detective van Tonder, who specialized in stalking the Indian activists.[61]

My mother, sisters and in particular my brother Peter helped us a great deal. Mac would pop in and give Adelaide some money. He said it was from the party. In spite of the structures being badly affected, there was still consideration to help comrades in need.

Issy was working as a bookkeeper for a small factory manufacturing women's garments. He persuaded the owner to let me have credit to hawk the garments – dresses and two-piece separates – during the hours allowed in the banning order. I carried the garments in a suitcase and tramped around the suburbs knocking at the doors of houses. Fortunately I knew a lot of people in the suburbs, mainly through selling *New Age* and *Fighting Talk,* as well as through my political involvement. Some were poor and needed garments, which I sold on credit.

Since I was not allowed to visit the factory, I could phone in the orders, while either Adelaide or Peter would go to the factory offices to make regular weekly payments. Apart from the much-needed income, one advantage of doing house-to-house sales was that I could talk to people about the political situation, hear about their problems, or indeed celebrate their happier news. This bit of income helped to pay rent, half of which was from Peter, and buy provisions as well as the medicines for Anand.

Issy and Adelaide thought I was the worst 'businessman' they knew. They thought I gave too much credit and did not mark up enough on the goods. Adelaide said I was easily charmed by some of the customers and was a soft touch. As for keeping accounts, Issy thought I was hopeless. He thought I was giving the factory owner too high a percentage of my sales income. No wonder the owner felt so pleased with my weekly payments. Issy showed me how to keep records and Adelaide kept a sharp eye.

In time I established a reasonable clientele, since the garments were affordable and stylish. I was rather pleased with my efforts until I met a woman who berated me for a garment I sold her. She had gone to a wedding function to find several women there wearing the same garment as hers. There was quite some embarrassment all round. She asked why I did not tell her that I had sold the same garment to several women in the suburb. I apologized and made a quick nervous retreat.

One afternoon I was walking in the High Street when I met a Coloured man who worked at the same furniture factory I had worked in. We stopped to exchange mutual greetings. He said he was sorry about the loss of my job and being under house arrest. I was most surprised at his sympathy. He was someone who was not remotely connected with or interested in anything political. He actually had an attitude problem to Africans.

A couple of other Coloured workers had told Harold Kingsman and me that this fellow reported to the White ticket collector that some African workers had entered the Coloured and Indian compartment of the train. The African commuters had entered the sub-sub-section of the train because theirs was overcrowded. The ticket collector made the Africans return to their overcrowded section.

Harold summoned the Coloured man with the allegation. He admitted what he did, adding that he had nothing against Africans. Harold was most unimpressed. He told this chap, who was a cabinet-maker, as punishment he would have to construct six wardrobes instead of the usual quota of four, failing which he would be fired. The man pleaded and begged. Harold refused to budge. At the end of the working day Harold and I checked the quality of the workmanship of the six wardrobes. We noticed all his fingers were blistered. It was clearly a painful lesson for him.

It was this man I met on the High Street. He took a ten-shilling note out of his pocket and offered it to me. I refused to accept the money. He insisted. I thought I should accept, because it seemed a genuine gesture and perhaps it was a recognition that our political opposition had some validity.

A young man by the name of Marcus Solomon from Cape Town arrived late one afternoon at our house in Fordsburg. He was brought there by a group of young Coloured men. I recognized one of them, who had a reputation for being a tough guy by the name of Jansen. They sat in the car.

Marcus Solomon told us he was on the run from the security police. He said he was a friend of Neville Alexander. Neville and several of his fellow political fraternity were in detention. He had managed to get away. He said the fraternity was the Yu Chi Chan club, a breakaway from the Unity Movement. He went on to tell me more details, stressing that the group in detention would be charged with advocating armed struggle.

I asked who sent him to me and what was expected of me. He said a Mr Dean in Cape Town suggested he met me. I already knew about Neville Alexander and his group in prison, and I had heard of Dean as a trade unionist.

Marcus asked whether I could help him slip out of the country. It was apparently known there that was an escape machinery operating in Johannesburg, and some people assumed I was in contact with it. I did not disclose to Marcus that I knew of its existence or that I was involved with its work.

Was this a set-up by the security police? I had no idea who this chap was. The men who brought him to us were in no way politically involved and the fact that he had gone into such detail made me suspicious. Adelaide also became uneasy about the request for help. I told Marcus that I could not help him. He looked disappointed. He thanked me and left to join his friends.

A week or so later I picked up a copy of *Cape Times*. There was a picture of Marcus Solomon. He had been captured, detained and later charged with

Neville Alexander and several others. They were all sent to Robben Island for ten years.

That report depressed me for a long time. I was in the machinery that helped political activists on the run to escape. Some did come from Cape Town. They had satisfactory credentials. If only Marcus had had that sort of reference I could have helped.

An Indian woman living in an upstairs apartment which was diagonally opposite had a commanding view of people visiting us. She often saw Winnie at our house. One day she commented to Adelaide, 'For an African woman she is very beautiful.' Adelaide tore off a few strips from this woman. No doubt she regretted what she had said.

The Rivonia Trial was in full swing. Quite often Adelaide would accompany Winnie to the trial in Pretoria. Winnie would wear the striking garments Nelson collected from various parts of Africa he had travelled to. She always looked stunning.

On the final day of the trial, after sentence was passed, she was surrounded by the press. Then she and Adelaide left Pretoria. On arriving at our house she slipped out of our back door and entered my mother's house. I followed. Keeping watch outside was Matselane, the woman who helped us with Anand. She was sitting with Anand on her lap. Also outside were those ever-alertful neighbourhood kids, who took their lookout positions.

We talked about the immediate situation, which had taken a dramatic turn. We were relieved that the accused got life sentences instead of the dreaded capital punishment. Winnie was completely calm, controlled and certainly more determined than ever to carry on the fight. The other immediate issue was that of the safety and care of her and the children,

I recall telling her to be extra careful since she was young and attractive and there would be attempts to undermine her through friendly infiltration. I reminded her of the division in her community in the Transkei, which was a Bantustan, where her father was a minister in Matanzima's puppet government, which had caused a great deal of conflict and tension within the families and clans. Chief Matanzima was Nelson's nephew.

When Winnie spoke to me about Nelson she never referred to him as Nelson, rather 'your brother'. Winnie knew that I talked about betrayals and treachery because there were people who testified against the Rivonia accused.

Just about a year or so before, Nelson Mandela was serving a five-year sentence for having left and returned to the country without a passport and in breach of his banning orders. Winnie received a message from an Indian chap who said he and some of his friends had a contact with a prisoner who could help Nelson escape from prison. Winnie told the chap she would think about it. They agreed to a date, time and place to meet for further discussion.

Winnie came to see us about the proposal. She said she did not know who this person was. I suggested she meet them and extract as much information as possible. But I added one proviso, that she took Adelaide with her. In the meantime I would alert some comrades. She should merely hear them out and not accept any plans. Winnie passed me the location and time of the meeting. She and Adelaide set off.

After an hour or so they returned. Winnie told me that she met a group of Indian men who were in touch with one Moosa Dinath, who was serving a long term of imprisonment. They said he was well known to the highest prison officers and he could arrange an escape from prison.

Winnie was sceptical and uneasy. I asked Adelaide what she thought about the idea. Adelaide said she recognized one or two of the chaps. She said they were a bunch of crooks. I said that this smelled like a plot to get Nelson out and in the course of the attempt get him shot on the pretext of attempting to escape.

I gave Winnie a brief profile of Moosa Dinath, who appeared to be a financial wizard. He had run an insurance company in the mid-1940s known as Universal Providers. He had a high profile in the Indian community at the time when there was a passive resistance campaign in 1946, so much so that he was elected as a vice-president of the TIC (we seemed to have made a habit of collecting shysters as vice-presidents). Moosa Dinath was a first-class fraudster and most likely was trying to cut a deal for himself at the price of Nelson's life. I advised Winnie not to bother to contact the men again.

Some years later Moosa Dinath made a comeback through his wife, Maud Katzanellenbogen, who befriended Winnie, resulting in her imprisonment and torture. An account of this experience is told in the biography of Mandela by Anthony Sampson[62] (I was listed as a co-conspirator in Winnie's trial).

In many ways Winnie was a remarkable person. She was always kind, sharing, extremely considerate, quiet and effective. She often brought gifts, cakes and food to us. She would update us on any visits she had to Robben Island.

One morning Winnie was on her way to work when she dropped in on Adelaide. When I got back from work Adelaide gave me an account of a horrendous incident that happened to one of our young neighbours. Whilst Adelaide and Winnie were chatting they heard hysterical screams and howling. They rushed out to see what was happening. They saw this woman engulfed in flames. Winnie grabbed a blanket, tightly wrapped it around the woman and speedily drove her to the Coronation Hospital. The woman, Rose, made a remarkable recovery and went on to have a child. Rose was the wife of a young waiter, Kista Moonsamy, who became a party member and an MK operative. Both became active members of the ANC and Kista became a local ANC councillor. Kista's son became one of Nelson Mandela's bodyguards.

When Mosie Moola, Abdulhay Jassat, Arthur Goldreich and Harold Wolpe escaped from Marshall Square on 11 August 1963 there was nerve-racking confusion, incompetence and no contingency measures in place. It was part luck and fortitude that made the escape possible. There was a sigh of relief when they were safely in hiding.

The security police were on full alert to recapture the men. Whilst there was excitement amongst the people, for the families of the escaped prisoners it was stressful, particularly for the wives and children. Neither was it easy for those behind the scenes who arranged the escape.

The next move was to plan for the men to cross the borders of South Africa. In the meantime, they needed a change of clothing, food and money. All the plans, including disguises, had to be carefully arranged. There were to be no telephone messages or written notes of any sort. Messages had to be carried by word of mouth. Meeting points were not to be held in any homes of known political people.

This is when the question of finding neutral homes for some of the family members to meet the organizers became vital. Finding a neutral house in a White suburb was a problem. Most of the White political families lived near each other in the northern part of Johannesburg, in areas like Berea, Yeoville, Observatory, Melrose and Houghton. The police knew all the houses of these families.

For one of the crucial meetings we found a family who were prepared to allow some of the spouses to meet. As it turned out, they agreed to allow our contacts to use their house a couple of times. The house of this couple was at right angles to the two houses next to it, which were occupied by Rusty and Hilda Bernstein, and on the other side Lesley and Ivan Schermbrucker. The back gardens of the three houses backed on to each other. This ensured a safe passage to the meeting point.

How did we come to meet this neutral family? Isaac and Elsie Yudelman ran the Random Bookshop in Rissik Street, opposite the offices of the *Rand Daily Mail*. I got to know them in about 1953. I used to frequent the bookshop, one of the few shops where we could meet, talk freely and discuss national and international affairs with them and some of their customers.

The Yudelmans were not involved in political organizations. They were actually from a conservative Jewish background. Apart from their warmth and friendship, they had a strong sense of justice. They clearly transmitted their cultured background to their children, who were also extremely pleasant.

Soon my brothers, comrades and friends frequented their bookshop, as did a number of budding African journalists like Nat Nakasa and Lewis Nkosi. During the Treason Trial hearings, several of the accused would pop into the bookshop.

Periodically I would get to know their part-time assistants Bernice Stoller, Monica Joffe and Ruth Polliakov (later Jacobson). They were students at Wits. During the State of Emergency in 1960, when Wolfie Kodesh was on the run, it was Ruth who found him safe accommodation.

Whilst we were in detention, the Yudelmans sent me a box of books, amongst which was the classic *Brighter than a Thousand Suns.*[63] For many years they took out an airmail subscription of the *New Statesman* for me. When the air rates increased, they asked if I minded a surface subscription! For all the years I read the London *Observer* this was from the generosity of the Yudelmans. When I fell on difficult times, they would let me have any book of my choice, sometimes even from the window display. I would read these carefully and have it returned on the Monday morning to put back in the window or on the shelves.

The shop was visited by lots of White people; many were introduced to me and turned out to be decent and progressive. One of the more progressive journalists I met at the Random Bookshop was Donald Wise. He was the *Daily Express* correspondent who was there at the time of the Treason Trial.[64]

Adelaide discovered at one of the police stations where I was detained that the police would mess up the food she had brought for me. This continued at the station I was shifted to. She reported the matter to Joel Joffe.

Mondeor Police Station was not far from Soweto and rather a long way from Fordsburg, so Winnie, who lived in Orlando township, offered to do the Mondeor food run for me. Elegantly dressed as always, she turned up at Mondeor and said, 'I have brought food for Mr Paul Joseph.' This did not go down well with the policemen on duty. They taunted her with derogatory remarks. She responded angrily and they assaulted her, injuring her wrist.

When this got too much for Adelaide she visited Bram Fischer in his chambers. On seeing him she burst out crying. Bram warmly embraced her. She described the behaviour of the police. Bram suggested she immediately inform Joel. Joel decided to ask his wife Vanetta to accompany Adelaide to the police station. When the two women arrived at the police station, immediately the police made attempts to separate them on account of their colour. Vanetta was having none of it.

They were kept waiting whilst one of the officers got on the telephone to a senior police officer. From the nature of the conversation, spoken in Afrikaans, about a White woman being at the police station with the wife of that Indian prisoner with food, he was clearly worried that she could be from the press.

The senior officer turned up. He was the station commander. He was polite as he greeted the women. He took the food and flask to his desk and from the drawer picked a white, starched napkin, a fork and a knife. He very carefully separated the food and was satisfied it contained nothing in the form of a coded message. The police had suspected that this was a widespread activity with political prisoners.

When the food was brought to me, I was surprised that it had not been tampered with. I had no idea of what had gone on at the reception desk. What I did experience was an increase in rough treatment. One night the police burst into my cell and pointed a gun at my face. They demanded to know what writing material I had and where it was hidden, as they suspected I was smuggling messages out. They checked all my clothes and every crevice, as well as the toilet cistern and pipes. They left with threats and in a huff.[65]

The next time I was shifted to another police station I was allowed only one half-hour exercise in 24 hours. The exercise ground was perhaps no more than about four yards square. I walked around the yard and crossed it diagonally. In the middle stood a huge sergeant. When I crossed the first time and passed him he shoved me aside.

When he made his next attempt to shove me I stepped aside. I asked whether I could speak to him. He agreed. I said I had done nothing except using the time to walk. Had I in any way upset him, I asked. He kept quiet. I then asked him whether he had a wife and children. He said he had. Would he mind if I arranged for him to collect some clothes from a friend who had a shop in the city. One myth the police had was that Indians are usually traders. I did not let on I was a factory worker. He immediately became friendly. The next day he drew out some daily papers from under his uniform and told me where to hide them.

In one of my interrogation sessions through the night, an angry security officer opened a window and shoved my head out. He threatened that if I did not answer there would be 'a solution'. At the time I was not aware that one of our comrades, Babla Salojee, had died in detention. Salojee allegedly 'fell by accident' from the sixth floor of Gray's Building. This was not the first death in detention. At another interrogation session, Swanepoel told me, 'Joseph, we have got you and none of your clever Jewish lawyers will get you out.'

During my detention I was frequently shifted to different police stations. In one such shift Swanepoel told me, 'Joseph, it seems that wherever we send you, you cause trouble.' I replied, 'I don't know how I can cause trouble. I am in isolation and not in contact with anyone but the police.'

After about ninety days we were transferred to Pretoria Central and placed in single cells. The White prisoners were confined to a separate part of the jail. We were under constant observation, being taken out one at a time to empty the slop bucket, use the toilet and shower and back in the cell to have the morning porridge. When taken out for the half-hourly exercise, we had to keep a pace of several feet from each other and not converse. Those who smoked were given a cigarette. The next half-hour exercise would be the next day. On Saturdays and Sundays we were not taken out. On those days, the warders would be off to watch rugby.

One night we heard some strange noises. Instinctively, we thought someone was planted in a cell to overhear our conversations. The noises sounded like heavy scratchings on the wall. We fell silent. The following morning as we were being led out of our cells after ablutions, we started walking in single file. Several yards from me I saw the outline of a huge person. As we got out into the light we were shocked to see Wilton Mkwayi,[66] our Deputy Commander of MK, walking with a limp. Wilton managed to convey that his limping was due to a bullet wound.

Over the next couple of days we were given more background to his arrest. One night Wilton was heading to a political engagement. Unknowingly, he walked into two gangs who were engaged in a shoot-out. He was hit in the thigh in crossfire. The only thing he could safely do was to limp to the house of a friend, Irene Kumalo, who was a nurse. That night she was not home as she was on duty at Baragwanath Hospital. He got into the house and lay on the bed.

The next morning the security police arrived. They had come in search of Irene, whom they had discovered was a friend of Wilton. This information was extracted from another detainee who was connected with MK. Alfred was his name.[67] We had worked in the same factory. I knew he was politically connected and we avoided political discussions. According to Wilton, Alfred was severely tortured.

Wilton was being widely hunted. When they burst into Irene's house to find out the whereabouts of Wilton, to their astonishment they found him slumped on the bed, his pistol on the bedside table. The police arrested him and then proceeded to the Baragwanath Hospital to detain Irene. Neither of their arrests was known to anyone. Wilton was taken in for interrogation and made to stand for fifteen hours before being taken to the hospital to have the bullet removed.

Within a couple of days I was taken out of my cell and led to the visitors' section, and within a few moments Adelaide was brought in. We were both delighted to see each other. Unusually the special branch officer seemed friendly. I asked him whether I could embrace my wife as we had not seen each other for a long time. We were separated by a glass panel with an aperture. The officer said he would ask his senior officer. As he walked away I told Adelaide that Wilton was with us in detention, and that he had been shot in the thigh. There was no time to go into details. The official returned to say permission has been refused. We were warned only to speak about family matters. Within minutes the visit was over. As I was being led to my cell, the officer asked me to become a state witness. When I refused, he immediately became unfriendly.

It was only after my release that I heard from Adelaide what she did with the information about Wilton's arrest.[68] She passed it on to Winnie, who in turn passed it on to a London contact. The London fraternity had a dilemma; how to make public the information that the deputy head of MK was under arrest.

Someone came up with the idea of persuading Colin Legum to get *The Observer* to carry a report. Then the South African newspaper correspondents would be able to wire the story from *The Observer* and in this way they would overcome the South African government's press censorship. It is conceivable that making the information public may have prevented Wilton Mkwayi from being subjected to further torture or even perhaps suffering the same fate as Steve Biko years later. But equally important, it alerted other MK cadres in the country.

19

Prison and house arrest

I first heard of Joel Joffe from friends in the movement and from press reports that he was the instructing attorney for leading figures in the Rivonia trial including Nelson Mandela, Walter Sisulu and several others.[69] He was tall and lanky, with a soft voice and a bit shy. On occasion when someone made a funny remark he would let out a little chuckle. He was ordinarily dressed, unlike many of the lawyers I knew or saw at courts who were prim and proper.[70]

Adelaide got to know Joel when she accompanied Winnie Mandela to the court hearings in Pretoria. It seems that Joel had heard of Adelaide, and about her visits to the Johannesburg prison where Nelson was awaiting trial. Later that year, in 1964, whilst still under house arrest, the security police called and I was put into detention.

When Adelaide got my clothes with blood stains from the Pretoria Central prison, she took them to Dr Zainab Asvat. My shirt had a burn mark on the collar. (It was actually caused by a fellow detainee in the exercise yard who mistakenly left his cigarette butt on my shirt.) Asvat suggested she inform Joel Joffe immediately.

My first meeting with Joel – I called him Mr Joffe – was when he turned up at the Turffontein police station with Adelaide to inform me that he was my attorney and that I would face two charges, one of furthering the aims of a banned organization, the ANC, and the other of furthering the aims of the banned CP. He told me that I would be formally charged in court in a day or two, and that the police would transfer me to the Fort.

Joel told me that Bartholomew Hlapane and Piet Byleveld had become state witnesses. This shocked me, as these two men had served on the district committee of the Johannesburg CP. Also serving on the committee were Dan Thloome, Bob Hepple, Esther Barsel and me.

I thought I would be charged along with Wilton Mkwayi, Dave Kitson, John Matthews, Isu Chiba, Mac Maharaj and Steve (Nandtha) Naidoo, as we were arrested in a swoop. Chiba was the contact between our MK unit and the regional MK Command. Isu and I had an agreement. In the event of arrests and if one of us got away then either one would alert the other. When the security police arrived at his house, Isu fled into the backyard and scaled the high fence, hoping to dash to my place to alert me. (In fact the police arrested me at the same time as he was being arrested.) As he leapt from the fence, he tried to hold his balance on landing by spreading his fingers on the ground. The force was enough to break his thumb. The police were on to him.

When he was taken for interrogation, one of the chief interrogators was a Major Britz. Major Britz was astonished when he saw Chiba. Chiba was the foreman of the dairy below the flats where Britz lived. He came in regularly for a supply of milk. Chiba was serving on the National High Command.

Mac was working closely with the National High Command. He was aware of the circumstances of the countrywide arrests and raids. The net was closing in. Mac and his wife Tim had driven down to Durban. When he returned to Johannesburg a number of people had been arrested there, including Dave Kitson, Lionel Gay, John Matthews and Bartholomew Hlapane. After my arrest, Adelaide walked all the way to Doornfontein to warn Mac. When she got there she found a number of police cars surrounding Mac and Tim's place. She got out of the area fast.

Later I learned from Daso that he had tipped off Mac about the arrests. Adelaide expressed frustration that even though Mac knew of the arrests he still returned to his place. Mac told me in prison that when he drove into the vicinity of his house and saw all the security cars, he said to Tim, 'I think we have had it.'

At the Fort I met several of my fellow accused. We had been shifted to several different police stations, then to Pretoria Central, again to different police stations and finally to the Fort. We had all been through some considerable torture, especially those of us who passed through the spade-like hands of Captain Swanepoel.

Now at the Fort, being together under a relatively mild regime, we could get visits from our wives or family members who brought us home-cooked food, a change of clothes and an update on our families. Once again, as she did during the State of Emergency in 1960, Adelaide had set up a rota of women to prepare food for some of the prisoners. Wilton and Naidoo had no immediate relatives or friends to provide for their needs. Mac was in a similar position, as Tim, his wife, was not allowed to come near the Fort after her release from detention.

In the course of our awaiting trial we were able to discuss a wide range of matters related to the charges of working for and furthering the interests of the ANC and the CP as well as MK. We also discussed the circumstances of each of our arrests. Wilton was particularly bitter about his arrest. He was adamant that Winnie Mandela was responsible for his arrest as well as those of Fikile Bam and Solomon Marcus. He could not substantiate his allegations. He sounded biased on the basis of Winnie's association with her driver, Brian Somana. I thought that, like many of us, he was caught up in the climate of suspicion fuelled by the stories put out by the security police.

Finally he reached the conclusion that when we got to Robben Island I should brief Nelson about Winnie's complicity. Though mindful that Wilton was the deputy commander of MK and I was obliged to accept his directive, I bluntly refused on the grounds of unsubstantiated allegations. Wilton was aware that Adelaide and I were close friends of the Mandelas, and when I reiterated my refusal he blurted out, 'Then you too must have had something to do with Winnie.' That statement convinced me that Wilton was wrong.

Joel decided to apply for a writ of habeas corpus, knowing full well the government had suspended the habeas corpus law. He calculated that merely by pressing for the application it would come to the attention of the public. This the government wanted to avoid. Adelaide made the application on the basis she feared for my safety and my state of health.

Joel also had the idea that if the security police did come to court to submit their application for refusal, he would be able to question them and require them to produce their log-book as to which police station they visited and at what time, as well as to the state of the detainee. The police realized they were in a trap, so they made no submission. Instead they agreed to pay Adelaide's legal costs.

Steve Naidoo and I were charged separately from Wilton Mkwayi, Isu Chiba, Mac Maharaj, Dave Kitson and John Matthews. Joel was their instructing attorney. They were charged with MK activities. Naidoo and I were charged with involvement with the banned ANC and the CP. The State were hoping to charge Naidoo with MK involvement but lacked corroborating evidence. After a number of appearances our case was postponed. Later I was charged separately. Joel was continuing to act for us.

Wilton and his co-accused were convicted and were sentenced, Wilton to life, Kitson to twenty years, Chiba to eighteen years, Matthews to fifteen years and Mac to twelve years. They were brought to the cells to collect their belongings, which gave us an opportunity to say goodbye. After the sentencing there was a tearful crowd and a few raised clenched fists. Mac asked to see his god-daughter, our younger daughter Tanya, to say goodbye. Adelaide took Tanya off her hip and passed the child to Mac for a goodbye kiss.

After further postponement I appeared in court. There was a strong exchange between Joel and the magistrate. Joel's contention was that there was deliberate intention in the frequent postponements, which constituted a denial of justice. The magistrate was irritated and threatened Joel with contempt of court. Joel challenged the magistrate to proceed with the contempt charge. The magistrate backed down.

Later I was taken to the prosecutor's office where several prosecutors were intoxicated. It was Christmas Eve. After some time they noticed me. The prosecutor said to me, 'Joseph, we are letting you go but we will come back for you. You may go.'

After my release I spoke to Joel about the habeas corpus application. He told me that at one hearing connected with another detainee he asked Captain Swanepoel in the witness box as to his whereabouts on a particular night. Swanepoel blurted out, 'I never assaulted anybody.'

Adelaide had been told by Joel I would be released. She and Tim dashed off to the magistrate's courts. They searched for me, but they could not find me. Adelaide phoned Joel, who suggested if I did not turn up they should phone again.

Meanwhile, as I walked down the road, I saw some familiar faces of people I knew living in the area. One woman on her doorstep asked, 'Were you not locked up in jail?' I told her I was and that I had just been released. She replied, 'You look so calm.' I walked further down the road to where some of my friends had a storeroom for the flowers that were sold from stalls around the city. They were delighted to see me. I asked for some flowers to give to some of the wives of my comrades left behind in jail and to the widow of Babla Salojee.

I walked the two miles with a load of flowers, first to Luxmi, Chiba's wife and then to Rokaya, Salojee's widow, and proceeded down Avenue Road to see Tim, and finally Adelaide. Adelaide's frantic face broke into joy. At last I was in the arms of a joyful wife, an excited Zoya and Tanya, my mother and sisters and Drushba, our pet dog, darting about excitedly. Later, neighbours popped in. Only Anand was not aware of what was happening. At the time it never occurred to me to announce that I was back in under house arrest. Neither was I in a mood to oblige by sticking to the rules.

In January of 1965 Steve Naidoo made a couple of court appearances. The same delaying tactics the prosecution applied. But this time they were in a quandary. The state witness, Lionel Gay, had fled to Botswana and was sitting on the banks of the confluence of the rivers Chobi and Zambezi waiting for permission to cross into Zambia.

When I discovered this I sent an urgent message to Vella Pillay in London to arrange immediate steps to get Gay out of Botswana, as the South

African police in collaboration with the Rhodesian police had the ability to spirit refugees back to Pretoria or Windhoek. Within a short time Gay got permission to enter Zambia. The Security Branch's only corroborating witness against Steve was Gay. Now he had disappeared, Steve was acquitted.

Joel had planned to emigrate to Australia and had to wind up his practice. Instead he had an urgent request from Hilda Bernstein, whose husband Lionel (Rusty) was one of the accused with Mandela and several other leaders. She urged Joel to take on the case. Joel accepted to be the Instructing attorney and immediately set about arranging for a team of eminent barristers and lawyers for the defence. The trial became a *cause célèbre* around the world.[71]

After that trial was over, Joel was asked to take on the trial of Wilton Mkwayi and his fellow accused. It was called the 'mini-Rivonia Trial'. In between Joel acted for several more people on political charges.

By this time Joel was much in the eye of the security police. He was deprived of his passport and accepted an exit permit, opting for the UK. His entry was facilitated by Dick Taverne QC, Privy Councillor and MP for Lincoln,[72] who was also a patron of the Lincoln branch of Amnesty International.[73] They remained friends from then on.

Joel arrived in London early in 1965 with his wife Vanetta, whom he met when she was a graduate teacher teaching him Afrikaans. They and their three daughters, Debbie, Abigail and Lisa, set up home in Colindale, London. Mark Weinberg, a talented financial expert and long-time friend of Joel's, had gone to London earlier and set up the Abbey Life Assurance Company. Abbey Life was aptly situated in St. Paul's Churchyard. Joel was invited to join the company. He started at the ground floor and rose to become one of its senior directors.

When Mac's wife Tim Omprakash was released from detention whilst the rest of us were still held, she had nowhere to go. Adelaide took her in. Both needed companionship and solidarity. Not long after, Mac and his comrades were sentenced.

Now there was Adelaide, Matselane (Rosie), Tim, Zoya, Anand and Tanya plus the pet dog Drushba. Our house always had a stream of relatives, friends, and comrades calling on us. It was also the meeting point for activists or for sending out teams of people to sell *New Age* or *Fighting Talk,* for leaflet distribution and house-to-house canvassing. When Winnie dropped by, as she often did, sometimes she would come with a friend or two and Adelaide would have ready a pot of curry and rice.

Any adults from the movement visiting us were always referred to as uncles and aunts by our children. So there were Aunties Tim, Winnie,

Shanti, Rookaya and Uncles Nelson, Mac, Wolfie, Percy, Mosie, Issy or Indres. Over the years many of the uncles and aunts disappeared, either put into jail, exiled or under banning orders. Zoya was puzzled but had a growing sense of what was happening. Adelaide always prepared meals or teas for the visitors, although after I was placed under house arrest there was much less cooking.

The security police were unaware that Tim was staying with us. Whenever they made their routine visits Tim was never there. Eventually they found out that she was working in a hospital. They reminded her that she needed a permit to work in the province. We secured a permit by using the name of Shanti Naidoo. The clerk at the Indian Affairs Department accepted the application in the name of Shanti Omprakash Naidoo. That gave Tim some months of employment.

One day the woman who had a commanding view of our flat from her balcony asked me to drop in for a cup of tea. She received me with courtesy, enquiring about our well-being and asking some questions which I quickly realised were leading to the ultimate question, how were we managing with the sleeping arrangements, since we were four adults and three children.

I said, 'Aunty, this is how it works. Matselane sleeps in the backroom cum kitchen. On the double bed I sleep on one side, Adelaide in the middle and Tim on her side. The only person who stays awake all night is Adelaide.' Her husband, who was a staunch Hindu, was quite furious and embarrassed and angrily said to his wife, 'I told you not to ask a question like that!' I did not tell aunty we had two folding beds for Matselane and Tim.

Tim was of valuable support to Adelaide and the children. Apart from her nursing experience, she also cooked well. The priority was Anand's state of health. Although Adelaide had always taken great care in ensuring the safest environment in our two rooms, the conditions we lived in were not conducive to a child with his disability, as he was prone to constant infection.

We had in the meantime made numerous enquiries about securing some kind of institutional care or help. Our enquiries reached a journalist, Hazel Fine, who conducted investigations into the plight of black physically disadvantaged children like Anand. She wrote a sensitive article in the Johannesburg *Sunday Express*, which had an equally sensitive editor. Hazel Fine understood the stress and strain in caring for children in that situation. She had a brother who was placed in one of the Rudolf Steiner institutions.

The article caught the attention of the health authorities and some social workers. The government agreed to set up an institution in Orlando Township (now part of Soweto[74]) on the basis of a semi-public subscription on a pound to pound contribution. When when the institution was established we applied, but our son was not eligible, since the law would not allow an Indian child in an African area.

In the meantime enquiries were being made on our behalf to institutions like the Cheshire Homes in Rhodesia (later Zimbabwe), India and England. Mac was in touch with our people in London. He was in contact with our key man in London, Vella Pillay, who was the recognized representative of the ANC and the CP and highly regarded by the Eastern European countries, the Soviet Union, the British Labour Party and a range of progressive organizations.

It seemed like there were some positive responses from the health authorities of the GDR. Tim contacted her sister Suri and Suri's partner Tony in London with a request that, if a place was found to secure Anand care, she would provide help for Adelaide and Anand to stay over en route to East Berlin. That was assured. I had heard of Suri and her brothers, who were prominent in the 1946 Passive Resistance Campaign.

It was only after my release that Adelaide told me Comrade Bram was involved in making arrangements for her and Anand. The only other persons who knew about the likelihood of the plans materializing were Tim and my brother Peter. Neither my mother nor sisters were informed, not for security reasons but because of the emotional stress of Anand being taken away. Adelaide and I agreed the opportune time to inform them would be when there was absolute certainty. Even then we knew something could go wrong if the security police got wind of our intention.

It also pained us that we were not able to disclose to some of our close friends who attended to Anand's and Adelaide's medical needs. As well as the doctors who gave their time, there was also the chemist Max Schlaghter, who gave us credit and immediate attention. The doctors would never accept payment. We felt there was a professional ethical principle involved and that they should accept payment, however small, but we could not convince them. In the end we gave up, with much appreciation.

Amongst the other friends who showed great concern and attention were Winnie and Nelson Mandela. Nelson would come over from Orlando Township to pick up Adelaide and Anand and drive all the way to the Baragwanath Hospital and back. Neither was it unusual for him to pop into our house late at night when he noticed the lights were still on. Instinctively then he knew Anand was not well. These visits by our comrades and friends were certainly a major factor in keeping up our spirits and confidence. The Mandelas adored Adelaide, and quite often when we were engaged in heated arguments she would say, 'Watch it. I will get Nelson for you.'

Adelaide told me that a number of people made discreet enquiries of my well-being and sent messages of support. Amongst the well-wishers were the Yudelmans.

There were other urgent matters of which she appraised me. There was the matter of Issy Dinat. The story of him being a suspect had resurfaced. This time it was much more widespread. Issy had come to see Adelaide in an outraged state. He believed he had traced the source of the rumours against him. He thought it was Yusuf Cachalia. He asked Adelaide to accompany him to Yusuf's home so as to raise the matter with him. Adelaide agreed to go with him on condition he kept a cool head and discussed the issue in a controlled way. She had also heard the rumours, which she treated as baseless. She was aware of the work that Issy and I were engaged in.

When Mac, Isu and I amongst others were arrested, Issy and Adelaide had visited Yusuf to seek help for 'Solly Matthews' (Mac). Apparently Yusuf gave them short shrift. On this occasion Adelaide accompanied Issy to Yusuf. Just as they got to the house, Issy had disclosed he had a gun. He said he would shoot Yusuf. This sent Adelaide into a flat spin and she prevailed upon him not to do anything foolish. He listened to her. Yusuf vehemently denied engaging in such rumours. Issy left not quite convinced. Adelaide was quite relieved that nothing untoward happened.

She did not relate this incident to anybody else lest it fuelled more problems, as questions of suspects, spies and informers were being bandied about and were clearly causing damage. In my own case over a period of years I had thrice come under a cloud. As stories were being circulated they seemed to acquire more exaggeration depending on who was putting out the stories and who was the intended target. In this sort of climate it could be used to settle scores. Innocent remarks or incidents were blown up out of context.

Not long after, Issy was detained under the 90-day detention law. Soon after his release we had a debriefing. Issy told me that he and some of the activists had been planning to spring me out of prison in Mondeor. Like the Dennis Brutus plan, this one was also abandoned. We covered quite a lot of ground. One of the loopholes in the detention process was that the security police did not take fingerprints or mugshots of their captives.

I was reasonably satisfied that Issy coped with his detention experience. I was confident that he could still make useful contributions in the struggle, since our structures were threadbare and we were in desperate need of help and resources. Issy had certain skills and daring (and, like most of us, also weaknesses).

I made a suggestion to Issy that he apply for a passport from a remote address. Should the authorities detect his political record, he should admit that he had had enough and wanted to get out. On the other hand his application could slip through the system and he could have a survival period to do political work. Fortunately no banning order was served on him. Whether this was a ploy or an oversight on the part of the security police will never be known.

Issy got his passport, which was concealed elsewhere and no one else knew. He continued his underground activities. He was working with Violet Weinburg, Bram Fischer and several other activists.

In 1964, word reached us that Mac's attempt to arrange Anand's medical treatment in Europe was successful. The news lifted our spirits. A major obstacle was that we were not in possession of passports and did not know whether the authorities would allow Adelaide to take Anand out of the country.

We had several Indian names, which the White authority always bungled, either with incorrect spelling or entered phonetically as it sounded to their ears. Quite often they entered names which had no connection with names in India. We decided that Adelaide should select some names and make a formal passport application through the Indian Affairs Department. She made one application for herself and Anand and a separate one for Zoya and Tanya.

Within a few weeks she got a notification that she was required to report to Gray's Building for an interview. The first part was to confirm the details as set out in the application. The next was to ask, did she know what communism was. Adelaide's response was 'What's that? What's communism? I don't know its meaning.'

The security officer seemed satisfied and entered in Afrikaans *Sy verstan nie wat is Kommunism. Sy viet niks* [She doesn't know what communism is. She knows nothing.] Adelaide read this upside down from the opposite side of the desk. A couple of weeks later the passports arrived with a set of names that we never used. We immediately had to find a hiding place. Where else except in the safe of the Random Bookshop?

In February of 1965 Adelaide was able to leave South Africa quietly with Anand for England and after a week or so go to the GDR. She and Anand flew to East Berlin, where an ambulance drew up alongside the aircraft to receive them, and drove them straight to a specialized hospital in Brandenburg. There they were warmly received by the doctors and medical staff. They assured Adelaide they would give Anand all the medical attention possible. Senior staff of the Afro-Asian Solidarity Committee told Adelaide that whenever she wanted to visit Anand, arrangements would be made. Their attention and assurance that Anand was being left in safe hands was quite an emotional experience.

I was back into house arrest and left with Zoya and Tanya. It was only after three months that the police discovered Adelaide's absence. They angrily demanded an explanation. I told them that her visit was purely for medical attention for our son and that she would soon return, as Tanya was still being breast-fed and Zoya also needed her mother.

When plans were made to get Zoya and Tanya out of the country, Issy was the key organizer. Amongst a handful of people in the know were my mother, sisters and brothers, and some of Adelaide's immediate relatives. I informed the Yudelmans and they asked a friend of theirs who was an airline hostess to keep an eye on the girls and step in if necessary to secure their passage. The girls were unaware of the air hostess's presence, neither was the friend who accompanied the girls. Later, the Yudelmans were among the very few people who knew what happened to me after the departure of our daughters.

Several months later there were more arrests and once again our structures were fractured. This time a group of people who later featured as the Fischer trialists, who included Violet Weinburg, Esther Barsel, Flo Duncan, Molly Anderson and Jean Middleton, were jailed. Issy was picked up on this under the 180-day detention law. This time he was given a very rough time but once again the security police did not take any fingerprints or mugshots of their detainees. Nor was a banning order slapped on him after his release.

Soon after my release Amina Cachalia broke her ban to visit me. I managed to contact Yusuf Cachalia and comrade Bram Fischer. We slipped into a safe house in Fordsburg, where I gave an account of my experiences at the hands of the security police, especially Captain Swanepoel.

Both Yusuf and comrade Bram felt that the security police would most likely take me in again, probably using the 180-day detention clause in which a person could be held without trial and be pressured to testify against an accused. It was felt this could present a danger to other comrades as well as to myself.

Both comrades well knew the particular circumstances of our family, especially Anand's medical condition. In view of that, I was advised to leave the country. I agreed, and set about making plans. But, with the virtual breakdown of organizational structures, that also seemed a remote possibility.

Third time lucky, with the help of Issy Dinat.

20

Escape

The first attempt was through Yusuf Cachalia, who arranged for a mutual friend to drive me to the Botswana border. We got well towards the border but this friend got nervous and seemed reluctant. He drove back to Johannesburg. Fortunately the security police did not come to check me and I slipped in safely.

The next attempt was through one of the Padiachee brothers, who were loyal supporters of the movement and had helped several of our activists with food and accommodation and secured their departure into exile.

I told Boya Padiachee of a contact I had in Durban who worked for a shipping firm who knew about the ships and timetables and could get me aboard a ship. Boya drove me to Durban. I met my contact, who seemed willing to help me but after a couple of days he contacted me. He had got cold feet.

So we drove back to Johannesburg. Boya went into my mother's house and confirmed that no police had come to check on me. Once again I slipped into safety.

Over the next few days there appeared to be a noticeable increase in police surveillance. It seemed the walls were closing in. One evening my niece was visiting our family. She had come from Durban on a school break. As we were chatting there was loud banging on the door. It was clearly the Special Branch. I asked my niece not to answer the door for a few moments until I had snatched my jacket and left through the back yard. I fled, making my way to Boya Padiachee some three miles away.

I got there and explained my plight. Boya immediately arranged for the use of a back room in the yard. He contacted my mother and spoke in Tamil to assure her that I was safe. My mother told him that the Special Branch had called a number of times in search of me. Boya got a message to Issy, who came around and assured me that he would work on a plan.

One night Issy turned up with a chap who was willing to assist me. We set off in the direction of Botswana. Some hours later we pulled up at what we thought was near the Botswana border. I was directed just to walk straight ahead. Eventually I would come to a row of raised parallel sets of wire held up by steel rods several feet apart and at intervals a steel pole spiked into the ground. Once over I should continue to walk, as that would be Botswana territory.

I was dressed in some warm old clothes, an overcoat and a felt hat, as the temperature tends to drop sharply at night. I had with me a compass but it was not luminous. Issy advised me not to risk striking a match, as it could be seen from a distance. The area was largely flat land. I had no water and had only eaten something earlier in the day. I walked for a considerable time trying to work out on which side was the Botswana border.

I got completely lost. It occurred to me that perhaps I was dropped off at a point that was not quite the suitably safe place intended. As I walked on I saw in the distance what appeared to be a ball of fire in the sky. The light was actually from a huge blast furnace. Then there was the barking of dogs. I realized I was still well within South African territory. I walked back. I was beginning to feel exhausted. A huge bird flew off the ground, and it occurred to me that there could be animals wandering around.

By now my eyesight seemed to have adjusted to the pitch darkness. Now I could see the plants, stones and rocks. I thought again that Issy and his friend must have made a mistake and in all probability had never been around this area. Exhaustion overtook me and I slept on the ground. I woke up at dawn when I had a better view of the lie of the land.

I came across a small shack made of corrugated fence and wood. I heard people snoring, so I gently knocked. After a while a door creaked open and a sleepy man appeared. I greeted him in bits of Afrikaans and English, as I knew no Tswana. I told him that I was from the Congress and needed to get to Botswana. He asked me to wait for a few moments. When he came out again he said he would lead me.

We walked for a while. Periodically he shook his head at the thought that I had walked for a long time. We came to a spot where there appeared a number of farm labourers and not far from them a White man driving a tractor. My guide showed me the fresh tracks of a South African army vehicle. I pulled my hat down to my ears. and followed him across the field where the labourers were at work and the tractor was ploughing up the land.

Apart from the labourers there were several men walking across the field, which my guide said was a common sight. I could be one of those chaps just walking across the fields. Like them I crept under and climbed over the wire fences. None of the labourers, walkers, or the tractor driver noticed anything unusual.

Once we were out of sight I gave him my overcoat and some money and thanked him very much. He bade me well and I thanked him again.

I got over the next lot of fences, which brought me into Botswana. Several hundred yards away I met a group of very young cattle herders. Issy had told me that should I meet any people I should ask for 'The *Makula* shop'.[75] The youngsters pointed in the direction of it. I walked for several more minutes until I saw a cluster of small buildings, one of which was the shop.

There I was received by a very polite, friendly man. I told him who I was and that I would like to make my way to Lobatsi. He welcomed me, saying he had expected me two weeks ago. Later he led me to the bathroom. I had a shower and he showed me to a bedroom, where I lay down for a while but could not relax, so I got up and had some tea. Later he asked me to join them for lunch.

Then he directed me to a nearby railway station; the line led to Lobatsi. I got on a crowded train which came from Johannesburg. I noticed some African men who looked as though they could be working for the security police on the lookout for likely political activists heading for Lobatsi. I had been warned about such agents travelling this route, and was careful to avoid glancing in their direction.

I got off at Lobatsi and made my way to a house where there were other exiles. I was delighted to meet Kesval Moonsamy, Eric Singh, and Basil Wheech, and relieved to see Steve Naidoo, M.P. Naicker and Jack Govender. The man who was in charge of the house was 'Fish' Keitsing. He was a fellow Treason Trialist and a Botswana national.

Later I was taken to the house where Dan Tloome – a senior ANC and CP activist – was staying. After that I visited the house where Maulvi Cachalia and his wife Mariambhai stayed. They too had fled into exile.

There were houses for PAC exiles and another for Unity Movement members. I was particularly keen to seek out Ghulam Nabbi, a Unity Movement member who came from a very poor family. I had heard that he was having problems, with no money even to buy food. I had arranged with a friend to pass on some cash to help him through. He was surprised that I had come to check on him. He later twigged that I might have been the person who sent him some money once before. I also made a visit to the house of PAC exiles, including some I had met when they were ANC members.

I discovered that Michael Dingaka and his wife Edna were living in the town part of Lobatsi. I called on them and periodically visited them. Michael was a Party member and one of our key men in MK. The security police were on the lookout for him. He had managed to evade arrest and slip into Botswana. Like Keitsing, he too was a Botswana national. I told him that he was on the wanted list as a VIP activist. He assured me he was aware and would be careful.

He often travelled to the ANC headquarters in Zambia through Rhodesia. The Rhodesians and the South African security had put a tag on him. On one of his return trips, he was stopped by the security police, handed over to the South African police and driven to Pretoria. There he was beaten and kept in solitary confinement. He appeared in court charged with acts of sabotage and involvement with MK. He was sentenced to several years of imprisonment.

Soon after my arrival I sent a cable to Adelaide in London, telling her that I was in Lobatsi. I also contacted Winnie Mandela informing her of my presence in Lobatsi and asking her to inform my mother and family. I took this measure to secure my safety in case the South African police snatched me back to South Africa.

The next step was to present myself to the British District Commissioner, so that he could record my presence in Botswana. He was polite and seemed very helpful. He was also keen to know at what point I crossed into Botswana. I said I did not know. Even if I knew I would not have told him, as that information and my presence would then be known by the South African and Rhodesian intelligence.

Adelaide acted immediately. She informed Amnesty International, the Defence and Aid Fund, Dick Taverne MP, who was a member of the Privy Council, Margaret and Colin Legum, and the ANC office.

Whilst I was in Lobatsi, an Englishman came to see me. He was Peter Mackay, who worked for the International Refugee Council. His job was to go to various points in Botswana to pick up refugees from Mozambique, Namibia and South Africa, drive them to the bank of the River Chobe to relative safety, and from there to secure them across the river to the Zambian side, when permission was given by the Zambian government. I was on his list, as well as two other South Africans. He arranged a meeting-point to pick us up. He arrived with a large covered truck, and after he collected us, he went off to pick up some Mozambicans and later some Namibians.

Peter Mackay was a very skilled driver in the part-desert and part-jungle towards the confluence of the rivers Chobe and Zambezi. He also knew how to deal with authority. He was polite, astute and quite jolly. We got on very well. He said he would have liked me to sit alongside him in the driver's cabin but was mindful that the other refugees might see it as a form of favouritism.

It was quite an experience driving through this part of Botswana, from

Lobatsi to Francistown, then to Kasangula.[76] The drive was spectacular. We saw just about all the animals except lions. There were times Peter would veer away from herds of elephants and buffaloes. When the elephants sensed danger, the huge male elephants would charge towards the truck.

After some thirteen hours of driving we arrived at Kasangula. I immediately jumped out and made for the river, when someone shouted 'Stop! There are crocodiles and hippos in the river!' We started building some grass huts, collected logs to burn at night and appointed two people to tend to the log fire. The fire was to stop the elephants wandering close to our huts. At night we would hear the villagers beating pots and pans to deter the elephants close to their dwellings.

We were told never to go to the banks of the river before dawn, as a range of animals would be drinking from the river. From what the villagers said, it was a fascinating sight to see the collection of animals drinking side by side. What was also interesting was to see the herds of hippos in the river. Again, we were warned not to venture anywhere near them. What we did not see were crocodiles.

We were told they keep well away from the hippos. We soon got to know what sort of time we should go near the river for dipping and washing, and to be alert. One morning a group of us went to the shallow side of the river to wash. I was the only one facing the river, the others were facing the bank. Suddenly a huge hippo emerged and charged towards us. I shouted and everyone jumped out, grabbed their clothes, and ran off. The villagers laughed at our plight. What amazed us was the sight of the villagers in their dugout canoes, skilfully paddling their way through the hippos without endangering themselves.

We sometimes heard elephants trumpet and walk away from our huts. Our huts were under the Marula trees. We discovered much later, when some of the village folk told us we picked the wrong site for our huts, that the leaves of the Marula have an alcoholic content. This was the why the elephants were trumpeting. We realized it was the log fire that kept them away. We accepted the village wisdom and took more care to make stronger log fires.

Where we were positioned was a sort of international point. We were on Botswana territory. On our right and fenced was Smith's Rhodesia. On the left was the Caprivi Strip in South African-controlled South-West Africa. Opposite the river on the right was Zambian territory. We were warned by the local Botswana police station not to venture near the Rhodesian territory. We clearly saw its armed soldiers. It was known that the Rhodesian police and soldiers had snatched and captured people from a liberation movement.

We got some food supplies from the International Refugee Council. They gave us ample supplies of Norwegian cheese, and allowance for bread, fish and vegetables. Occasionally we could buy rice.

Sitting on the banks of the river at sunrise or sunset was a beautiful experience. For me, Kasangula is still in my memory as one of the most beautiful sights I have seen. We used to see the pontoon plying between Zambia and Botswana. I soon got to know the men who handled the pontoon. Sometimes they would invite me to join them, but I was not allowed to set foot on the Zambian side, since I had no official permission.

One day a chap arrived off the pontoon and walked towards our hut. He broke out into a huge grin that was unmistakably that of Desmond Francis. He had come from Livingstone on the Zambian side, where he had a teaching job. He had heard that I was in Botswana and had come with a supply of food and newspapers, excitedly received. It was two years or more since I had last seen him. This was the first of many visits he made to me at the river's edge.

Desmond was seven years younger than me. The family lived in the same neighbourhood as us. His grandparents in Durban were the descendants of the indentured workers brought to work on the sugar plantations along the coast of Natal. The labourers were contracted for periods of five or ten years. They were paid ten shillings a month, lived in compound rooms and were given some provisions.

On expiration of their contracts, workers could ask to renew their contract, be shipped back to India, leave the plantations and accept a plot of land or, in some cases, leave for the Transvaal or the Cape. Desmond's parents opted to move to the Transvaal and fend for themselves.

Desmond was one of ten children. The father became a waiter, some sisters entered the garment factories, the eldest brother had managed to complete a training course in teaching. Desmond attended primary school and later college and finally a teachers' training college. He became a school headteacher.

He started showing a political interest and was discreet in the way he expressed it. He was sensitive to the events related to the social, economic and political deprivations caused by the firmly established racial system. Sometimes when we met, he would pull out a banned book from the back of his pants. If it was not a book, it would be a political pamphlet.

One day Desmond and I were walking in the direction of Wits, where he had an appointment at the dental department. As usual he was attended by the dental students under the supervision of qualified dentists.

Opposite the University in Jan Smuts Avenue we stopped to cross the road, when suddenly we heard a loud crash. A section of a building of steel and concrete in construction collapsed on a number of African workers, who were trapped under the rubble.

There was no sign of an alarm being raised. Neither did we see anyone heading to the collapsed site. We shouted to some of the White workers, who each had a labourer alongside them. The labourers could not leave to provide help to the trapped workers. We kept shouting at the Whites to no avail. We left in disgust. That seemed to be the turning point in Desmond's life.

This incident was soon followed by the Sharpeville massacre, the banning of the ANC and the PAC, the imposition of the declaration of a State of Emergency and in swift measure the scooping up of political activists from all the anti-apartheid opposition components; the ANC, the PAC, former CP members, some Liberals and segments from the Unity Movement were amongst those arrested. All told, about two thousand people around the country were scooped up.

Desmond was deeply affected by these events, which followed in quick succession. Many of those detained were people he knew or had heard or read about. He showed a keen interest to assist. Initially he was invited to join a study class. We soon discovered that, whilst most of our activists shared political interests, there was a need for us to participate in the discussions. It became a process of mutual benefit, since no one could claim they knew enough. The changes taking place in the country threw up many complexities, which needed to be understood. Having gone through some aspects of national, colonial, class, gender and socialism questions, the participants were enthralled by the discussions on Marxism. The most fascinating for them was on dialectics.[77]

Desmond was one of several teachers at the recently established Nirvana High School in the Indian Group Area of Lenasia. Amongst these teachers there was Don Muljee, Fakir Saleh, Solly Vania, Billy Nannan, and Bobby and Tommy Vassen. We also had a crop of other teachers in other schools.

The head of the Nirvana High School was a Mr Rathinsamy, who was a progressive and someone I had been in touch with for several years. He kept a low profile and may only have had a notion of who were the politically aware teachers.

The initiative of drawing teachers, students, factory workers and waiters into the movement was taken mainly by the Transvaal TIYC, which in turn had several of its members in the underground CP. After a period of time it was proposed by some of the MK cadres that Desmond be considered for recruitment into MK.

Some of our MK cadres considered that Desmond should be sent abroad for training, as we were aware the survival capacity of all our activists could be shortened at any time and there was therefore a need to send people out as well as training some people in the country. Desmond was considered a suitable choice to send abroad as he was single, and his family were not entirely dependent on his income. Mac Maharaj did the communication in code to our contact man, Vella Pillay, in London. Vella acted on behalf of the CP, ANC, Indian Congress and MK. His full-time job was economic adviser to the Bank of China in London.

In one of my chats with Desmond, I told him that his task was to be sent to a country for special training. He was not to get involved in any discussion on the Sino-Soviet split that was then very much talked about. I explained that his task was to undergo whatever course that was arranged and, on completion, to return to the country.

When he reached London, he was met by Vella Pillay and Yusuf Dadoo. It was arranged that he be sent to Czechoslovakia. In the meantime, he had to wait. At some point he received £300 from South Africa, from his school pension fund. For some unexplained reason he passed the money to Vella.

As the weeks went by, Desmond was kept waiting. Neither Dadoo nor Vella saw much of him. He was in limbo. He had virtually no money for himself. Fortunately, he was in contact with my brother Daso, who had just got out in time.[78] In London, Daso found a job in the mailroom of the International Defence and Aid Fund (IDAF). He got a job for Desmond and Benny Bunsee. The work was not well paid and quite boring but it did manage to see them through for a time.

Then Desmond came across a situation vacant in an educational journal. The situation called for a qualified teacher in a school in Lusaka. He applied, and soon enough he was accepted and headed for Lusaka. It was about two years or more since I had last seen him. He made frequent visits to us in Botswana.

I spent about three months in Botswana before my application for political asylum, made through Adelaide in London, was accepted and permission came through to enter Zambia. I made my last trip on the pontoon. This time I could set foot in Zambia. Once there, I spent some time with the locals, who were very helpful. Whilst chatting with them I remarked that we had not seen any crocodiles. They pointed to the spot where we had camped on the opposite side of the bank, and said they used to see us washing there each morning. They then told me that it was actually the breeding point for the crocodiles. They said we were lucky because quite often the crocodiles got on to the bank to sun themselves. Talk of miracles!

By sunset I managed to get a lift to Livingstone. I asked to be dropped at the police station. There I declared my position as that of a refugee from South Africa. They asked where I would be staying for the night. I asked to be locked up. They looked surprised. I said that it was for my safety. They agreed.

The next morning I made enquiries about Desmond's place and managed to get a message to him. He was very excited to collect me from the police station. Later, he drove me off to Don Muljee's house. Don was one of our activists, who managed to get out in time when the security police came looking for him. Don and his wife Bhabi set up home in Livingstone and Don got a teaching job. I soon met several South Africans. Some were politically involved and others non-political, holding professional jobs.

Within a few days I was asked to present myself at the British High Commission to go through the procedure for obtaining documents to enable me to travel to London. I was allowed a seven-day stay in Zambia and directed to the immigration department. The department was headed by an official called Richardson. He was a surly, unpleasant official who, I learnt, was about to retire and already had a job lined up with the South African immigration department.

Whilst in Lusaka I met the ANC representative Tennyson Makiwane, whom I knew from political involvement in Johannesburg. He saw me off at Lusaka airport.

Part 2: Exile

21

London Beginnings

I arrived in London in August of 1965[79] as a refugee. At Gatwick Airport I was met by Adelaide, Suri and Tony Naidoo, and another old-time friend, Wolfie Kodesh. The immigration official was abrupt, and took a long time to process my documents, including a letter from the High Commission's office in Lusaka consenting permission for me to enter the country. He rudely asked me why I had to come to England and 'cause trouble here'. I told him that I thought Britain was the most democratic country in the world and that was why I chose to come.

On the way to London Adelaide told me that after a long wait she asked a staff member whether all the passengers from that flight from Lusaka to Gatwick were cleared. She was told yes, except for a gentleman who seemed to be having a problem. She then asked to see a senior officer and asked him to help. He shrugged his shoulders and was about to walk off, when she stopped him. 'In that case I am going to contact Mr Dick Taverne QC and Member of the Privy Council.' She added, 'I have here a copy of a letter from the Home Office granting him entry.' The official stopped in his tracks and then walked to where I was waiting. Adelaide's intervention sorted out my entry.

Once in London, like Joel Joffe, I was helped by Dick Taverne, as well as by Canon Collins, and Colin and Margaret Legum. I was an adoptee of the Lincoln branch of Amnesty International. By the time I arrived Adelaide had found a small flat in Powis Square, Notting Hill Gate. Some friends whom Adelaide had met through Charles Bloomberg,[80] Mo and Irving Teitelbaum,[81] helped pay the rent, and unstinting support from Suri and Tony Naidoo made life bearable.

Soon after I arrived I was told by an ANC official not to take on a job in London, as J.B. Marks had suggested I was to be sent to India to represent the ANC. This never materialized owing to a series of incompetences. So after some weeks I contacted Joel, who invited me to join Abbey Life. Joel phoned me to come over to the Abbey office for an interview.

I was offered a clerical job which included dealing with the post, replenishing the vending machine, fixing the toilets and a couple of times operating the switchboard when the operator could not get in on time. I also ran messages and delivered confidential documents to legal firms and brokers.

Initially I was paid a weekly wage in cash. Later the company arranged banking and our wages were paid monthly. I had never had a cheque book. As a factory worker or waiter I always got paid in cash. After I got my salary paid into the bank I got my first cheque book.

I went into a fancy Indian clothing shop to buy Adelaide a saree. She was thrilled and wanted to know how much the saree cost. As she flicked through the pages of the cheque book it appeared blank until she got to the middle of the book to see the stub. She was amused. So much for the change from a wage-earner to salaried staff.

The office culture in the City was very relaxed. Some offices started at nine but law firms started at ten. My hours of working were from 8 a.m. to 5.30 p.m. When heads of departments started work at 9.30 a.m. their mail was on their desk. There was a notable increase in productivity.

My responsibilities increased as the company's business volume increased. I initiated systems of controls and order as the files contained documents of client confidentiality, so much so that even senior staff had to go through the system of control; even Joel had to wait his turn one afternoon until the check was satisfied that he was on the staff. The woman at the counter did not know he was one of the directors. The next morning Joel said he was so pleased at the tight controls.

The company was keen that I attend some internal and external courses in management. I was invited to several, which was a boon for me. My responsibilities continued to increase. The post room needed messengers. The company's records needed reorganization. I was given those responsibilities. In time we had a department of about thirty people. I was made supervisor.

Whilst a fair number of Abbey Life staff were South Africans, there were also some Americans and English. Most of the South Africans had a political background coming from the ANC, PAC, CP and a couple of Liberals. The company had not set out deliberately to recruit political people. They wanted people with skills, efficiency and reliability, and that suited the new recruits. As it turned out, none of of the political people engaged in political activity during working hours. Essentially they carried out their work responsibilities. All wanted to improve their lives and many did so.

I once saw Joel take a visitor around the company. He made a comment to the effect that 'Some of our best workers are communists.' I laughed up my sleeve. I thought we should be working to overthrow the capitalist system yet here we were bolstering it.

I avoided getting engaged in political discussions, mainly because I was there to do a job. But somehow word got round that I was a political person and had spent time in jail. Some of the staff were people who were sympathetic, some were openly Conservative, some Labour, but most were non-political. Some did reflect biased views about African, Asian and Caribbean people. This was not particularly surprising as I was in the heart of the country that once had the largest colonial empire.

I got to know a young, bright and exceptionally handsome man from East Pakistan (now Bangladesh), who was being trained by Mark Weinberg, specializing in whole-life annuities and advising clients with large sums of money. His name was Aziz Khan and we became good friends. He seemed to know about my South African background. He was very interested, since he was involved in a movement to break away from Pakistan. I, too, was supportive of their cause. Aziz often turned up at fundraising socials.

One day I spoke to him about South Africa's hold over Namibia, then known as South-West Africa. South Africa held on to this mandated territory with all its might. The question about its right to do so was raised by some countries and by a particularly outstanding man, the Reverend Michael Scott, at the International Court of Justice. It dragged on for years.

Later, Aziz went along with Mark Weinberg and Joel to set up Hambro Life Assurance Company in Swindon, where Aziz became a director.

One of the most impressive characters to have joined Abbey Life was Pranlal Sheth. Pranlal was a distinguished barrister in Kenya who had defended political leaders at the time of the Mau Mau campaign for independence. In the mid-1940s he was involved with Makhan Singh and Pio Gama Pinto in organizing the dockworkers in Nairobi and in helping Dr Yusuf Dadoo and Nana Sita bolster support for the 1946 Passive Resistance campaign in South Africa.

He became a close confidant of Jomo Kenyatta and Oginga Odinga. In Kenya, Pranlal was one of the lawyers invited to draw up the constitution in preparation for independence. In the course of time a cleavage developed between Kenyatta and Odinga. Odinga approached Pranlal for legal advice. When Kenyatta heard of this he took exception. He sent some of his police to arrest Pranlal and had him deported to India – illegally, since Pranlal was born in Kenya.

Pranlal stayed in India for a short while and then made his way to London in the hope of finding employment, since he was a London-trained barrister. He tried very hard for about fourteen months when one day he bumped into Ruth First. They had met in Nairobi when she went to collect material for the autobiography of Odinga which she ghosted.

When she heard from Pranlal about his plight, she said she would contact a friend. The friend was Joel Joffe. A couple of days later Pranlal got a telephone call from Joel, asking if he would like to come over for an interview. Joel got him into the legal department.

In a matter of months the company directors discovered they had landed a gem in taking on Pranlal, who had expert knowledge of company law and could write sound legal opinions. The company no longer needed to send its work out to barristers around the city, thus saving themselves additional costs. In time Pranlal became company secretary and head of its legal department.

As the company expanded it took on African, Caribbean and Asian staff. They worked in harmony with all the different nationalities and were promoted on merit. Abbey Life could be accorded pioneer status in employing people from different ethnic backgrounds. Its prestige in financial circles grew so much that Barclay's Bank asked for speakers from Abbey Life to give talks to their management and staff.

Pranlal was the first to give a talk. By then he was deputy chair for the Commission for Racial Equality. Barclay's asked for a second talk. This time Pranlal asked me to do it. He seemed pleased with the feedback he got.

At about that time Abbey Life took on some Asians, including a number of women from Uganda who had been expelled by Idi Amin. The women had no experience of clerical work but with close attention and support they became proficient. Pranlal and his wife Indumati were also doing a lot of community work for the needs of East African Asians.

Ruth Jacobson, a friend of ours from South Africa, asked if I could help a South African who had come to London with his wife and two boys and was staying with them. Ralph Sepel, a lawyer, had been detained in South Africa then let out without charges. Sepel decided to leave South Africa when the men were charged in what became known as the Rivonia Trial, as he realized it might come out that he was involved politically rather than in his professional capacity in negotiating the sale of a farm in Rivonia. I did not know the Sepels in South Africa (though later Ralph told me that it was through Bram Fischer that he heard of me).

I followed up Ruth's request and Leon Brenner did the interview. Ralph was taken in to head the legal department. His rise to administrative director and later as managing director (after the departure of Mark Weinberg) was meteoric. He later went off to form another insurance company called

Albany Life – another example of 'from Bolshevik to banker'!

Apart from Ralph Sepel we had Pallo Jordan, Issy Dinat, Aziz Pahad, Billy Nannan, M.B. Yengwa, Fred Dube, Steve Naidoo and Enver Carim and a seasonal holiday crop of students like Thabo Mbeki, Stephen Lazar, Jairaj Singh, Steven Friedlander and Vusi Make.[82] The company, largely through Joel Joffe, found employment for South Africans for humanitarian reasons as well as for talent and ability. In fact they were considered an asset for the company.

At the time I started work at Abbey Life there were only 27 staff. I came across some very genuine and decent people, who helped and inducted me in the nature of the insurance industry. Some of the staff were exceptionally considerate. Two of the staff, Gillian Spencer and Marion Williams, would travel all the way from Kent to take our young girls for an outing so as to give us a break. They would return from the zoo or Regents Park with delight, to a lunch with Adelaide.

There were also some interesting, amusing and dodgy characters working in the company.

I got to know an underwriter by the name of Teddy Jones (not real name). He was the spitting image of Stan Laurel. When he returned from the pub after lunch he was jolly and funny. After work he would head for the pub before heading home to Kent.

One day he did not return home. His wife was concerned but did not fret. He disappeared for a few days. It turned out Teddy was so drunk that he got on to a boat-train and landed up somewhere in Europe. When he returned home he told his wife that the BBC had sent him to Prague to cover the Soviet invasion of Czechoslovakia – a story which neither his wife nor the rest of us at the office believed. Still, one could not but like Teddy. I enjoyed his company.

Another character was a former beach photographer from Brighton, Derek Barnard. Derek was also an actor and then became an insurance broker with a great deal of success. His acting ability was certainly the key to his success. He was snapped up by Mark Weinberg to become an Abbey agent. His reputation and success made him one of the top earners.

He retained his house in Brighton and travelled to the offices in London each way by taxi. His day would start with a personal barber who came each morning to shave him. He later acquired a house in Little Venice where he lived with his wife Kay. They were a marvellous couple and always received us with great warmth. Derek was an acute observer and a very fascinating conversationalist. His personality and presence could be felt in any company.

One day he arrived at the ward at the University College Hospital to visit Adelaide, who was a patient there. He sort of waltzed across the ward calling out 'Hello, Adelaide'. He held her hand and kissed it. The nursing staff and some visitors stopped in amazement.

Derek and Kay enjoyed good food and often accepted Adelaide's invitations. Derek could hold his drink and was always steady. He never landed in Eastern Europe. He did visit the Soviet Union and on his return he came to see me to confirm, 'I saw the future and it does *not* work.' He obviously had detected my socialist leanings. He nevertheless supported the anti-apartheid struggle and on occasion bought tickets for fundraising events.

Another member of the staff was a young woman by the name of Patty. She asked me whether I would speak to her branch of the Young Conservatives. I agreed, and a date was fixed in a place in Surrey.

The hall was quite full and Patty said this was rare. It was their first meeting on apartheid. At the outset I said that if any statement I made on South Africa seemed factually incorrect, exaggerated or otherwise questionable it should be challenged.

After the talk there followed a series of questions. One was whether I would prefer black magistrates and judges to deal with matters pertaining to black people. At that time the apartheid government was working on the separate development of the Bantustans. The whole concept of apartheid was virtually endorsed by the Conservative Party. I countered the questions by demanding justice on the basis of equality regardless of colour.

The next morning Patty came to see me at the office. She said the feeling was that I spoke well except that 'I spoke lies'!

The next invitation was from a young chap, Ken, in our print room. He said his youth group would like me to talk to them about South Africa. Ken lived in Barnet and the composition of the young people was clearly working class. This was their first meeting on South Africa. They asked questions which were honest and innocent. They seemed satisfied and pleased.

One of the typists in our department was a young woman who I discovered was of English and German parentage. Whenever she spoke to me she never looked me in the eye. She sort of addressed me slightly sideways. She was finicky and made petty complaints.

She sat in the main well of the office and would converse audibly to the staff next to her. On one occasion she spoke loudly enough as to seem to direct her comments towards me. She said she did not like Pakistanis and carried on in that vein. A senior clerk tried to warn her off, 'Do you realize that Paul can hear you?' She ignored the woman's caution and immediately set off on another track, 'Pakistanis I can stand, it is Jews I dislike.'

I asked a senior typist to accompan the young woman to my office and bring a notebook to record the interview. I asked her what she thought she was doing degrading Pakistanis and Jews. I reminded her that the owners of the company were Jewish. She had no explanation, neither did she apologise. I gave her a written warning.

After lunch she did not return to her desk. An hour or so later I got a telephone call from someone claiming to be the woman's husband, saying that his wife was distressed at the way I spoke to her, that I had made overtures to her to take her to the pub and that he would come over to sort me out. I replied that before he came over I should tell him I do not drink neither do I frequent pubs during lunchtime or after hours. Also that he had no legal basis to enter the premises since he was not an employee.

I contacted the personnel manager, who by now had received a copy of my memo and the written warning. I told him about the threat from the husband. He said he would inform the security. About a week later the husband phoned me to apologize and ask for her wages.

A female member of staff had some difference with male colleagues. The next day I had a telephone call from a man saying that I had upset his girlfriend and that he was going to come over 'to knock your turban off your head'. So from being a Pakistani I had graduated to being a Sikh.

A young White woman joined the staff as a typist. She was an Afrikaner and came from Pietersburg, the same town as Vanetta Joffe, in the then Northern Transvaal. She was friendly and a very competent typist. We got on very well.

This relationship struck some of the English typists as rather odd. One of them said she did not understand why I was so friendly with the Afrikaner woman, since I, as a black person, had suffered so much from their ill treatment. My response, to her annoyance, was that this woman did me no harm. She had come to work, and in a work relationship there needed to be a friendly relationship. I explained to the English typist that we were struggling against a racist regime which had the support of both Afrikaners and English-speaking people. We always distinguished, our struggle was not against White people as such but against the system which used them against us. In any event, the system had its origins in England and Holland.

I did not disclose my chat with the English typist to the Afrikaner woman. She eventually left on the best of terms. Reflecting on that experience, one could say that it was a miniscule attempt at reconciliation.

As the company expanded, it took over virtually the whole building of 1–3 St. Paul's Churchyard. Part of the ground floor, with a service lift, was used as a canteen. The company was looking for a caterer who could provide hot drinks, sandwiches, grills, etc. The boardroom would be used for lunch exclusively for the directors and assistant directors. They would be served with grilled steaks, salads and fruit.

One of the applicants was an Italian, Lucien Saliba. He appeared to have wide experience in catering. I was asked to sit in for the interview. He did a presentation which sounded reasonable in terms of cost factors, the exception being that the grilled items would have to be paid for by the staff.

Saliba prefaced his presentation with what he could prepare – burgers, etc. – and assured us that it would not have the additives of wood shavings which he knew was the case in Glasgow. He also informed us that he once worked for a firm that made sandwiches three years in advance and froze them. Our jaws dropped. He hastily assured us he would not do any of that for us.

We decided to award him the contract and he assured us he would do his best. Soon Lucien had a couple of young Italian lads and a young woman to help with the catering and the usual chores in a restaurant.

There was something nice about Lucien. He was a little paunchy, of average height, with neatly combed black hair and eyebrows. He had an amusing repartee and a stylish way of casting himself around with some elegance.

Maria, his wife, occasionally dropped in. She was tall and attractive, a hairdresser by profession. Lucien told me that Maria's sister was married to a count.

One day Maria visited the restaurant. She saw the young woman assistant dashing around. Maria stood arms akimbo in the kitchen doorway and, eyeing the young woman, narrowed her eyes. She spoke in Italian to her. The woman seemed a bit intimidated. The next day the woman did not turn up for work. I asked Lucien what had happened to his young assistant. He threw his hands up, raised his brows and sighed.

Lucien's reputation in the boardroom rose as the quality of his food improved. He ensured that each director got a fair-sized steak, accompanied by salads and a glass of wine.

There were occasions when Joel came in late and there was no steak for him. Lucien quickly figured out that one director had more than one steak. Joel never complained. Thereafter Lucien's timing for Joel's entry was so precise that he had his steak. Joel was unaware of this precision.

When Joel had to go into hospital for an operation, Lucien turned up for a visit with a huge steak. That was one time that Joel was unable to eat it.

On one visit to our home Lucien, after using the toilet, came down to tell me that while he was there he glanced at copies of *The African Communist* and *The World Marxist Review*. He said the best place for such journals was in the toilet.

Whenever Adelaide and our three daughters went into the city to visit Abbey Life, I would arrange a little lunch in Lucien's kitchen. They relished his cooking. He became a good friend of ours. When we had our house-warming party, Lucien helped with the food and he, his wife and his daughters were amongst the guests. Their presence and Lucien's food preparation caused a sensation. We saw quite a lot of him. Eventually he gave up living in London and he and Maria went back to live in Italy.

On one of his visits to London we reminisced about people and incidents at Abbey Life. We talked about a chap from Nigeria who was a snappy dresser and a real charmer. When the war broke out in Biafra he seemed quite distressed, since he came from that part of Nigeria.

After a couple of weeks he used his charm to con some of the female staff about the hardship his family was suffering in Nigeria. He also conned his way into getting his lunches on credit, saying he had to send his money home. Lucien was obliging. When the war ended, our conman disappeared without a farewell.

The next time Lucien arranged to visit us he hobbled in because of a damaged leg. I went through the courtesies of enquiring about Maria and his daughters. He started sobbing and pulled out a large white handkerchief, the sort that President Kaunda used whenever he sobbed. I asked him what the trouble was. He sobbed again, saying, 'My Maria, she left me.' We were very sympathetic and naturally asked, 'But why, Lucien?' Back came the reply, 'My Maria, she said I belong to the Mafia', taking out the handkerchief and gently sobbing into it. By the end of the evening Lucien hobbled back into the car, assisted by a friend, who drove to South London. We never saw or heard from him again.

The directors at Abbey Life decided to bring in a team of experts on what was then called time and motion to streamline the firm's organization and productivity. They sent out notices to all the staff. The news was received with apprehension and anxiety. The workers feared this sort of investigation could lead to a loss of jobs.

I talked to lots of workers, especially those in our department. They agreed I should present their fears to the senior directors. I proposed we first let the time and motion people come, observe what they did and what sort of questions they asked, and then if we were worried we could tell the company.

In the meantime I learned that the firm of time and motion experts was being paid a substantial sum of money and that the head of the team was flying in by helicopter from Cheshire to be around each week.

We discovered within a week how the team was operating. They would pick the brains of the workers, the section heads and the supervisors. This, we suspected, would be regurgitated in impressive language and the recommendations applied.

I decided to speak to Joel about the workers' fears. I told him that we workers could work out new systems and increase productivity without external pressure. That way the company would save a lot of money, and all the data, information and work plans could be obtained through us, on the understanding there would be no job losses. Joel agreed and the contract with the time and motion people was terminated. There was relief and joy at the news. The staff put in an improved and quality performance.

When Mark Weinberg, Joel Joffe and Sydney Lipworth left Abbey Life to join Hambro Life, the new leadership of Abbey Life decided to bring in another team of time and motion experts. The team was led by a man who was rated a 'whizz kid' in the business.

This time I briefed the staff in our department. I said that we should give the time and motion team our full co-operation, put out our best performance and keep the department as tidy as possible (we already had the reputation of a clinically clean department). I proposed that the team should not enter the department without informing us, and that they only talk to individual staff in the presence of a section head or another member of the staff. The team agreed and was pleased with the arrangements.

The team was brought in on an outside contract; later the company put them on the payroll. After several weeks they submitted their report and proposals to the directors. An assistant director called me in to discuss that part of the report pertaining to our department. It showed that our department had a 94 per cent turnaround in productivity.

I proposed that we have a staff meeting of the department. He agreed, and within days a meeting was held. I chaired the meeting to give an account of the report. The staff were thoroughly pleased. The assistant director complimented the staff. The meeting opened to questions. A young member of the staff expressed her satisfaction and then popped the direct question, 'What's in it for us?'

The assistant director showed a reluctance to respond. I informed the meeting that in several weeks the staff assessment was due and that I had a copy of the budget review for the year, which included salary increases, 'I will ensure that whatever your entitlement you get every penny.' The assistant director became edgy and said to me under his breath, 'You can not say that.' I replied, 'Yes I can. It is allowed for in the budget proposal.' The staff applauded. It had not dawned on the assistant director that the staff in our department had the highest ratio of union members. The assessments went well and the increments were received.

Then followed a visit from the head of the team. He highly commended the efficiency, the co-operation and the friendly manner in which they were received in our department. He then went on to relate how he had worked in several parts of the world, including South Africa. I expressed interest about his stint in South Africa and asked who he had worked for. He was reluctant to disclose which company. It suddenly dawned on me and I exploded, 'You fucking bastard. You must have worked for the South African government to computerize and streamline the Pass Laws which put our people into prison.' The second thought that flashed through my mind was, 'Hell! I have blown it. I have put my job on the line with this outburst.' He was silent and then stuttered, 'They told me that you would get this out of me.'

Within several days I heard that the team head was off the premises. He was apparently outraged that some of his teammates were made redundant. He stormed into the personnel department demanding an explanation. The personnel director gave our 'whizz kid' the sack. I was told he fled to Hawaii.

When Weinberg and Joel left Abbey Life, Joel was sure my job would be safe under Ralph Sepel. It did seem like that for a while, until Ralph left to start Albany Life Assurance. I stayed on until there was talk that Abbey Life was going to relocate to Bournemouth. We were offered very attractive perks, most importantly a choice of a good house, or to accept redundancy. I discussed the proposal with Adelaide and our young daughters. Everything was weighed up.

We were invited on a day's outing to Bournemouth. On our return the children asked for our impressions. It seemed the girls had already decided against the move. From the family discussion it was clear that relocation would have a negative effect on all of us. We had adapted to life in London. When the company asked for our decision we stated our reservations, adding that we had come to the conclusion Bournemouth was a town for the newly-weds and the nearly-deads. Besides, it was a lily-white town.

I think I was fortunate in working at Abbey Life Assurance, where I met all sorts of people and had a range of experiences. Also fortunate was the location of the company, which was sited in a richly historical part of London. Often I had visitors and relatives from abroad who would meet me either at lunchtime or after work and I would take them to the fascinating parts of London, where there was hardly a day without some event taking place.

Our association with Joel and Vanetta and my work at Abbey Life Assurance Company were most enriching. Engagement itself may not resolve our major problems in the face of political persecution, famine, unemployment, racial discrimination and the violation of justice and liberty, but it can at least bring improvement of the quality of life, and in that respect, Joel Joffe stands out in my life.

One Sunday the Joffes invited us to lunch at their home in Swindon. Joel arranged for someone to pick us up in London. To my amazement the chap who came to collect us was Dorf Seligman, who I had last seen in the summer of 1953, when I was returning from the World Youth Festival in Bucharest via London. On board the ship I had got to know Dorf, who was a fellow passenger. He was working for the BBC as a musicologist.

The voyage lasted for eleven days, during which time we developed a pleasant friendship. In the course of the trip we talked around various subjects, particularly on books about England, South Africa, America and Russia. I did not disclose that I was involved in liberation politics or that my colleague Henry and I had no passports or travel documents. Dorf detected that we had some political leanings but he never pressed us. We did, however, share a firm conviction that racial discrimination was not acceptable.

A couple of days before we sailed into Table Bay, I asked Dorf if he would mind taking some books which I had purchased in London, as I was not sure whether customs would allow me to take the books through. I assured him that the books were not banned, even though some of the subject matter would raise some eyebrows. He willingly took them.

I did not see Dorf until we were allowed through. Customs took a woodcut and some booklets on art, architecture and municipal housing from me. These I got back through the office of Sam Kahn, MP and solicitor, after a couple of weeks. Dorf gave me the books he brought through and we bid each other goodbye.

So imagine my surprise when some twelve years later, this time in London as a political refugee, I meet Dorf Seligman again.

Dorf recollected the story of the books he brought through customs. Whilst waiting for customs, he said, an official came to him to say he must leave the queue. Dorf got nervous. It turned out, however, that the official was a friend of his parents, who got him through without the usual formalities.

When we arrived at Liddington Manor, the Joffe's house, Joel received us, commenting, 'I see you know each other. Was it not Dorf who got you your Marxist literature off the ship?' The books were Palme Dutt's *The*

Crisis of Britain and the British Empire[83] and a textbook by Karl Marx.

Some years later, a rat had nestled at the back of our bookcase. It had nibbled quite a chunk out of Palme Dutt's book but chewed very little of the textbook. That reminded me of a reference made by Engels in his book *Anti-Dühring*,[84] about leaving Dühring's remarks to the nibbling criticism of the mice. The Palme Dutt book I threw away, and the Karl Marx textbook was amongst a pile of books the Special Branch carried away.

When Dorf drove us back to London I had another mild shock, Dorf and Joel were cousins.

Most of the buildings around St. Paul's Cathedral, where the Abbey Life Assurance Company was situated, were church property. One of the smaller buildings housed the offices of the International Defence and Aid Fund, which Canon Collins founded. It started off as Christian Action.[85]

IDAF became the central organization to provide legal and welfare aid to the victims of apartheid, especially those involved in the political struggles against the brutal apartheid regime. The Canon had a network of lawyers and clergy – some in South Africa – to filter substantial funds for legal defence and welfare needs.

One of the people Canon Collins often consulted was Joel Joffe, particularly on legal matters. The Fund was having difficulty in finding lawyers to defend people charged with political offences. A large number of lawyers were either banned under the Suppression of Communism Act, or imprisoned or exiled, while others were not too keen to get embroiled for fear of repercussions.

At one point the Canon sent for Joel to discuss a particular problem. One of the lawyers who was prepared to take on political cases was Joel Carlson. Carlson was formerly a state prosecutor who specialized in dealing with Africans under the Pass Laws. By Carlson's own account, the process of prosecutions was like a conveyor belt system. The guilty ones were sent off to farms to serve their terms of imprisonment like slaves. The story of the farm labour scandal was broken by the Reverend Michael Scott, Ruth First and Henry Nxumalo.[86] Carlson eventually became disgusted with the prosecution of Africans under the Pass Laws and decided he would go over to the side of the victims. He took on political trials.

IDAF was advised to be careful of Carlson. Stories were being put out that he was milking IDAF by charging excessive fees. Sometimes the stories seemed to come from reliable sources. This was the Canon's dilemma, hence his request to see Joel Joffe for advice.

At about the same time, the Canon, the Legums and I, amongst several other people connected with IDAF, received a letter claiming very convincingly that Carlson was not genuine. I was suspicious, and was sure it was a ploy by the South African security service. One of the biggest trials that Carlson had taken on was that of Winnie Mandela and 21 others, who were put into detention and tortured. I had been in touch with Winnie before her arrest and I was listed as co-conspirator in her trial.

After Joel's meeting with the Canon, Joel asked to see me in his office. He was not aware of my contact with Winnie at that stage. He told me about the Canon's reluctance to retain Joel Carlson for political trials, and asked me what could be done in the light of the information that had seeped through to the Canon.

I argued that if it was true Carlson was ripping off IDAF, and had wormed his way into the confidence of Winnie and her fellow accused because there was a serious lack of lawyers available, should not the release of the imprisoned be our first concern in spite of the higher charges? It seemed that Carlson's reputation of having been a state prosecutor and now a civil rights lawyer was what had dented his reputation. I would go for the freedom of the accused.

Joel agreed with my view and Carlson got on with his work as defence lawyer. He succeeded in getting Winnie Mandela and her co-accused acquitted, and went on to get Namibian prisoners freed.

It turned out that the whole smear campaign was indeed engineered by the security police with the assistance of Moosa Dinath, the convicted fraudster. But the heat was now on Carlson. He got out in time and settled in the United States. There he wrote a stunning book about his life, *No Neutral Ground*.[87]

It was known that South African intelligence worked in conjunction with their counterparts in certain European countries. The ANC, Anti-Apartheid Movement (AAM) and IDAF offices were bombed, rifled and burgled, staff were stalked and assassinations of leading people took place in Paris, Harare, Lusaka, and Maputo.

One of their agents, Gordon Winter, wrote a book, *Inside BOSS*[88] (Bureau of State Security), detailing his work of infiltration in various organizations in London. He put Abbey Life Assurance on his radar. He was convinced Mark Weinberg had anti-apartheid views, hence his employment of South African political exiles, naming me in particular. He left out Joel Joffe! Winter used his ex-wife to become friendly with Weinberg. This instruction came from Pretoria. As it turned out neither Weinberg nor Joel was involved in any way with political movements either in South Africa or in the UK.

Gordon Winter was totally discredited when a number of people named in the book sued for defamation. The publisher Allen Lane paid up to

£15,000 in one case and, in the lowest case, £50. Winter disappeared and later emerged in Ireland.

22

Life in London

We lived in Powis Square, in the Royal Borough of Kensington and Chelsea, from 1965 to 1968. Powis Square was seedy and run down. It had been the centre of the Notting Hill race riots in 1958. Tensions were not quite settled but were calmer, thanks to a number of progressive and friendly people in the area who helped to protect African, Caribbean and Asian families.

The mid-1960s was the height of 'flower power', the anti-Vietnam protests and the anti-apartheid campaigns. This all added to the atmosphere of friendship and conviviality, especially on Saturdays as crowds poured into the area for music, food, antiques and fruit and vegetable stalls in and around Portobello Road.

We made friends with the local leaders and activists, a mixture of communists, Labour, socialists and community workers. They campaigned for play spaces, holiday projects for children in the area and for childcare so as to allow stressed mothers some free time. We did not join any political organizations except the Notting Hill People's Association, which did an amazing amount of work on behalf of people living in deprived conditions. Two people who made an impact and touched our lives and that of our children were John and Jan O'Malley. We still maintain a close and warm relationship.

Having come from a slum in Fordsburg in Johannesburg to a slum in Notting Hill Gate was a bit nostalgic. For added coincidence our landlord was a South African of Indian origin. They were a fine family. Sometimes they invited us for dinner or tea and entertained us generously. Their three daughters enjoyed playing in our flat with ours including the newly-born Nadia.

There were a number of people living in the flats above us. One was occupied by a very pleasant Caribbean man, who was a plumber by day and a brothel keeper by night. We got on quite well.

One of the gatherings we had in our flat was for the screening of *The War Game*, which was about a nuclear attack. The film was prohibited from viewing in cinemas but several copies were in circulation and we drew a large crowd to watch it in our front room. This was followed by a lively anti-war discussion.

One of the highlights of my time in Powis Square was Muhammad Ali's visit to The Tabernacle, a local church. He got a tremendous reception and the crowd was overwhelmed with excitement. People were desperate to shake hands with him. I was lucky enough to be amongst those who did. When I got home, I told Adelaide all about it and vowed that I would never wash my hand again.

One evening when I got home Adelaide told me that Joel had dropped in to visit her. He had heard she was not too well. Whilst Joel was there he used the outside toilet and then went into the bathroom, which was under the stairs. It was winter time and we used oil heaters. I later heard that Joel was shaken by the cramped conditions in our Powis Square flat.

Not long after Joel's visit Pranlal Sheth, Abbey Life's legal adviser, called me to his office to inform me that the company's mortgage committee had decided to consider applications for staff loans, and that our names were the first to be proposed. There was a unanimous vote that we ought to be considered. I had a feeling that Joel's visit to the outside toilet had something to do with it!

Somehow this news spread through some of the offices. I soon discovered that the persons most likely to have intelligence information would be the door commissioners or the postal messengers.

One such messenger was Tom, who still had some years to go before retirement. Tom came from the East End of London. He had a tough working life. He was loyal to Queen and country. Whenever he chatted to me he would talk about how he knew Pakistanis who slept fourteen to a room. I never responded, believing that any comment would not change his mind.

When our mortgage application came through he burst into my office with anger, 'Here, Paul! What's this I hear? You are going to get a loan from the company to buy a house!' adding, 'I've worked all my life and got nothing.' I asked him to sit down to tell me why he was so angry about my getting a mortgage. He related to me how he had worked all his life, at times for five shillings a week, 'And here you come along to this country and in a short while you get yourself a house!'

I waited for him to be a bit calm and then asked whether I could ask him a few questions. He agreed. I asked him whether he smoked, drank or made bets. He said he did. I asked him whether he ever saw me go to the pub, smoke or gamble. He said he did not. I told him that I knew something about the lives of the working class in England. I had read up quite a bit on British history. I knew that theirs was not a happy lot. I also knew about the history of the trade union movement, the co-operative and the socialist movement as part of my political involvement in South Africa. Finally I said to Tom, 'Now we are trying to get a comfortable place to live and you still object. You say we live fourteen to a room and now we want to improve our lives and you are angry. What should we do Tom?' Tom looked sorry and apologized for his outburst.

It would be another ten months before we could find a place. A couple of times Joel came with us to view houses in Mill Hill. There was one particularly beautiful house at a reasonable price. The owners seemed pleasant but politely turned us down. Joel wrote them a tactful letter hoping to persuade them. The reply was negative. We had similar experiences in other areas. It seemed when we phoned for a viewing the name Joseph seemed acceptable until we turned up. Suddenly the house was sold or an offer was being considered.

We found a house advertized in an evening paper. The house was not far from Sheila and Percy Cohen, so we asked Sheila to view it. She thought it a bit shabby but worth looking at. We asked Joel to join us at the viewing. It seemed to us that the house was a solid structure and that with a bit of work and at the price it might be worth it. Joel advised us to buy it.

It was the second shabbiest house in the street, but we settled for it. I took two weeks' leave to work and clean up the house. We got help from Jack Coates, a carpenter who had built us a couple of beds. Then we discovered woodworm in the floorboards and under the stairs, which the surveyor had overlooked. The former owner refused to share the cost of dealing with the woodworm. Jack suggested we get a specialist firm to give an estimate. The estimate pinpointed all the affected parts. Jack pulled out all the floorboards and replaced them with new ones.

In 1968 we eventually moved into our new house in Vineyard Avenue, leaving behind lovely memories from Powis Square of friends like the O'Malleys, Eddie Adams and his wife June, and the children's playmates. It was a cold October day when we moved into the house, which had no central heating. All we had was Nadia's cot, a little radio and clothes.[89] A friend brought Adelaide and the children, who had been staying with Ramnie and Issy, who had moved into the neighbourhood. Steve Naidoo and other friends helped us move and brought us rugs, blankets and bits of furniture. Some months later we cleared the back garden. It would be a year before we could afford central heating and to lay down carpets.

We were now ready for a house-warming party. We invited our friends, some of my colleagues, especially from the mortgage committee, Pranlal and Indumati Sheth, and, of course, Joel and his wife Vanetta. We also invited a friend who surprised everyone present. Sir Robert Birley was headmaster of Eton College until 1963, and was visiting professor at Wits from 1964 to 1967. Sir Robert had done a great deal for South African political prisoners like Nelson Mandela, for us and for many others, either by getting the Home Office to allow entry into the UK or by helping to obtain jobs and scholarships. Many of his former pupils went into government or were business executives or academics. Quite often just a phone call was enough.

When we moved from Powis Square it was with regret. Although our flat there was small and a bit uncomfortable, we adapted very easily. We very much enjoyed our time there. We left with fond memories.

There had been a constant stream of friends dropping by for social and political reasons. We gained tremendous experience in these relationships and support for the South African liberation movement. Powis Square became the launching pad to continue our activities in Mill Hill East.

In North Kensington we had a Labour MP. Now in the ultra-Conservative Barnet we were hemmed in by Margaret Thatcher in Finchley Central and John Gorst in Mill Hill. The possibility of getting public support seemed bleak.

One drizzling and cold Saturday morning an elderly man handed me a leaflet at a street corner in Ballards Lane. It was asking people to support the struggle against apartheid. I introduced myself and complimented him on supporting the liberation movement in South Africa. He was Albert Tomlinson, one of the few Labour councillors in Barnet. He was tall and distinguished looking with a gentle manner. He had been a conscientious objector during the Second World War and a member of the Bloomsbury set.

I invited him and a few of his friends round. We initiated the Barnet branch of the AAM. It became one of the most flourishing components of the AAM in the country. Whilst Adelaide was involved, she was also active with women's groups and the Workers Educational Association. She introduced the study of Afro-Asian fiction in the women's literature study group.

The lesson we learnt from that experience was never take any situation for granted.

Anand

Over the years Adelaide and I took turns in visiting our disabled son Anand in Berlin. Sometimes I would take Zoya and at other times Adelaide would take Tanya or Nadia. It was such a joy seeing Anand being so well looked after.

In 1967 my brother Peter arranged for my mother to fly to London, and we arranged to take her to visit Anand. Getting travel documents for her was very complex. After nearly sixty years of residence in South Africa she was denied a passport. On compassionate grounds she managed to secure a certificate of identity. This did not guarantee the rights which a passport provides.

On arrival in London there was some bureaucratic resistance until I explained she was en route to visit her grandchild in hospital in Germany. After a week in London, Zoya and I accompanied my mother to Branden-burg. She was tearfully delighted to see Anand.

On 10 October 1970 I got a telephone call from Eric Singh, who was in exile in Berlin and worked closely with the Afro-Asian Solidarity Committee and the ANC. He had been told by the Brandenburg Hospital authorities to inform us that Anand had died. I was shocked, since only a few months earlier we had visited him.

I decided to telephone Minnie Sepel, a long-time South African friend, to be with Adelaide until I arrived home to break the news to her. Whilst she was there, however, someone from the London ANC office received the message from Berlin and telephoned Adelaide. It was all a very distressing experience for our family.

The next day I sent a cable to my mother to inform her of Anand's death. The cable was held back for a couple of days and then it was just shoved under her door. When my mother found it, she could not read the contents. She took it to a neighbour a couple of doors away. I was convinced that this was the work of the security police, who periodically called on my mother and sisters with probing questions about us.

Within a few days I made arrangements for Adelaide, Zoya and me to travel to Brandenburg. Tanya and Nadia were cared for by Herby Pillay's mother, who kindly offered to stay with the girls at our place.

We were received by representatives of the Afro-Asian Solidarity Committee and driven to the hospital, where we were warmly and sympathetically received. The senior doctor invited us into her office. She was fluent in English and had been amongst the medical staff at the hospital when Adelaide first arrived with Anand. She asked for the nurse who had taken care of him to be present, and then she explained the circumstances and the cause of Anand's death.

Anand had not died from any medical condition, but from a mishap when the nurse was feeding him. He choked on the liquidized food and the nurse, who was young, panicked. She rushed out to get oxygen. By the time she returned Ananda had died. She was devastated. She had been attached to him. She said he was an exceptionally beautiful boy. She could not get over his death.

We understood the nurse's plight and assured her that we accepted the death was an accident. We embraced her. We thanked the medical team for the years of support for Anand and their kindness whenever we visited the hospital.

We were led to the burial ground, where some of our exiled comrades came to share our sorrow. Vic Syvret, a senior exiled trade unionist, officiated at the funeral. It was a very painful experience.

On our return we had messages and letters of sympathy from friends and relatives in London and South Africa. From Robben Island messages came from Nelson Mandela, Mac Maharaj, and Ahmed 'Kathy' Kathrada. Adelaide arranged for a memorial gathering in our house for some of our friends and relatives like Suri and Tony Naidoo, Adelaide Tambo, and M.B. and Edith Yengwa.

Some years later I had in mind that we should have a headstone in memory of Anand and that as a family we ought to make a trip to the Brandenburg Hospital. I contacted Eric Singh. After the collapse of the GDR the atmosphere had become a matter of concern. There were racial tensions and it was unpleasant. We read and heard of assaults and abuse of Africans and Asians. Eric advised us not to go, especially with our daughters, as they could be targeted. We took his advice.

That was when we thought we should call our house 'Anand Bhavan' (House of Happiness) in memory of our son. As well as in all our memories and thoughts, Anand is also remembered in Zoya's eldest child and our first grandchild, Shura, which was Anand's second name.

Employment after Abbey Life

Joel contacted me and suggested I should consider working for Oxfam. If I was interested he would arrange for an interview which would include Adelaide. I had always supported Oxfam. We spent a lovely and interesting day at the Oxfam head office in Banbury. Everything was attractive except at the time Oxfam salaries were somewhat below our requirements. The idea was that anyone working for Oxfam would have a spouse with a higher income. Adelaide was not in a job. Regretfully I turned down the job.

In 1975 Raymond Suttner was given a long prison sentence as result of his activities in the SACP and his involvement in MK. I followed the trial with great interest and was so impressed at the powerful statement he made in court that I wrote to his mother, Sheila.[90]

When Sheila came to London some time later we invited her for dinner at our house. In the course of the conversation she learnt that I was job hunting. She immediately offered to put the word around. She told me that she knew a Gerald Rabkin in South Africa who was now running a huge import, export and domestic ware business. Several days later I got a telephone call from Rabkin asking that I come over to his warehouse in Old Street for interview.

I was offered a job as a traffic manager. It turned out that a traffic manager need not know how to drive a vehicle (I could not drive) but was responsible for organizing the distribution of goods through the company's vehicles and the hiring of drivers to deliver the goods across the country and to Ireland. I accepted the offer.

Terms and conditions were not set out in the form of an employment contract, neither was there a job description. Everything was by word of mouth. I was told the staff were entitled to two weeks' annual leave. There was no pension scheme. As my salary was about a third less than my former Abbey Life employment, I also took on an evening job at the Southbank complex as a car park attendant. It meant working five days and six nights a week, but at least at the Southbank I often got complimentary or reduced-price tickets for the shows and displays, and very generous helpings from the caterers.

Some of the staff at the warehouse had worked there for many years. The warehousemen were bitter, rude and often abrupt with other staff and me, and at times even with customers. Nevertheless they were hard working. I steered a gentle path with these men. They gradually opened up to me. I found out that their mood swings were based on their disenchantment. The former owners had promised them that they would be looked after when they retired. By now they were on the verge of retirement and would not receive a penny.

One day it was announced that the company was being sold. Our boss had developed an undisclosed illness. The company was sold to a multinational based in Zambia. Within a few days the directors of the parent company arrived. Our new bosses were Greek, Lebanese, African, German, English and Asian. I now had the unique distinction of being exploited by all nationalities and not just the goddam South Africa Whites.

Our new CEO and senior directors were two Ismaili Asian brothers from Tanzania. The new bosses spoke English with an East African Indian accent, which was no barrier to reaching the high echelons of international finance.

They were shrewd and calculating in their dealings.

A few years later came the staggering news that the company was to relocate to Manchester, one of the reasons being that labour was cheaper than in London, and warehouses were cheaper to buy or rent. None of us was young enough to consider relocatation. Although our new bosses had made generous promises for a good pay-off for redundancy, when the time came most got very little redundancy payment.

None of the staff had any company pension scheme. I had made representations several years earlier but had been told that we should make our own provisions. One of the warehousemen was 57 years old and was devastated at the loss of his job. He could not find any employment. The last I heard of him he was heading for a breakdown.

One day I bumped into the warehouse foreman. He said with regret, 'If I had known how shabbily we were going to be treated, I would have stolen over the years.'

When I got my pittance of a redundancy payment, I told the CEO that I did not think they would make it in Manchester. He looked astonished. I said I would give him a few years. Sure enough, in a few years' time he sold a hotel he owned to save his business. In time, the business, I was told, collapsed.

Oxfam

At about the time of my retirement I decided I would give my time to Oxfam on a voluntary basis. I contacted Joel, who by now was Chair of Oxfam. He was delighted. I filled in an application form and handed it in to the Finchley Central branch. I got a letter from a lovely chap called Chris Marsden, who was based in the Burnt Oak branch, asking me to join that branch, which I did, not disclosing that I knew Joel or anything about my background. I was keen to be just a volunteer.

I cleaned the toilets, swept the shop, took out the rubbish, made tea for the staff and carried the bags of donations. Initially I was to do only a few hours a week. Then I decided to do a full day's work. I was trained to handle the till and keep the books. As I got more interested I did three full days a week. I was put through a course by the personnel department. Eventually I was offered a paid part-time manager's job, but I did not want that. Soon I was recruiting and training volunteers. Some got to take on responsibilities and, in one case, a volunteer took on a permanent job at head office in the human resources department. I was very impressed by the quality of experience of many of the retired and young volunteers. I learned a great deal about people's experiences in their working life.

I also learned how some people came as volunteers but soon enough helped themselves to what was in the shop, or worked in league with other volunteers in other charities in dodgy scams. I was able to detect some of these people and tactfully got them out of the way. I also discovered then that ten per cent of all charities are subjected to pilfering, if not by volunteers then by customers.

Later I was asked to help out at two other shops in Edgware and Mill Hill. I found Oxfam open and transparent. It gave regular information to volunteers and to the public about its projects in this country and abroad. I was pleased about its positions on the arms trade and on wars, violence, and famine caused by governments, besides the disasters caused by natural forces. I often talked to people as to why they became volunteers. Most were concerned about the plight of people in other parts of the world. Many were well educated. Some had given up lucrative jobs, some were widowed, some disabled and some were in need of a social and friendly environment.

I was informed that Oxfam would periodically arrange for volunteers to visit countries where Oxfam programmes were being applied, since they realized the importance of volunteers being equipped with first-hand knowledge.

One such programme came up and I was asked to do a presentation. On completion there was a choice of going to an African, Asian, South American or European country. I chose a European country, giving as my reason that in the minds of people the perceptions are that only African or Asian countries are suffering from poverty, misery and starvation. I thought that by going to a European country I could change that by telling people that poverty, starvation and a range of deprivations are also experienced in Europe. That, coming from a black person, I thought would be more effective.

I was sent off with two other volunteers to Bosnia and Serbia at the time of the conflict in the former Yugoslavia. I was shocked. I met and spoke to many of those affected by the conflict, which left in its wake bombed-out homes, schools, offices and workplaces, people with terrible injuries and the loss of many lives. The whole of civil society in the former Yugoslavia was torn apart. The damage to women was horrendous. Thousands were raped, assaulted and left destitute, unable to care for their families. Begging was common.

Given all that, there was a strong desire to rebuild their lives, villages, towns and cities. People were grateful for the support Oxfam was giving to provide water purification, assistance with medical needs and help with the construction and repair of damaged dwellings.

On my return I addressed a number of meetings of Oxfam volunteers at some of the branches, and a meeting of the management of the London branches. I also arranged for meetings in the homes of friends in Mill Hill and Finchley and got one of the weekly newspapers that covered the borough of Barnet to carry a full-page report, as well as a report in a daily paper. I also wrote an open letter to all my friends and contacts in various parts of the country. I was pleased with their response and their support for Oxfam either in cash or in kind.

23

Exile politics:
comrades, friends and enemies

On my arrival into exile in London, Colin and Margaret Legum became close friends, much to the annoyance of some of my left-wing friends, who saw Colin as some sort of government agent and an anti-communist journalist. The issue I was most concerned with was to engage a network with people who were against the apartheid system, regardless of ideology. The Legums earned the wrath of the apartheid government. They were on the list of names banned visiting South Africa.

At no stage did we ever enter into discussion on ideological differences. What was important was what we could achieve. They quietly did a lot for the anti-apartheid struggle. Colin was an important opinion-maker and Margaret an important contact to highly-placed people. She secured entry permits, jobs and accommodation for South Africans. After the end of the apartheid government, the Legums visited South Africa and in Soweto Margaret made contact with Irene Kumalo, who had been allowed to marry Wilton Mkwayi on Robben Island. They became the best of friends.[91]

Soon after I arrived in London I met up with Savery Naidoo.[92] I first met Savery when he came to Johannesburg to study at Wits in 1949. Within a short time he became very popular on campus. He also got involved with the activities of the TIYC. Several of its members were also at the university. Together with some of the White left-wing students they campaigned for Savery as a candidate for the Students Representative Council. His election to the SRC was a rare achievement for a black student. His activities caught the attention of the security police. Almost immediately he completed his studies he was denied re-entry to the Transvaal province.

One day Savery and I were having a chat about some of the people we knew on Robben Island. I told him the story of Marcus Solomon, the young man from Cape Town whom I refused to help escape because I thought he might be a police spy, and who was then sent to Robben Island for ten years.

Savery listened quietly and sighed on completion of my story. He asked me what else I could tell him about Marcus Solomon. I said there was nothing more but my regret and that I hoped he would forgive me.

Then Savery said, 'Can I tell you something about Marcus Solomon? He is my half-brother.' I was flabbergasted. I had known Savery for over thirty years. I thought I knew much about his family, only to discover he and Marcus shared the same mother. As Savery talked I could see the strong resemblance between him and Marcus, both handsome and gentle.

Some years later, after Marcus was released from Robben Island, he was given a passport. He came to London with his eleven-year-old daughter. They came to dinner, but sadly Savery had died a few years before. When Adelaide and I visited Cape Town, soon after the unbanning of the outlawed organizations, we had a lovely reunion with Marcus.

In the months before the Rivonia Trial, for some days Julius First did not come to the factory. Then after a few weeks his picture appeared in the papers with a report that he was being sought by the police in connection with some political case before the courts. Julius had managed to evade arrest. It was later reported that he was a conduit for funds to an illegal organization (the ANC).

Julius eventually made his way to London. When the police could not track him down, his son Ronnie was detained. Ronnie was one of the directors of the firm, so the police assumed that he would have known about monies going through Julius's accounts. But it could also have been as a reprisal and hostage for not capturing Julius. Certainly Ronnie First's name did not feature in evidence in the Rivonia Trial.

Although Julius was an industrialist, he still retained an acute interest in political events, and where possible gave valuable support. He stood bail for large numbers of people charged with treason in 1956. He also ensured some of us detained during the State of Emergency in 1960 were able to draw our salaries.

What was hardly known was that he allowed the illegal CP to hold a conference in his factory to raise funds for the ANC and MK.

Once in London the First family occupied a house in West Hampstead and after some time found a suitable-sized house in Camden Town. Tilly and Julius lived in the basement flat and the rest of the family occupied the floors above. We often visited Ruth and Joe and popped in to see Tilly and Julius. It was only from then on I stopped calling Julius 'Mr First'.

Tilly was very fastidious in the way she ran their flat and arranged the teas she served. She did most of the chatting, and occasionally clashed views with Julius in a light-hearted fashion.

Julius died at the age of 80. At the funeral I saw their son Ronnie. He still looked striking and handsome. It was a warm and friendly meeting. I had last seen him in early 1964 when the security police called at the factory office to serve a banning order on me and I had to leave the factory premises immediately.

Julius First was an unusual person who was a Communist in his young days, became a factory owner and still retained his loyalty to the freedom struggle. He was highly respected by Nelson Mandela, Walter Sisulu, Oliver Tambo, Moses Kotane, J.B. Marks, and a handful of activists. His lifelong support for Ruth and Joe was a major factor in enabling them to make their remarkable contribution to the cause.

Tilly continued to live on in the flat and needed care. Eventually arrangements were made for her to fly out to South Africa, where Ronnie arranged for her care until she died at the age of 94.

After Ruth's assassination and burial in Maputo in 1982, the London office of the ANC had a memorial gathering. Chairing the event was Ruth Mompati, who was the ANC's chief representative in London. Commiserating with Tilly, Mompati said that she was not just the mother of Ruth, she was the mother of all of us. That was perhaps one of the most poignant statements of the event.

Daso, Desmond Francis and Bennie Bunsee were working at the IDAF offices. My brother told me that he and his friends were increasingly feeling resentful at the manner in which one of the senior staff members was commanding them to do certain tasks. He said she sounded like a White madam; it seemed at times they were back in South Africa in a sort of master and servant relationship.

I suggested that perhaps he should speak to Joe Slovo, and if Joe felt they had a genuine criticism, I was sure it could be quietly resolved. Daso spoke to Joe, who agreed to look into the matter. Within a few days there was a change in the staff member's attitude. From then on their relationship with her went smoothly.

I mention this incident since it was a form of behaviour and attitude that many of us came across in our relationship with White comrades back in South Africa. This was not particularly new; Moses Kotane had raised it many years before. Joe mentioned the style of work and attitude of White comrades when he delivered his keynote speech at the Party's sixtieth anniversary celebrations held at Conway Hall in London. I recall what he said was something to this effect, 'When the socialists arrived in South Africa from Europe they came with their White baggage.' Many of us encountered experiences not only with White liberals but also from White comrades.

For example, in London Adelaide got involved in the ANC's Women's League. Among the many activities were women's study classes. At one of the classes an African comrade made a contribution. When she had finished, a White comrade took it upon herself to say, 'What this comrade means is...' Adelaide made an immediate intervention, 'Excuse me. You need not explain what the comrade said. We understand clearly the English she spoke and it is about time you Whites stopped speaking on our behalf. We can speak for ourselves.'

At one of our dinner parties we invited Joe and Ruth. It was a welcome dinner for Hugh Lewin, who was released after a nine-year sentence for his part in the African Resistance Movement (ARM), and for his wife Pat Davidson. Pat was part of Bram Fischer's legal team in the Rivonia Trial. Pat was in the car travelling with Bram and his wife Molly to Cape Town when they went off the road. The car plunged into a river and Molly drowned.

Hugh turned up with a bottle of KWV, a much celebrated and sought-after brandy. The gift was from Bram Fischer, doing a life sentence. Hugh also had brought a bottle of KWV for Joe and Ruth from Bram.

We did not tell Joe and Ruth that we had also asked another couple to dinner. We asked the Lewins to pick up this couple, who were living not far from them in South London. They were Bill and Celia Pomeroy, who were amongst the leaders of the Huk guerrilla movement in the Philippines. They were captured and sentenced to life imprisonment, and pardoned after ten years. They came into exile in London.

In a way it was honouring three couples involved in the struggles for freedom. When the Lewins and the Pomeroys arrived they were received with great excitement and joy. It was one of the happiest dinner parties we had in our house.

When Adelaide was in need of specialized medical treatment, the ANC arranged for her to be sent to a hospital in the Caucasus specializing in mineral treatment. The hospital complex also had Moses Kotane for treatment. For Adelaide it was a boost and a bonus because she had last seen Moses during the State of Emergency in 1960, when she acted as his courier, during which time they developed a close friendship.

During her stay there Joe made a special trip to see Moses, and visited Adelaide to assure her that our three daughters and I were coping. On his return to London Joe came to see me to assure me that Adelaide was doing well and getting the best treatment.

Not long after I arrived in London I was placed in a SACP group in North London. To my surprise this group consisted of some seventeen people. In

South Africa I was in a Party cell of only four. In our group we had Ruth First, Harold Wolpe, Thabo Mbeki, Reg September, Jack and Rica Hodgson, Fred Carneson and several other people. Sometimes I felt I was in a branch meeting. Clearly the way the SACP functioned in London was relaxed and easy. Whilst this did have its advantages, it also had its disadvantages in terms of discipline.

The group meetings were interesting, with lots of discussion and argument. Quite often we sat through boring and tedious speeches by Soviet leaders. At times we discussed the articles in *The African Communist*, the Party's theoretical journal.

Adelaide and I visited South Africa after the unbanning of the major organizations. We took the opportunity of locating some of the workers I knew in Julius First's Anglo-Union furniture factory. The first of course was Harold Kingsman. That was quite an emotional meeting.

Later I located Abu Bakr Lachporia, who had been an apprentice French polisher. He became a successful businessman running his own French polish shop. He handed over his business for the day to his foreman so that he could take us around, calling on other workers from the factory.

On another visit to South Africa Abu Bakr told me that his main pastime was playing bridge. His team was pitched against another team led by Ronnie First. Both were startled, as both had been at Anglo-Union, Ronnie the boss and Abu Bakr the French polisher. But most incredible was that the teams of players were multiracial, something which would not have happened in the apartheid days.[93]

Apartheid was brought to an end by the power of the resistance movements, which consisted of many components in the liberation forces, made up of the ANC, the PAC, the Unity Movement, the Black Consciousness Movement, sections of the Liberal Party and the African Resistance Movement, as well as outstanding individuals — civic, religious, social, trade union leaders, teachers, and others.

When Nadine Gordimer won the Nobel Prize for literature in 1991, we in the Barnet AAM were so delighted that we organized a celebratory meeting in Muswell Hill. We got the support of Bloomsbury, Gordimer's publisher; they had a stall displaying her work at the celebration. We invited two speakers, Bettie du Toit and Dr Ivan Toms.

Bettie du Toit was an Afrikaaner mill worker who became the first woman to be banned under the Suppression of Communism Act. She went into exile first in Ghana, then in London. Her memoir, *Ukubamba Amadolo*,[94]was published in 1978 with a Foreword by Nadine Gordimer.

Dr Toms was a frontline protester against conscription by the apartheid regime to get young Whites to fight in Namibia and help suppress any resistance by black people in South Africa. Toms had been arrested and terrorized by the apartheid regime. He was a distinguished physician and campaigned for resources and medical attention for the victims of HIV/AIDS. There was a nasty campaign against him because he had openly declared he was gay. He led the anti-conscription campaign. Eventually Toms was allowed to pursue further studies in his field at Sussex University. He was much acclaimed by the ANC and by the United Democratic Front (UDF).[95]

The speeches by Bettie du Toit and Dr Toms were truly a tour de force in honour of Nadine Gordimer and the virtual end of apartheid.

Some years after I arrived in London, I wandered into the bookshop of the National Film Theatre. I picked up a copy of the *London Magazine* and there to my astonishment was a short story by Ahmed Essop.

When I eventually returned to South Africa after the end of apartheid I made the rounds of meeting my comrades, friends and relatives. I spent a lot of time with Ahmed and his wife Farida in their lovely house and garden. By then I had read just about every book he had written.

In the course of visits I was invited to the house of the departing Consul of the Indian government, at which there was a farewell party.

Nadine Gordimer was at the party, and we managed a short conversation amidst the large number of guests. She talked about Ahmed Essop and I was pleased when she remarked, 'He is a very underrated writer.' Later he won some literary awards.

There are many unsung heroes in our struggle but one I must pay tribute to is the aforementioned Desmond Francis. When I visited his school after I crossed the River Zambezi over to Zambia, I had met a Mary Haines from Southampton. In 1968 I got an urgent letter from her. She had married Desmond. Desmond was arrested in Livingstone and handed over to the South African Security Police. He was seeing off his mother and an aunt who had come to spend time with him and Mary in Zambia. At the end of their visit he drove them to the railway station on the Rhodesian side of Livingstone. After helping with their luggage and settling them in the carriage, Desmond alighted from the train. He was stopped by two White Rhodesian police, and escorted to the railway station office.

There he was questioned and shown copies of *Sechaba* – the ANC's official journal – and some political tracts which were found in the boot of his car. He was kept for several hours, by which time Captain Swanepoel arrived. He was driven to Pretoria to the Compol Buildings, the interrogation centre.

After that he was taken and placed in solitary confinement and brutally treated.

Mary and I worked as best we could to raise Desmond's illegal detention and treatment. We thought that his marriage to a British citizen could be a basis for an intervention (for the South African police it was resentment that he married a White woman, which they mentioned). Mary also wrote to her MP in Southampton. I contacted *The Daily Worker* and Philippa Ingram broke the story in the UK. I also wrote a letter to the *New Statesman* and contacted Amnesty International.

Desmond was later transferred to Maritzburg in Natal. There he was told to testify against a number of other political prisoners. Desmond took the opportunity of informing the court about the torture he underwent and the effects of solitary confinement, as well as his marriage to a British citizen. He also told the court that he did not know any of the accused and was not in a position to state anything.

The prosecutor conceded and Desmond was let out. But, unknown to the security police, he had smuggled out a message that a group of Namibian political cadres were in prison, a fact not known to any outsider. I received the message and the story was released for the first time to the outside world by *The Daily Worker* and again Philippa Ingram broke the story.

Some years later, when Desmond met some of those Namibian comrades, they were delighted and thankful for his daring to smuggle out news of their plight.

In 1977, Desmond, Mary and their young sons, Shuni and Krishna, set off for Southampton, where they set up home, found teaching jobs and soon became part of the community. They got involved in the AAM and the ANC. Desmond was invited by E.S. Reddy, the UN Secretary for the Committee on Apartheid, to testify on the question of torture and imprisonment by the apartheid government.

Desmond's political involvement also embraced the solidarity movements of Vietnam, Palestine, Cuba and Sri Lanka's Tamil people. On a visit to India he was appalled at the treatment of the Dalits. He identified with them.

But the high point of his political life was his visit to South Africa in 1990. After barely a few days there, the police arrived at his mother's house to take Desmond off to the police station. The government was still in the hands of the apartheid regime. They told Desmond that he did not have a visa and therefore his stay was not legal.

He was allowed one call, which he made to Adelaide. Like Desmond, Adelaide had travelled to South Africa on a British passport and did not have a visa but had not encountered any problems. She contacted John Carlin, who was *The Guardian* correspondent on South Africa.

Carlin phoned the head of the police station in Lenasia to enquire the basis for Desmond's detention. He was given the same rubbish about him not having a visa. Carlin set out Desmond's British status and asked that he be released, otherwise he would contact The British High Commission's office. The police relented and Desmond was let out. He headed for Adelaide's brother Gladster's house, where he spent the night.

During the 1980s, Desmond underwent a personality change. He discarded the Western style of dressing. He now wore a colourful lungi which carried a large imprint of Nelson Mandela in ANC colours. He wore *pata patas* – sandals cut out from tyres – that were commonly worn by African municipal and domestic workers. He grew a long beard and long hair and wore African beads and bangles. He was a notable figure on the streets of Southampton, London, Johannesburg and in India.

Desmond died from a heart attack at the age of 77. He was on his way from his home in Southampton to Halifax, Yorkshire, to be with his son and daughter-in-law and the two grandchildren.

His funeral was attended by a large number of people. He was much loved, and adored especially by children in the schools where he taught. Some said that 'the man wearing a Mandela lungi who was a familiar figure in Southampton' had died. One man said he remembered Desmond was his teacher some twenty years ago. He had heard by chance of Desmond's death.

Apart from his political involvement in the liberation of South Africa, and his legacy as an unusual teacher, he also left a legacy of photographs from his student days in apartheid South Africa and of the day Nelson Mandela was made President of South Africa. The photographs are a unique collection and hopefully someone will catalogue them and ensure these photographs are preserved for future generations.

There were two things he did before the end of his life. The first was to arrange with a bookshop in Southampton a launch of Beverley Naidoo's book *Death of an Idealist. In Search of Neil Aggett*,[96] the young doctor who was driven to his death by the apartheid police as a result of isolation and torture. Aggett was the first White political activist to die in detention.

The other was his response to the news of the death of Nelson Mandela. He lit a large number of candles and placed them alongside a portrait of Nelson Mandela. The house of Desmond and Mary looked like a shrine. A large crowd came to pay their respects to Mandela.

Desmond had a capacity for easily making friends with people on the buses, trains and in the streets, at gathering or workplaces. This friendship could be for a few minutes, for hours or for years. He had the sort of charm and warmth that attracted people, who would readily acknowledge him.

Apart from the funeral in England, there was another event a few days later in Johannesburg. The initiative was taken by Ramnie Dinat (Naidoo). A number of relatives, friends and comrades joined in paying tribute to Desmond's contribution to education and the liberation movement.

24

Amnesty International

When I entered the UK as a political refugee, immediately I made contact with Amnesty headquarters in Mitre Court and the Amnesty group in Lincoln. On one of Adelaide's prison visits when I was first detained in 1964 she talked about 'friends abroad' who were concerned about my and the family's welfare. It was only after my release I learned that she was referring to an AI group in Lincoln, England. In a letter to Adelaide they sent £5 and said that I had been adopted as a prisoner of conscience.

When Adelaide quietly slipped out of the country with our disabled son, and stopped in London en route to Berlin, she contacted the Lincoln group. She arranged that on her way back from Berlin she would stay over for a couple of weeks in London and would make a point of going to Lincoln for a visit.

They accorded her a very warm welcome. She met all the members of the group, including Dick Taverne QC (then an MP, now a member of the House of Lords), who was patron of the group and with whom she developed a long friendship.

The Lincoln group invited me to speak on Human Rights Day on 10 December 1965. From then onwards we kept in regular touch with them, particularly with Anne Scorer and a German man called Walter.

I continued keeping in touch with Mitre Court, where I had offered any help they needed in their work. Quite often I was asked to advise them and assist their South African desk. The desk was headed by a Swedish woman, Karen Hamberg. Amnesty made it a practice not to have a national head from the particular country it was working in. This was done to maintain objectivity. Those of us who were involved were only in an advisory capacity.

In the course of my visits I got to know a fair number of people, including Mo Teitelbaum and Ian Macdonald, who later became a QC. Mo was a pillar of support to some of the South African refugees, especially towards us as a family.

After Karen Hamberg another Swede, Bengt Albons, took over from her. Both were committed to their work and developed a strong friendship with us that continues up to this day.

At that time Amnesty still had a policy not to support anyone charged with violent struggles or campaigns. This posed a dilemma for many of its supporters where violent struggles were being carried out, including Algeria, Vietnam, Namibia, South Africa and Mozambique. Amnesty was steadfast in its position.

A request came to Amnesty from the Oxted Amnesty group in Surrey. They wanted to hear a South African speak on the political situation. Mo Teitelbaum proposed that Amnesty should ask me to address them. The Oxted group had adopted the Mandela family and Mandela as a prisoner of conscience when Mandela was sentenced to five years' imprisonment for breaking his banning order and leaving and re-entering South Africa without valid travel documents.

When Mandela was charged at the Rivonia Trial for heading MK, the Oxted Amnesty group were obliged to abandon their support for the Mandela family, as Mandela was no longer considered a prisoner of conscience.

I had heard of the stockbrokers belt in Surrey, but up to then had never been anywhere near it. Oxted's houses were palatial, with manicured gardens and beautiful tree-lined streets. I believe the secretary of the Amnesty group was a Mrs Payne, in whose house the group was meeting. She was a refugee from Germany. I was cordially received, and joined her and her husband for dinner. They invited me to sleep over on account of the time and distance back to London.

After dinner we sat in the lounge, and soon a number of people arrived. One gentleman with a sort of senior officer's moustache appeared in a striped suit. He turned out to be a retired colonel in the British army.

I gave my talk, setting out the historical stages of the Indian, African and coloured people's struggle for freedom and how all these struggles started off peacefully throughout the sixty years of struggle and were often met with violence by the state. I explained that after Sharpeville all avenues of peaceful struggle came to an end, at the cost of deaths, injuries, banishments and imprisonments. To worsen the situation the government proscribed the ANC and the PAC. These organizations were the main channels for the African people to express themselves.

The ANC decided to continue the struggle and so was born the formation of MK. I gave a brief outline of the views of some of the ANC leaders like Chief Luthuli, Oliver Tambo and Nelson Mandela on this profound change in policy. I may have spoken for about forty minutes and then fielded questions.

After the questions and answers were over, the retired army colonel addressed the gathering. He said he had listened carefully to what I said. For him it was an unusual experience and I was the first black person he had heard give a factual, true and accurate account of the situation in South Africa.

As a result he moved that the Oxted Amnesty group rescind their decision and re-adopt the Mandela family and Nelson Mandela as their prisoner of conscience. The entire meeting was in agreement and the secretary was asked to convey the decision to Amnesty headquarters.

It caused a sensation in Amnesty International. The issue came up on the next agenda. The motion to change its policy on the question of the violation of due process and human rights of those involved in violent forms of freedom struggle was defeated. But the discussion on the subject continued to occupy the attention of Amnesty supporters. I believe that Amnesty did later make some change to its policy.

Increasingly, I got to know more and more Amnesty people as employees, volunteers and supporters, who in the main were committed, loyal and understanding of the various struggles for freedom and justice around the world.

Organizations like Amnesty and bodies involved in solidarity or civil rights movements in the UK would attract intelligence agents from the Home Office and Foreign Office or from countries in which democratic rights were abused and opposition to oppressive policies were challenged.

One day a young volunteer whom I got to know as a particularly intelligent and genuine person told me that someone who visited Amnesty approached him saying that he would like to help people in South Africa against apartheid. He said he knew of a source where arms could be obtained, and asked my friend to enquire how best he could arrange for the delivery of arms. He had in mind the ANC.

Having heard him out, I suggested he arrange for a meeting with his contact within a few days. In the meantime I briefed some of our senior people in the ANC. They agreed that I should have the initial meeting with the contact to get a clearer understanding of what he was proposing.

The contact turned up, and after a discussion I indicated I would be interested but would need time to discuss with my people and suggested that we met again in a few days time. He agreed.

This time I hid a tape recorder in the office. The contact did not turn up. After a day or two I saw my friend at the Amnesty office and told him what happened. I explained that his contact was an intelligence operator. He was shocked and embarrassed that he had put me through this experience. It was clear he had been taken in. It proved how even intelligent people can be politically naïve.

Unity Movement

As repression increased in South Africa, Amnesty International adopted more prisoners of conscience and gave support to their families.

The adopted prisoners came from a range of different political opposition movements. One in particular was the Unity Movement of South Africa, led by I.B. Tabata and Dr Ahmed Limbada. They were both veteran leaders of the original Non-European Unity Movement of South Africa, founded in 1943 and based in Cape Town. The Tabata-Limbada faction broke away and set up their base in Lusaka, Zambia.

Earlier, round about 1963, there had been another breakaway group, led by Neville Alexander. They had a strong Maoist influence and were known as the Yu Chi Chan ('Guerrilla Warfare') Club. They were based in Cape Town. The breakaways were based on differences over the ways of challenging the apartheid regime by armed struggle.[97]

In 1964, Neville Alexander and several members of the Yu Chi Chan Club were charged with seeking to overthrow the government. They were sentenced to several years on Robben Island.

In the 1970s a group of the Tabata-Limbada activists was rounded up in South Africa and charged with intent to commit acts of violence to overthrow the government. Following their detention in solitary confinement, they were put on trial. They managed to secure legal defence services from a firm of lawyers in Durban, N. Pillay & Partners.

Apart from legal assistance, there were welfare needs for the prisoners and their families. But more important was to get the evidence from former prisoners on the effects of solitary confinement and torture.

One of the detainees was Sonny Venkatrathnam, whose wife Theresa worked for N. Pillay & Partners. Sonny also at one time had worked for the same firm. The principal of the firm was Navi Pillay. Her husband, Gabriel Pillay, was amongst the original Tabata-Limbada group of detainees. After application for habeas corpus, he was released without charge and was able to continue his work in the legal practice.

Navi Pillay was a freshly qualified lawyer and taking on a political trial was a totally new challenge. Fortunately she had the advice and assistance of a brilliant lawyer, Rowley Arenstein, sometimes referred to as 'the Joe Slovo of Durban', who was a banned lawyer. N. Pillay & Partners were able to employ him as a legal clerk.[98]

On the advice of Arenstein, it was proposed that Navi and Gabriel (or Gaby, as he was widely known) travel to London to take 'evidence in Commission' from former prisoners, now in exile, on the effects of solitary confinement and torture. Unknown to the South African authorities, Navi and Gaby left for their first trip ever abroad. They barely knew people except by name. They knew of the existence of IDAF but none of its personnel.

On arrival the Pillays initially contacted the South African civil rights lawyer Albie Sachs, who at that time was lecturing in law at Southampton University. He was unable to assist on account of work commitments and his distance from London. He suggested they approach Joel Joffe, who was at the time based in Swindon. He, too, could not afford the time to assist. He suggested that I be contacted, since I was based in London and was known to many of the exile community, some of whom were former political prisoners.

I got a telephone call from Navi Pillay, who gave me a brief rundown of her mission. I remembered reading about her when she made the habeas corpus application to the court on behalf of her husband. I suggested she came over to our house in Mill Hill where we could talk in private.

She turned up with her husband, who was carrying an attaché case and was very smartly dressed. I naively assumed he was the head of the legal firm and the woman was a legal clerk. I was embarrassed when I discovered that it was the other way around.

The Pillays were thoroughly pleased with the response they got from all those who made signed statements of their experiences during detention. Much to their surprise they got evidence from most of the former prisoners. Most were ANC and CP members, many wearing both caps. Their surprise was based on the history of long-time differences between the Congress Alliance and the Unity Movement. But we worked on the principle that, regardless of the political differences, we all experienced the same repression and violence from the same apartheid regime.

Navi said that any of us prepared to give evidence in Commission could apply to the court for an indemnity should our presence be required. The evidence obtained in Commission was made available to the court as part of the defence case, although the court was not likely to use our statements, as they ignored the defendants' complaints. It had no effect. The men were duly sentenced to several years' imprisonment on Robben Island.

Whilst the visit of Navi and Gaby was not successful, it was not entirely in vain. It did lead to positive gains in securing funds for the defence of those imprisoned as well as for the welfare needs of the prisoners and their families. The next step was to request support from Amnesty International in getting the prisoners adopted as prisoners of conscience by Amnesty groups.

Some time later Tabata and Limbada came to our house to thank us. They visited us a number of times either for tea or to dine. On several occasions they visted us socially with their respective wives, Jane Gool and Bibi. Adelaide always asked them to stay for a meal.

One day Tabata and Limbada dropped in for tea. When they left Adelaide noticed an envelope on the piano. She ran after them calling out that they had left something behind and waving the envelope. When she caught up with them Limbada said, 'Adelaide, that's for you..'

She returned to the house and opened the envelope. In it was an open Lufthansa air ticket to Lusaka and an invitation to come for a holiday in appreciation for the support we had shown for their imprisoned comrades. When I got home from work, I found Adelaide quite emotional at their kindness. She took up the invitation and flew with great pleasure to Lusaka.

The next time Tabata and Limbada came on a visit, Tabata mentioned that the ANC had asked him to speak at a memorial gathering for J.B. Marks. I looked a bit surprised. He gently said, with a smile on his face, 'The difference with you young chaps is you see each other as enemies, whereas we of our generation see each other as political opponents.'

That was another salient lesson I have never forgotten.

Sonny Venkatrathnam

Sonny Venkatrathnam was one of those adopted by an Amnesty group, in Ealing, West London. They campaigned on his behalf for several years.

When the prisoners on Robben Island complained about not being allowed access to literature, Sonny and a fellow prisoner, Kader Hassim, who was also a lawyer, drew up a petition. It was addressed to the Robben Island Prison Commanding Officer with their demands for improved conditions and their rights to literature. It was signed by several fellow prisoners.

Prior to its submission a copy was smuggled out and sent to me. I passed it to IDAF, who in turn sent a copy to the United Nations. The petition was taken up by the firm of N Pillay & Partners, who made application to the Supreme Court, using the petition in their submission. The application succeeded.

As a consequence of this, plus the efforts of Helen Suzman, the only Progressive Party MP, and the efforts of a number of international bodies, the Red Cross was allowed to visit Robben Island. Thereafter the life of the prisoners became more comfortable and bearable, with decent food, sports activities and access to literature, and the writing and receiving of more letters.

Karen Singh

One day I got a telephone call from a chap whom I had known when he was about twelve or so years old. His name was Karen Singh, the son of Debi Singh, a senior member of the NIC and a well-known trade union leader. Debi was a fellow accused in the Treason Trial. Karen had come on a visit to London with his young wife and was staying with Dr Zainab Asvat. He was anxious to meet friends of his late father.

I was delighted to hear from him and immediately invited them over. They were a handsome couple, elegantly dressed. At dinner we chatted about friends and people in Durban. After the evening was over I walked them to the tube station. I told him I hoped he had not recorded this evening's engagement in his diary. The visit, I told him, was purely social and not political. He agreed and as they left they gave the clenched fist salute, to which I responded.

Some months later I received a cutting from the *Daily News*, a Durban paper. It was a report that the police had carried out a series of raids in the homes of leaders and activists. The police also busted a rally called by the Black Consciousness Movement. All those arrested were involved in organizing a rally at which a speaker from Frelimo in Mozambique was billed to speak. They were charged with incitement.

Amongst those arrested was Karen Singh. The police found a diary in which was noted a visit to the homes of Dr Dadoo and Paul Joseph. The cutting was brought by a young articled clerk, Pat Naicker, who lived in our neighbourhood. It was sent by her mother with a letter angrily pulling up her daughter for socialising with me. Did she realize the risk involved, she wrote.

Sometime later I got a phone call from Karen. He was in London and wanted to see me. We arranged to meet, as I was keen to probe his involvement. I took him for a walk along Dollis Brook with a notion that he might be wired. He said he was asked by the Black Consciousness Movement (BCM) to go abroad to seek financial support for their trial. Some of them were given bail. He was the only one who had a passport.

He said he was aware that N. Pillay & Partners were getting funds from abroad, especially from London. He said he had got to know some of the female staff at the Pillay offices and they were very pleasant. He told me that after London he would be visiting Stockholm to seek funds. He showed me the indictment charging him with incitement. It contained his speech.

The speech was brazenly couched with violent intent and was one of clear incitement. The distinct impression I got was that the speech had been deliberately written for him by an agent provocateur. I did not indicate any alarm at the contents.

I then asked him to explain why he had kept a diary of his visit to Dadoo and me in spite of what I had advised him on his first visit. He gave no explanation other than that he was foolish.

He said he would be meeting some people in Stockholm. I was curious as to how he had obtained the names of people there. I followed this up by contacting the Durban lawyers. It appeared that Singh and a friend had burgled the offices of N. Pillay & Partners.

I saw him off at the tube station then went over what he had said. There were too many flaws to make his account plausible. So I contacted Joe Slovo and reported my talk with Singh. I also forewarned my Amnesty friend in Stockholm that Singh had said he was visiting and suggested he did not introduce him to the Stockholm Amnesty people.

Singh left Stockholm only getting a drawing by an artist showing a black man breaking his chains. The motif was later used by the Black Consciousness Movement on their letterheads. I got a letter with the motif from the BCM, thanking me for helping their organization.

When their trial started Karen Singh was not amongst the accused. He became a state's witness. The Amnesty Group in Stockholm contacted me on receipt of a letter from Singh's wife, asking for financial assistance. They asked me whether they should support Singh. I replied that since Singh was a state witness the state should provide them with financial support. The group politely turned down Singh's request.

But the links with Amnesty in London and Stockholm grew stronger. Both in the UK and in Sweden Amnesty and IDAF gave sterling support as well as sustained media coverage and information to campaigning groups. It was a tremendous boost to the morale of the prisoners.

I am still a member of Amnesty International.

Reflections

Although for years the apartheid government enjoyed the support of Western military, intelligence and finance, our confidence was instilled in us by people like Nelson Mandela and Chief Luthuli.

Many years ago Mosie Moola said to me, 'The struggle for freedom is hard and difficult. To hold on to that freedom will be much more difficult and much harder.'

I am still mindful of his words.

It often occurs to me that many of our people who went through the fire of apartheid in the grim times now show tremendous weakness in dealing with the host of problems in the free South Africa, such as corruption, abuse of office, HIV/Aids, the shooting of miners on strike and the government's violation of its own laws.

An interviewer on a BBC programme asked one of the leading South African political figures in relation to the Marikana shootings, 'What has happened to the Freedom Charter?' and received the reply, 'That has been put on the back burner.' My reaction to that was, 'I hope the Freedom Charter will not be burned to cinders.'

Appendix 1

Thursday 13 August 2011

Today I felt a compulsion to go to 13 Lyme Street, Camden Town, to stand in front of the house in which Joe and Ruth, Tilly and Julius had lived. The English Heritage plaque reads:

> **Ruth First 1925-1982**
> **Joe Slovo 1926-1995**
> **South African freedom fighters lived here**

I spent several minutes remembering the four people. Ruth and Tilly, with their striking features, the elegance in their dressing, and their sharp intellects. Joe, easy-going and erudite and a great raconteur. Julius, quiet but very perceptive.

A unique family for whom I had a special affection.

When I got back I told Adelaide where I had gone. She nodded and understood why.

Appendix 2

Bob Hepple

24 October 2015

Yesterday I attended a memorial service and celebration of another long-time friend and comrade, Sir Bob Hepple, at Clare College Chapel in Cambridge. Bob was Master of Clare College.

Having read Bob's account of his life *Young Man with a Red Tie*[99] and some earlier accounts of his prison experience, I got to understand more about the strengths and weaknesses of people. He admitted candidly he could not take the pressure and the intimidation of solitary confinement and the threat of capital punishment. He agreed to be a state witness. This he disclosed to his barrister, Bram Fischer, who in turn informed his fellow accused in the Rivonia trial. He was let out. Before that the accused managed to reach a consensus that, if given a chance when released, Bob should leave the country.

In the end, he fled the country without having to testify against his comrades. He did not, however, escape the stress and trauma of leaving his fellow accused and family. What plagued him was the talk of him having betrayed the movement. This followed him for a long time. The problem was accentuated when Kathy Kathrada published his book *Letters from Robben Island*[100] in 1999. In one of the notes he smuggled out to Sylvia

Neame he said that Bob had let out too much and told the police about a hideout in a certain cottage called Mountain View. That story caused a great deal of damage to Bob.

After the service for Bob, I travelled with Sir Nick Standlen, a retired High Court judge, on the train from Cambridge to Kings Cross. We talked about Bob. I said that, despite what Bob went through, he managed to achieve so much in his academic life in Cambridge. He wrote books on racial discrimination and law and was invited by the new government of South Africa to help draw up labour laws (as indeed he did for Namibia) and, more importantly, he was enthusiastically and warmly embraced by Nelson Mandela.

I said I doubted if there was anyone who could claim they came out of prison unscathed. We have all been damaged to some extent. Sir Nick said to me that when he met Albie Sachs, Albie told him that he had not got over his experience in jail. I said that we are dealing with human beings. Whatever the weaknesses, we should judge people in the context of the historical time they made their contribution in the struggle.

Appendix 3

Joel Joffe
Letter dated 25 June 2017 sent to Joel Joffe's family
Several weeks ago I asked some neighbours whether they would mind doing a printout of the song 'Hava Nagilla' and putting me through the paces of singing it. What I had in mind was to visit Joel and sing it to him. I remember Joel saying on his *Desert Island Discs* programme that his grandfather wrote the song in Palestine.

That brought back memories of my time in the Young Communist League. We often got invited to the Jewish Workers Club in Upper Ross Street, Doornfontein, Johannesburg. There we would meet members of youth movements like Mapam and Hashomer Hatzair, and old folk who were Bundists, Communists and left-inclined Zionists. Some of these older people came from Russia during the Czarist period. Some lived during the revolutions of 1901 and 1917. Our visits were heightened by the singing and dancing, especially when it came to the singing of 'Hava Nagilla'.

As word reached me that Joel's health was in decline, I held back. Then we got the message that Joel had died. The news was shattering, as it was for Zoya, Tanya, Nadia and our grandchildren.

When our grandson Arjuna came from school his mother Nadia told him of Joel's death. He immediately came over to embrace and comfort us.

As he held us he said, 'Mama and papa, Joel is not dead, for what he did for people will live on. Joel still lives in you.'

NOTES

1   The Saint Thomas Christians are a community of Christians from Kerala who trace their origins to the evangelistic activity of Saint Thomas in the first century. It is one of the oldest Christian communities in the world.

2   Arundathi Roy, *The God of Small Things*, New Delhi, HarperCollins, 1997.

3   By the time I was fifteen years old I was frequenting these courts as a spectator, witness or an accused in the many political trials from the days of the African mineworkers' strike in 1946 to well after the Treason Trial in 1956, and events related to the breaching of banning orders or detentions.

4   In the early 1960s it became John Vorster Square.

5   I learned only in 1953 that Red Square in Moscow had nothing to do with revolution or blood. The word *krasna* in Russian means red or beautiful.

6   Enver Carim, *The Golden City*, New York, Grove Press, 1969.

7   (Dutch origin) Devil's Passage, either manmade or a natural cut between mountains. This one is near Polokwane.

8   The *SS Mendi* was a South African ship carrying 823 men of the 5th Battalion the South African Native Labour Corps. The majority were drowned when another ship collided with her in thick fog.

9   Weekly paper founded in 1937. It became a leading voice in the South African struggle against apartheid, especially in the 1940s. It evolved into *New Age*.

10   Spellings are as published in the 1972 edition of *The Southern Africa Indian Who's Who*.

11   'Spear of the nation.'

12   The COD was formed in the early 1950s by anti-apartheid Whites. It was closely aligned to the African National Congress.

13   The Unity Movement was founded in 1943. Strongly influenced by Trotsky's concept of revolution, it established a strong base amongst Coloured and African intellectuals in the western Cape.

14   John Eaton (Stephen Bodington), *Political Economy; a Marxian textbook*, New York, International Publishers, 1949.

15   In the 1940s *The African Bookman*, established by Julian Rollnick, was active in Cape Town, providing reading matter for the often newly literate urban South Africans until it closed in 1948.

16   Harriet Beecher Stowe, *Uncle Tom's Cabin*, Boston, John P. Jewett, 1852.

17   Tolstoy Farm was a community started by Gandhi in the Transvaal in 1910, inspired by his correspondence with Tolstoy. It became the headquarters of the campaign of *satyagraha* ('truth force' through passive resistance) which he led at that time. This campaign was a reaction to the discrimination against Indians in the Transvaal.

18   Attached to the Jubilee Social Centre was the Jan Hofmeyer School of Social Science. It was intended only for Africans but did allow Coloureds and Indians to study. It offered no degrees, only diplomas in social science. The head of the school was an American missionary, Dr Ray Phillips, seemingly a progressive but who was clearly guiding the students away from radical studies of the acute social problems of Africans

under apartheid. One of the students who attended the school was Winnie Mandela.

19   1960/61, shortly before the Sharpeville massacre.

20   The first place where the pass laws were introduced was Mauritius, then British Guyana and later South Africa.

21   In the 1960 census there were only eight Indians recorded as living in the Orange Free State. By 1965 there were only five left. Three had gone to Liverpool. The three were the aunt, uncle and cousin of Mac Maharaj, the dashing and daring underground operator in the ANC and CP.

22   In many towns in the Transvaal (now Mpumalanga, and the area called Polokwane and the Reef, as well as parts of Gauteng) where there was no sizeable number of Indians to warrant an 'Asiatic bazaar', the authorities would confine them to a particular street or locality. All the property they lived in was leased from the local authority. There were only two towns in the province, Mackenzieville in Nigel and the Indian area of Barberton, where freehold properties were allowed. Through the Group Areas Act Vrededorp was cleansed of its Indian, Coloured and African communities. Indian traders were allowed to set up their shops in a complex in Fordsburg and in their sophistication the White Johannesburg Council called it 'The Oriental Plaza'. See P Pranshankar Someshwar Joshi, *The Tyranny of Colour. A Study of the Indian Problem in South Africa*, Durban, E.P. & Commercial Print. Co., 1942.

23   The apartheid government passed the Group Areas Act on 27 April 1950. This Act enforced the segregation of the different races to specific areas within the urban locale. It also restricted ownership and the occupation of land to a specific statutory group.

24   Sarah Gertrude Millin, *King of the Bastards*, New York, Harper & Brothers, 1949, and London, William Heinemann, 1950.

25   This story of Margery and Sidney was one the most painful of the many stories I came across that were a result of racial oppression.

26   Lindiwe was a social science graduate. She came from a well-know family. Her father was once president of the Transvaal ANC. One brother, a doctor, was married to Chief Luthuli's daughter. Lionel, her other brother, became an internationally acclaimed filmmaker and actor.

27   The Third World Youth Festival was held in Berlin in 1951.

28   Julius Fucik, *Notes from the Gallows*, Santa Barbara, Peregrine Smith, 1948.

29   The reference to nationalities has always been somewhat complex in the context of South Africa. At the height of the UDF a notion was put out that there are no such groups, we are all one people, i.e. Black. At the time it sounded appealing but in the post-apartheid years it was not a reality. In many ways the ANC messed up this important factor, hence there are not many Indians , Coloureds or Whites who joined the ANC. No real practical effort has been made to wind down the separate areas that exist for the different groups. I would hope that in time from the melting pot a national concept might emerge. It is a process that needs to be worked on by the people themselves.

30   Pius would have got his education from the night school movement initiated by the CP.

31   One of the CP leaders.

32   The Second World War resulted in a strong reaction from the Jewish community against Nazism and its vile terror against the Jews. The revival saw a surge of support for the left-wing cause and the liberation organizations of black people against racial

discrimination. One of the organizations that flourished was the Jewish Workers Club in Doornfontein. We in the YCL found it an enlightening experience to meet and socialise freely with White people.

33   Gillian Slovo, *Every Secret Thing. My Family, My Country*, London, Little, Brown and Company, 1997.

34   The building had a cinema, two exclusive restaurants (for Whites only), and was the chambers for the barristers. It was the first of its kind in Johannesburg.

35   This was a strange restriction applicable mostly to people from Eastern Europe, especially from the Baltic states, Poland and Russia.

36   Africans who were charged with infringing the Pass Laws were being sent as slave labour to White-owned farms. A detailed account of the scandal can be found in Sylvester Stein, *Who Killed Mr Drum?* London, Corvo Books, 2003; originally published in *Mayibuye*, an ANC publication, in 1999.

37   *The White-Haired Girl*, co-directed by Wang Bin and Shui Hua, 1950.

38   The Drill Hall in Johannesburg was erected as a mark of British military might after the brutal South African War (1899-1902). In 1956-57, the Treason Trial brought 156 leaders of the Congress Alliance to the Drill Hall before the trial was moved to Pretoria. From the 1960s until apartheid's demise, the Drill Hall was used as a conscription centre for the apartheid government.

39   Uncle Sam was a well-known wheeler-dealer, who drove fancy cars, gambled for high stakes, and was a flashy dresser.

40   The mother of Margaret Legum.

41   The PAC was a breakaway group from the ANC. Led by Robert Sobukwe, they disapproved of the ANC's close assocation with the SAIC, the CP, and Whites who were willing to forge links with the ANC, for example the Liberal Party. Later there was a small segment which broke off from the PAC. Calling themselves the Pan-Africanist Freedom Movement, led by Peter Tsele, they disintegrated when Tsele died in a car crash.

42   We always knew him as Isu. He is more widely known as Laloo. His full name is Ishwarlal.

43   In my opinion Dr Dadoo was sometimes too tolerant in accommodating differences.

44   Dr Dadoo left South Africa in 1960 at the request of the movement to obtain international support.

45   Unknown to me at the time, both my brothers also did favours independently for the movement.

46   Early in the 1980s it was widely reported that they defied the Group Areas Act by occupying a formerly White-owned property. Together with the rest of the Indian flower sellers they organized a petition against the council's attempt to dislodge the flower sellers from the city. The petitions were signed by thousands of White people too. The council failed in its attempts. The Indian flower sellers were no longer restricted.

47   My brother knew that next door to the premises was a chap who was on nodding acquaintance with Mac. Daso and Issy locked themselves in the room. As they were busy stuffing the bags with documents and various items there was a knock on the door. There was no exit and the room was on the first floor. The men broke out in a sweat. Daso suggested to Issy that since there was no escape possible they might as

well open the door. When Daso opened the door there was this acquaintance, who asked 'Can I help?' They thanked him very much and assured him they could manage. Daso thought it was conceivable that the man next door had an inkling that Mac was political, and was sympathetic.

48 The CP sent a message telling him to turn down the offer. To some of us the police offer was laced with threats of a trial, intimidation and an attempt to sow seeds of dissension.

49 A fair amount of this episode has been written. The best and most reliable account was by Dennis Herbstein, who wrote it up for the *Sunday Independent* 16 July 1994.

50 This was also a sensitive issue which needed careful discussion between Nelson Mandela and Chief Luthuli.

51 Isu did not know that Sheriff was being bankrolled by a Market Street merchant, Ahmed Laher. One day Kathrada pointed out Ahmed Laher to me, saying, 'That is one of your vice-presidents of the TIC.' I was confounded, as I never saw him at any meetings, so I could not understand how he got elected. I discovered a couple of years later his name was put forward by Yusuf Cachalia.

52 I was arrested on the declaration of the State of Emergency in March 1960 and held up to the end of August. I was amongst a handful who were finally released.

53 Lilliesleaf Farm is now a museum, as part of a complex with an adjacent hotel in which the rooms are in the names of the Rivonia Trialists. The hotel is one of a chain of Marriott hotels around the world. The ANC seems to have gone along with the whole scheme. Without doubt it is important to retain the history of this episode in the nation's history, but it should have been done without the hotel project. It means that, for instance, the Freedom Charter is no longer the property of the ANC but of the owners of the Marriott hotel chain.

54 It was alleged that he was the person who informed the security police of the high command hideout.

55 Bulgarian and Soviet Communist leader who served as head of the Communist International (Comintern) from 1935 to 1943 and as prime minister of Bulgaria from 1944 until his death. When I was working at Julius First's furniture factory, after knock-off time, some of us would thumb lifts home. Sometimes cars, vans or lorries driven by Coloureds or Indians would oblige. One day I came home in a hearse for a laugh. We would also thumb White motorists, who never stopped. One day, however, a White motorist actually did stop to offer us a lift. My friends and I got into the back of the car. As we sat down I quipped to Abu Bakr, 'See Abu, there are some good White people.' The driver said, 'No. I am not from here.' He was from Yugoslavia. Then he added, 'My wife comes from Bulgaria, she is a niece of Georgi Dimitrov.' With that kind of talk, I invited him to visit us at home.

56 Gray's Building housed the security police political department on a number of floors. The rest of the building was commercially occupied.

57 Adelaide once told me that someone at a women's meeting asked how she could join MK. Adelaide said, 'You don't ask to join. MK will find you.'

58 I first knew of John Harris by repute as an ardent member of the South African Liberal party. It was much later than I actually got to know him, largely through his effort to help build up SAN-ROC together with Denis Brutus, George Singh, Reg Hlongwane, Chris de Broglio and several others. Through this committee they were to make a frontal attack on the Apartheid South African presence in every international body.

Special targets were the International Olympic Committee (IOC) and the Federation of International Football Associations, as well as the rugby and cricket bodies. Dennis Brutus was the chair of SAN-ROC. In 1961, when he was banned from gathering, his place was taken by John Harris, who went in his place to attend the IOC meeting in Switzerland.

59   One night in the interrogation room I was in, I heard screams and pleas. I asked whether somebody was being assaulted. One security man said to me, 'The sounds are your imagination, they are in your head.' The screams sounded like Ivan Schermbrucker, a CP member. The next morning I smuggled out a message about what I had heard the night before. On my release Adelaide told me it was actually Hugh Lewin. On the same night the police broke John Harris's jaw and damaged his testicles. The police said he injured himself when he tried to escape from the security car.

John, Hugh and several others who were members of ARM were rounded up and imprisoned soon after the bomb explosion in Park Station. Hugh was imprisoned for seven years and Eddie Daniels, a Coloured, was sentenced to fifteen years, which he served on Robben Island.

60   After the completion of my first ninety days' detention I was transported to Pretoria Central prison. As I got out of the car I noticed two White women in front of the huge prison doors. I recognized one woman as Adelaine Hain, whom I had met with her husband Walter some years before at a meeting in the Indian quarter in Pretoria; the other woman I discovered later was Ann Harris, John Harris's wife. Many years later when I came into exile I met Ann at the house of the Hains in London.

61   He eventually became an alcoholic and was kicked out of the force. He went to a Muslim prayer meeting and eventually converted to Islam and married an Indian Muslim woman.

62   Anthony Sampson, *Mandela, the Authorised Biography*, New York & London, Harper Collins, 1999.

63   Robert Jungk, *Brighter than a Thousand Suns: A Personal History of the Atomic Scientists*, New York, Harcourt Brace, & Company, 1958.

64   Donald Wise filed his report to the *Daily Express*. It gave a graphic account of the police brutality. The headline to his report was 'Guns Blaze at High Noon'. When he next came to court we quietly acknowledged each other.

65   Adelaide told me that after Vanetta accompanied her to the police station, she said that she was ashamed of being an Afrikaner because of what was being done. Adelaide told her there were some good people amongst the Afrikaners so she ought not to feel that way. She mentioned Bram and Molly Fischer as examples.

66   Wilton Mkwayi was born in the Ciskei. His working life was in Port Elizabeth. He became an active trade unionist, having joined the CP and the ANC. He was amongst those arrested in 1956 and charged together with 156 leaders and activists for high treason. One day during the marathon treason trial when he was going into the court, the police cordoned off the area and stopped the public from entering the vicinity of the Court House. Wilton was chased away. He took the opportunity and disappeared, quietly carrying on political activity. He was next almost caught at Rivonia, but was mistaken for a labourer.

67   Alfred was a sander at the furniture factory. In the cabinet workshop was a worker who

also ran a general dealer's store in Newclare. This man, Seymour, and I got on very well. He once told me that Alfred had approached him to obtain a quantity of glycerine. He was perplexed as to why Alfred wanted it. I shrugged it off, telling him that all I knew about glycerine was that it was used for medicine. I did not report to our MK unit what I had stumbled on. I remember Alfred as a strikingly handsome man, well spoken and neat. I was extremely sorry when Wilton told me how Alfred was arrested and tortured.

68 Wilton told us that he was quite embarrassed about the circumstances of his arrest. When he finished his military training in China, the Chinese instructors told him that if ever he got caught, it must never be in the company of a woman. Now he was caught in the house of a woman friend. He said he did not know how he was ever to explain the circumstances of his arrest to the Chinese comrades.

69 Joel Joffe was born on 5 May 1932 in Forest Town, Johannesburg, his father having moved there from Doornfontein when it still had a thriving Jewish community of bakers, tailors, shopkeepers, and workers in the garment industry. His father was a reasonably successful merchant. Joel went to the Marist Brothers' school and then to Wits. Amongst his contemporaries and friends were Mark Weinberg (knighted in January 1987), Sydney Lipworth (knighted in January 1991) and Arthur Chaskalson, who was appointed President of the Constitutional Court by Nelson Mandela and later became Chief Justice of South Africa. Joel himself was awarded the CBE in 1999, and made a life peer in February 2000.

70 Sydney Kentridge (Sir Sydney Kentridge as from1999) was the best dressed, whereas Vernon Berrange was flamboyant in his attire.

71 Much later, when Joel was living in London, he wrote a most moving and highly acclaimed account of the Rivonia Trial. Joel Joffe, *The State Vs. Nelson Mandela, The Trial That Changed South Africa, London,* Oneworld Publications, 2007.

72 Taverne was made a life peer in 1996.

73 Adelaide got to know Dick Taverne through the Lincoln branch of Amnesty. He dealt with the Home Office to facilitate my entry into the UK

74 The name Soweto drerives from South West Township.

75 Local slang for Indian shopkeeper

76 Kasangula is the name of the border post at the meeting of the two rivers. The border post on the Zambian side has the same name.

77 In the case of Billy Nannan he was swept off his feet by Sartre's writings on existentialism. The works of the masters were hotly exchanged. When Billy was brought out from isolation to testify against Wilton Mkwayi, Mac Maharaj and others, he was asked how he met Mac Maharaj. He said it was through Paul Joseph. When the prosecutor asked how he met me, Billy said, 'It was through borrowing books.' The prosecutor asked 'What sort of books?' Billy replied, 'On existentialism and dialectics.' The prosecutor asked 'Exist what?' The prosecutor was bewildered and gave up! Sitting in the crowded court gallery was Professor Sir Robert Birley, former headmaster of Eton College who was Visiting Professor at Wits. He was astonished and so impressed that, after Billy's release, he offered him a teaching job at a prominent high school in Holland Park in London.

One of the stories that came out during Billy's detention was that he helped an Afrikaner warder in the rudiments of maths. The warder was so impressed with Billy's method of teaching that he asked in Afrikaans, 'Are all you coolies so clever?' Billy answered,

'No I am not. You should speak to the ones in the street.' The response was in fluent Afrikaans.

78   The police got on to the unit where Daso helped produce the propaganda material. The chief operator of the unit was Mac Maharaj.

79   When I eventually slipped over the border, I wrote to Adelaide to enquire about work in London, even if it meant construction work on the Victoria Line tunnel. She showed the letter to friends, who shook their heads at that suggestion.

80   Charles Bloomberg was a South African journalist, a long-time friend involved in the left movement. He was a political historian specializing in the Broederbond, the secret pro-apartheid group within the Nationalist Party and Government during and after Second World War.

81   The Teitelbaums who were a couple involved in the Workers Revolutionary Party, made generous financial contributions for the welfare of the Mandela family as well as to the Anti-Apartheid Movement.

82   In 1999 Mbeki became President of South Africa. Aziz Pahad, Deputy Minister of Foreign Affairs, Pallo Jordan, Cabinet Minister (Arts and Culture), Issy Dinat, a Chief Executive of the Krugersdorp Council and Enver Carim became a successful author. His novel, *A Dream Deferred* (London, Allen Lane, 1973), was described in the *Times Literary Supplement* as 'particularly convincing on the corrupting effect of power on sexuality'. Pranlal Sheth became an executive director and was later awarded a CBE. Jairaj Singh became the deputy head of Pimlico School and Stephen Lazar a successful medical doctor.

83   Palme Dutt, *The Crisis of Britain and the British Empire*, London, Lawrence and Wishart, 1953.

84   Friedrich Engels, *Anti-Dühring*, Leipzig, 1878.

85   Denis Herbstein, *White Lies. Canon Collins and the Secret War Against Apartheid*, Cape Town and Oxford, James Currey Publishers, 2004.

86   Freda Troup, *In Face of Fear. Michael Scott's Challenge to South Africa*, London, Faber & Faber, 1950. Ruth First wrote extensively in *New Age* and in books. Henry Nxumalo wrote on the subject in *Drum* magazine and in the *Guardian*.

87   Joel Carlson, *No Neutral Ground*, London, Davies-Poynter, 1973.

88   Gordon Winter, *Inside BOSS: South Africa's Secret Police,* London, Penguin Books, 1981.

89   Our youngest daughter, Nadia, was born in 1966 in St Mary's Hospital Paddington when we lived in Notting Hill Gate.

90   Apparently Raymond thought the message came from Michael Joseph, the well-known London publisher.

91   Irene died. Following Wilton's release from Robben Island, he later became a senator and lived in the Cape. He died at the age of 68.

92   Savery Naidoo came from East London in the Eastern Cape where he attended the well-known Lovedale College. He spent a considerable time in Port Elizabeth and often visited Cape Town.

93   Although Blacks and Whites playing bridge was not illegal under apartheid, it was not part of the social convention.

94   Zulu for 'Hold your knees' or go-slow, the alternative workers' action to illegal strikes.

95   The UDF was an alliance of most of the anti-apartheid groups and organizations which functioned openly from 1983 to 1991. It was another major force in the overall defeat of apartheid.

96   Beverley Naidoo, *Death of an Idealist. In Search of Neil Aggett,* London, Merlin Press, 2012.

97   The Unity Movement fragmented over a period of time into four factions. As with the PAC, many of the Unity Movement members joined the ANC. Others became disenchanted and just faded out.

98   Later the government banned Arenstein from working as a clerk in any legal firm.

99   Bob Hepple, *Young Man with a Red Tie,* Johannesburg, Jacana Books, 2013.

100 Ahmed Kathrada, *Letters From Robben Island: A Selection of Ahmed Kathrada's Prison Correspondence, 1964-1989,* East Lansing, Michigan State University Press, 1999.